Your
Treasury of
Inspiration

Love & Best Wishes,

John & Mary Ann

Summer of 1981

Your Treasury of Inspiration

**An album of favorite selections
for daily inspiration and enjoyment.**

An Anthology of 1200

PRAYERS • SCRIPTURE PORTIONS

MEMORABLE QUOTATIONS • HOMEY SENTIMENTS

• INSPIRATIONAL POETRY AND PROSE

Compiled by Eleanor L. Doan

Illustrations by Nancy Munger

ZONDERVAN PUBLISHING HOUSE
OF THE ZONDERVAN CORPORATION
GRAND RAPIDS, MICHIGAN 49506

Acknowledgments

Grateful acknowledgment is made to the following publishers,
authors, and other copyright owners for permission to use
the copyrighted selections in this book.

ABINGDON PRESS for "The
Secret" by Ralph Spauld-
ing Cushman from *Spiri-
tual Hilltops,* copyright ©
1960; and "Life's Com-
pleteness" by S. G.
Fisher from *A Treasury
of Sermon Illustrations,*
edited by Charles L.
Wallis, copyright © 1950
by Pierce & Smith.

AMERICAN TRACT SO-
CIETY, Oradel, New
Jersey, to reprint "The
Incomparable Christ."

SYBIL LEONARD ARMES,
Dallas, Texas, for "I Take
Hands Off My Life" and
the poem "Altars" from
The Radiant Trail (Nash-
ville: Broadman Press
1947) p. 4. Used by
permission.

ATHENEUM PUBLISHERS
for an extract from *The
Captain* by Jan de Hartog,
copyright © 1966 by
Littra A.G. Reprinted by
permission of Atheneum
Publishers.

BEACON HILL PRESS,
Kansas City, Missouri, for

"Home" by Kathryn
Blackburn Peck from *In
Favor With God and Man.*
Used by permission.

BIBLE SOCIETY RECORD
(1865 Broadway, New
York, N. Y. 10023) for the
poem "Know the Bible in
your mind . . . ." Reprinted
by permission.

A. & C. BLACK LTD.,
London, and THE MAC-
MILLAN COMPANY,
New York, for the excerpt
from *The Philosophy of
Civilization* by Dr. Albert
Schweitzer, copyright
1923.

GEOFFREY BLES LTD. for
the excerpt from *Four
Loves* by C. S. Lewis and
for Romans 12:2 from
*Letters to Young
Churches* by J. B. Phillips.

THE BOBBS-MERRILL
COMPANY, INC. for a
stanza from "Wet Weather
Talk" from *The Biograph-
ical Edition of the Com-
plete Works of James
Whitcomb Riley,* copyright
1913 by James Whitcomb

Riley and 1940 by Lesley
Payne, Elizabeth E.
Miesse, and Edmund H.
Eitel. Reprinted by per-
mission of the Bobbs-
Merrill Company, Inc.

BRETHREN PRESS,
CHURCH OF THE
BRETHREN, Elgin, Illi-
nois, for "The Touch of
the Master's Hand" by
Myra Brooks Welch.

CARLTON C. BUCK for
"Above Mediocrity" from
Quiet Time Verse.

CHRISTIAN CENTURY
FOUNDATION for the
poem "God Immediate"
by Raymond Kresensky,
copyright 1931 by Chris-
tian Century Foundation.
Reprinted by permission
from the February 25,
1931 issue of *The
Christian Century.*

CHRISTIAN PUBLICA-
TIONS, INC., Harrisburg,
Pa., for "God's Best"
by A. B. Simpson from
Songs of the Spirit.

THE CHRISTIAN SCIENCE
MONITOR for "Dirt

Farmer" by Arden Antony,
from the September 26,
1938 issue.

CRESCENDO PUBLISHING
COMPANY, Boston, for
"A Prayer" by Max
Ehrmann from *Poems of
Max Ehrmann.* Reprinted
by permission.

COVENANT PRESS for "The
Home-Going" by Helga
Skogsbergh from her
collection of poems *Songs
of Pilgrimage,* copyright
1962 by Covenant Press.

WILLIAM S. DEAL for the
quotation from *How to
Grow Old Gracefully.*

DECISION Magazine for the
quotation by Billy
Graham made in an
address to the World
Council of Churches
Consultation on Evange-
lism in Switzerland and
which appears in *The
Quiet Corner,* copyright
© 1965; and for the
quotation by Bishop
William Connor Magee,
which appeared in the

Contents

To the many known and unknown authors from centuries past as well as those of the twentieth, my sincere appreciation.

Also, my heartfelt thanks to the scores of friends* worldwide whose interest in enriching the content of this anthology prompted "favorite" contributions.

ELEANOR DOAN

In Appreciation

*These friends are:

Colena M. Anderson
Margaret J. Anderson
Francena H. Arnold
Dr. S. Barton Babbage
Dr. J. Sidlow Baxter
Sallie Lee Bell
Rev. John R. Bisagno
Dr. E. M. Blaiklock
Rachel Borne
Al Bryant
Rev. Carlton C. Buck
Alex Burns
Dr. Emile Cailliet
Betty Carlson
Rev. Morry Carlson
Dr. Thomas Carruth
Marie Chitwood
Margaret W. Clarkson
Rev. Clay Cooper
Fayly H. Cothern
Dr. T. T. Crabtree
Matsu W. Crawford
Dr. W. A. Criswell
Elna Worrell Daniel
Dr. William S. Deal
Rev. Richard DeHaan
Rev. Mack R. Douglas
Rev. Charles DuMond
Rev. Merrill Dunlop

Kathy Ecenbarger
Mrs. V. Raymond Edman
Oscar C. Eliason
Richard Engquist
Dr. Ted W. Engstrom
Margaret Epp
Dr. W. Herschel Ford
Gloria Foreman
Rev. C. W. Franke
Marjorie Frost
Dr. Frank E. Gaebelein
Rev. Stanton W. Gavitt
Dr. Armin R. Gesswein
Dr. Virtus E. Gideon
Dr. and Mrs. Billy
    Graham
Dr. Manford Gutzke
Rev. John E. Haggai
Jack Hamm
Dorothy Haskin
James C. Hefley
Dorothy Howard
Dr. David Hubbard
Gladys Hunt
Dr. John E. Huss
Rev. Earl Jabay
Mr. and Mrs. Gordon
    Jaeck
Ruth Caye Jones

Barbara Jurgensen
Dr. James Kelso
Rev. Clyde Kirby
Dena Korfker
Mrs. Richard E. Landorf
Bruce Larson
Dr. Robert G. Lee
Dr. Addison Leitch
Dr. Harold Lindsell
Dr. Herbert Lockyer
Dr. Raymond
    McLaughlin
Rev. Don Mainprize
Miss Sylvia Mattson
Dr. Aaron Meckel
Phyllis Michael
Professor Herbert J.
    Miles
Chaplain Herbert
    Moehlmann
Dr. Jess C. Moody
Cora R. Moore
Anna B. Mow
Mable H. Nance
Dr. Clyde Narramore
Vida Munden Nixon
Kenneth W. Osbeck
Dr. Cecil Osborne
Ray Overholt

Rev. Richard Peace
Douglas C. Percy
Rev. John Pollock
Bruce Porterfield
Rev. Arnold Prater
Eugenia Price
Dr. Paul S. Rees
James W. Reid
Rosalind Rinker
Anna Schroeder
Steve Sloan
Dr. Oswald J. Smith
Cordelia Spitzer
Mildred Stamm
Rev. Ira Stanphill
Rev. George Sweeting
Bessie Sykes
Dr. Merrill C. Tenney
Mr. N. B. Vandall
Grace Vander Klay
Rev. Glenn Wagoner
Adel P. Wasserfall
Grady Wilson
Dr. T. W. Wilson
Dr. Walter L. Wilson
Dr. Sherwood E. Wirt
Rev. Lon Woodrum
Dr. P. J. Zondervan

Daily along life's path there is
need for Inspiration —
to encourage and comfort,
to challenge and motivate,
to strengthen love and devotion,
to charm and bring laughter,
to enrich faith, and
to quicken an awareness of God's
presence.
    Within the pages of this album,
inspiration may be found:
It may come from the finest
    of literary selections or from the
    warmth of some homey verse;

Preface

It may be experienced from read-
    ing the creed of a statesman,
    words of a hymn, or a portion
    of Scripture from the mind
    of God;
It may even come from the heart
    of a child, the reflection of
    a parent, the reminiscing of a
    teacher, or the pen of an
    unknown poet.
    The inspiration drawn from this
album will have an influence . . .
from life to life of the awareness
of God in whom "we live, and
move, and have our being"*
. . . diffusing a lasting beauty —
of which the poet wrote: "A thing
of beauty is a joy forever: its
loveliness increases; it will never
pass into nothingness."**

Eleanor L. Doan
Glendale, California

* Acts 17:28
** John Keats

INSPIRATION

Inspiration is such a fragile thing ... just a fragile thing. Just a breeze, touching the green foliage of a city park. Just a whisper from the soul of a friend. Just a line of verse, clipped from some forgotten magazine ... or a paragraph standing out from among the matter-of-fact chapters of a learned book.

Inspiration ... who can say where it is born, and why it leaves us? Who can tell of its reasons for being ... or for not being?

Only this ... I think that inspiration comes from the Heart of Heaven to give the lift of wings, and the breath of divine music to those of us who are earth-bound.

MARGARET E. SANGSTER

Achievement & Success

He has achieved success who has lived well, laughed often, and loved much; who has gained the respect of intelligent men, and the love of little children; who has filled his niche and accomplished his task; who has left the world better than he found it, whether by an improved poppy, a perfect poem, or a rescued soul; who has never lacked appreciation of earth's beauty, or failed to express it; who has always looked for the best in others and given the best he had; whose life was an inspiration; whose memory a benediction.

BESSIE A. STANLEY

Success is the persistent achievement of a worthy, challenging goal.

MACK R. DOUGLAS

99

---

*For success, try
aspiration
inspiration
and perspiration.*

Success is to be measured not so much by the position that one has reached in life as by the obstacles which he has overcome while trying to succeed.

BOOKER T. WASHINGTON

●

**Something attempted, something done
Has earned a night's repose.**

HENRY WADSWORTH LONGFELLOW

No one ever gets very far unless he accomplishes the impossible at least once a day.

ELBERT HUBBARD

Whenever you hear of a man doing a great thing, you may be sure that behind it somewhere is a great background. It may be a mother's training, a father's example, a teacher's influence, or an intense experience of his own, but it has to be there or else the great achievement does not come, no matter how favorable the opportunity.

CATHERINE MILES

If you have anything really valuable to contribute to the world, it will come through the expression of your own personality — that single spark of divinity that sets you off and makes you different from every other living creature.

BRUCE BARTON

A PSALM OF LIFE

Tell me not, in mournful numbers,
Life is but an empty dream! —
For the soul is dead that slumbers,
And things are not what they seem.

Life is real! Life is earnest!
And the grave is not its goal;
Dust thou art, to dust returnest,
Was not spoken of the soul.

Not enjoyment, and not sorrow,
Is our destined end or way;
But to act, that each tomorrow
Find us farther than today.

Art is long, and Time is fleeting,
And our hearts, though stout and brave,
Still, like muffled drums, are beating
Funeral marches to the grave.

In the world's broad field of battle,
In the bivouac of life,
Be not like dumb, driven cattle!
Be a hero in the strife!

Trust no Future, howe'er pleasant!
Let the dead Past bury its dead!
Act, — act in the living Present!
Heart within, and God o'erhead!

Lives of great men all remind us
We can make our lives sublime,
And, departing, leave behind us
Footprints on the sands of time;

Footprints, that perhaps another,
Sailing o'er life's solemn main,
A forlorn and shipwrecked brother,
Seeing, shall take heart again.

Let us then be up and doing,
With a heart for any fate;
Still achieving, still pursuing,
Learn to labor and to wait.

HENRY WADSWORTH LONGFELLOW

Footprints in the sands of time were not made by sitting down.

Specialize in doing what you can't.

THE FAMILY OF SUCCESS

The Father of success is named Work.

The Mother of Success is named Ambition.

The oldest son is called Common Sense and some of the boys are called Stability, Perseverance, Honesty, Thoroughness, Foresight, Enthusiasm, and Cooperation.

The oldest daughter is Character. Some of the sisters are Cheerfulness, Loyalty, Care, Courtesy, Economy, Sincerity, and Harmony. The baby is Opportunity.

Get acquainted with the Father of success and you will be able to get along with the rest of the family.

SUNSHINE MAGAZINE

Self-trust is the first secret of success.

RALPH WALDO EMERSON

Those who would bring great things to pass must rise early in the morning.

MATTHEW HENRY

THE LOST MASTER

"And when I come to die," he said,
"Ye shall not lay me out in state,
Nor leave your laurels at my head,

Nor cause your men of speech orate;
No monument your gift shall be,
No column in the Hall of Fame;
But just this line ye grave for me:
   'He played the game'."

So when his glorious task was done,
It was not of his fame we thought;
It was not of his battles won,
But of the pride with which he fought;
But of his zest, his ringing laugh,
His trenchant scorn of praise or blame:
And so we graved his epitaph,
   "He played the game."

And so we, too, in humbler ways
Went forth to fight the fight anew,
And heeding neither blame nor praise,
We held the course he set us true,
And we, too, find the fighting sweet;
And we, too, fight for fighting's sake;
And though we go down in defeat,
And though our stormy hearts may break,
We will not do our Master shame:
We'll play the game, please God,
   We'll play the game.

ROBERT W. SERVICE

Triumph is just umph added to try.

HOWARD CRIMSON

Success comes from mastering defeat.

The man who makes no mistakes does not usually make anything.

BISHOP WILLIAM CONNOR MAGEE

It is one thing to itch for something and another to scratch for it.

Only one life
'Twill soon be past.
Only what's done
For Christ will last.

You can do anything if you do not care who gets the credit for it.

HARRY A. IRONSIDE

Dare to be wise; begin!
He who postpones the hour of living rightly is the rustic who waits for the river to run out before he crosses.

HORACE

Adversity

Welcome each rebuff
That turns earth's smoothness rough,
Each sting that bids not sit
   nor stand but go!
Be our joys three-parts pain!
Strive, and hold cheap the strain;
Learn, nor account the pang; dare,
   never grudge the throe!

ROBERT BROWNING

•

**Great minds have purposes, others have
   wishes.
Little minds are tamed and subdued by
   misfortune;
but great minds rise above them.**

WASHINGTON IRVING

**I am an old man and have known a great
many troubles, but most of them have
never happened.**

MARK TWAIN

**Most of the shadows of life are caused
by standing in our own sunshine.**

RALPH WALDO EMERSON

If the pattern of life looks dark to you,
And the threads seem twisted and queer,
To the One Who is planning the whole
   design,
It's perfectly plain and clear . . .

For it's all part of God's loving plan,
When He works in His threads of gray,
And they'll only make brighter
The rose and gold of another happier day.

•

TO ONE IN SORROW

Let me come in where you are weeping,
   friend,
And let me take your hand.
I, who have known a sorrow such as
   yours,
Can understand.
Let me come in — I would be very still
Beside you in your grief;
I would not bid you cease your weeping,
   friend,
Tears bring relief.
Let me come in — I would only breathe a
   prayer,
And hold your hand,
For I have known a sorrow such as yours,
And understand.

GRACE NOLL CROWELL

**In the hour of adversity be not without
hope
For crystal rain falls from black clouds.**

NIZAMI

Have courage for the great sorrows of
life and patience for the small ones; and
when you have laboriously accomplished
your daily task, go to sleep in peace.
God is awake.

VICTOR HUGO

**Difficulties are stepping stones to
success.**

*Never a tear bedims the eye
That time and patience will not dry.*

BRET HARTE

THE CONQUEROR OF MY SOUL

*Out of the light that dazzles me,
Bright as the sun from pole to pole,
I thank the God I know to be
For Christ — the Conqueror of my soul.*

*Since his the sway of circumstance,
I would not wince, nor cry aloud.
Under that rule which men call chance,
My head, with joy, is humbly bowed.*

*Beyond this place of sin and tears,
That life with him — and his the aid
That, spite the menace of the years,
Keeps, and will keep me, unafraid.*

*I have no fear though strait the gate:
He cleared from punishment the scroll.
Christ is the Master of my fate!
Christ is the Captain of my soul.*

DOROTHEA DAY

COME, LORD JESUS

*Because of little children soiled,
And disinherited, despoiled,*

*Because of hurt things, feathered, furred,
Tormented beast, imprisoned bird,*

*Because of many-folded grief,
Beyond redress, beyond belief,*

*Because the word is true that saith,
The whole creation travaileth —*

*Of all our prayers this is the sum:
O come, Lord Jesus, come.*

AMY CARMICHAEL

LORD TAKE AWAY PAIN

*The cry of man's anguish went up unto
    God,
"Lord, take away pain! The sorrow that
    darkens
The world Thou hast made, the close
    circling chain
That encircles the heart, the burden that
    weighs
On the wings that would soar!
Lord, take away pain from the world
    Thou hast made,
That it love Thee the more!"*

*Then answered the Lord to the cry of His
    world,
"Shall I take away pain?
And with it the power of the world
    to endure,
Made strong by the strain?
Shall I take away pity that binds heart
    to heart,
And sacrifice high?
Would you lose all your heroes that lift
    from the fire,
White brows to the sky?"*

*"Shall I take away love that redeems at
    a price,
And smiles at its loss?
Can you spare from your lives that would
    climb into mine,
The Christ on the cross?"*

FROM THE WALL OF A DENVER HOSPITAL

If I could only see the road you came,
With all the jagged rocks and crooked
   ways,
I might more kindly think of your misstep
And only praise.

●

**The people we have the most trouble
with is ourselves.**

Adversity is the path of truth.
LORD BYRON

HUMILITY

I asked God for strength,
   that I might achieve —
I was made weak,
   that I might learn humbly to obey.

I asked for help
   that I might do greater things —
I was given infirmity,
   that I might do better things.

I asked for riches,
   that I might be happy —
I was given poverty,
   that I might be wise.

I asked for all things,
   that I might enjoy life —
I was given life,
   that I might enjoy all things.

I got nothing
   that I asked for —
But everything
   I had hoped for.

Despite myself,
   my prayers were answered.
I am, among all men,
   most richly blessed.

AN ANONYMOUS SOLDIER
OF THE CONFEDERACY

Great truths are greatly won. Not found
   by chance,
   Nor wafted on the breath of summer
     dream,
But grasped in the great struggle of the
   soul,
   Hard buffeting with adverse wind
     and stream.

Grasped in the day of conflict, fear and
   grief,
   When the strong hand of God, put
     forth in might,
Plows up the subsoil of the stagnant
   heart,
   And brings the imprisoned truth-seed
     to the light.

Wrung from the troubled spirit in hard
   hours
   Of weakness, solitude, perchance of
     pain,
Truth springs, like harvest, from the
   well-plowed field,
   And the soul feels it has not wept
     in vain.

HORATIUS BONAR

●

SORROW

Go, bury thy sorrow,
   The world hath its share;
Go, bury it deeply,
   Go, hide it with care.
Go, bury thy sorrow,
   Let others be blest;
Go, give them the sunshine,
   And tell God the rest.

●

TRUST

Build a little fence of trust
   Around today;
Fill each space with loving work
   And therein stay;
Look not through the sheltering bars
   Upon tomorrow,
God will help thee bear what comes,
   Of joy or sorrow.

MARY FRANCES BUTTS

Awareness

MOMENTS OF AWARENESS

So much of life we all
pass by
With heedless ear,
and careless eye.
Bent with our cares
we plod along,
Blind to the beauty,
deaf to the song.

But moments there are
when we pause to rest
And turn our eyes from
the goal's far crest.
We become aware of
the wayside flowers,
And sense God's hand
in this world of ours.

We hear a refrain,
see a rainbow's end,
Or we look into the heart
of a friend.
We feel at one with
mankind. We share
His griefs and glories,
joy and care.

The sun flecks gold thru the
sheltering trees,
And we shoulder our burdens
with twice the ease.
Peace and content and
a world that sings
The moment of true
awareness brings.

HELEN LOWRIE MARSHALL

True happiness comes from the knowledge that we are of some use in this world.

TIME

Like the speed of an arrow that is shot
from a bow,
Like the glance of a sunbeam on
mountains of snow,
Like the lightning that flashes a moment
then dies,
So swift move the wheels of time as
it flies.

You cannot build your happiness on someone else's unhappiness.

A child may be as new to the world as snowdrops in January, and yet already have a good and keen and deep understanding, a full mind and a hospitable heart. He may be able to think hard, imagine richly, face trouble, take good care of himself and of others, keep well, and live abundantly.

WALTER DE LA MARE

GOD'S EXPRESSIONS

Look without!
Behold the beauty of the day,
The shout
Of color to glad color,
Rocks and trees,
And sun and seas,
And wind and sky:
All these
Are God's expression,
Art work of His hand,
Which men must love
Ere they can understand.

RICHARD HOVEY

We live in the present,
We dream of the future,
But we learn eternal truths
from the past.

MADAME CHIANG KAI-SHEK

This is maturity:
   To be able to stick with a job until it
   is finished;
   to be able to bear an injustice without
   wanting to get even;
   to be able to carry money without
   spending it;
   and to do one's duty without being
   supervised.

You must know how to flower where God
has sown you.

JAN DE HARTOG

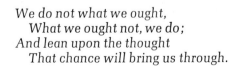

We do not what we ought,
   What we ought not, we do;
And lean upon the thought
   That chance will bring us through.

MATTHEW ARNOLD

We get from people what we give;
We find in them what we bring;
We discover that the changes in them
   are really changes in ourselves.

THE SECRET

I met God in the morning,
When my day was at its best,
And His presence came like sunrise
With a glory in my breast.

All day long the Presence lingered,
All day long He stayed with me;
And we sailed in perfect calmness
O'er a very troubled sea.

Other ships were blown and battered,
Other ships were sore distressed,
But the winds that seemed to drive them
Brought to us both peace and rest.

Then I thought of other mornings,
With a keen remorse of mind,
When I too had loosed the moorings,
With the Presence left behind.

So I think I know the secret,
Learned from many a troubled way —;
You must seek Him in the morning,
If you want Him through the day!

RALPH SPAULDING CUSHMAN

I find the doing of the
will of God leaves me
no time for disputing
about His plans.

GEORGE MACDONALD

Twice happy is she
   content with her task,
Who still keeps her
   vision beyond.

SARAH K. SMITH

Act is the blossom of thought.

**Look at self and be disappointed.
Look at others and be discouraged.
Look at Christ and be satisfied.**

ASSURANCE

Everywhere
I find the signature,
the autograph of God,
and he will never deny
his own handwriting.
God hath set
his tabernacle
in the dewdrop
as surely as in the sun.
No man can any more
create the smallest flower
than he could create
the greatest world.

JOSEPH PARKER

**The days that make us happy
make us wise.**

JOHN MASEFIELD

AWARENESS

To live content with small means.

To seek elegance rather than luxury.
    and refinement rather than fashion.

To be worthy, not respectable,
    and wealthy, not rich.

To study hard, think quietly,
    talk gently, act frankly.

To listen to stars and birds,
    to babes and sages, with open heart.

To bear all cheerfully, do all bravely,
    await occasion, hurry never.

In a word, to let the spiritual,
    unbidden and unconscious grow up
    through the common.

    This is to be my symphony.

WILLIAM ELLERY CHANNING

Beauty

DIRT FARMER

He finds beauty among these simple
    things;
    The path a plow makes in the rich,
      red loam,
Gay sun-gold in ripe wheat — a plover's
    wings —
    A cow-bell, tinkling as the herd comes
      home.

He treads the soil, with earth-love in
    heart;
    Watches the young crops spring from
      fertile ground,
Loves the warm rain that makes the peach
    buds start,
    Land — and a man — in close
      communion bound!

ARDEN ANTONY

Beauty is an expression of orderliness in
nature as seen in
    the regularity of spaces between waves
      on an ocean,
    ripples on a pond,
    growth marks on a shell, or
    cross marks on a hawk's lost feather, or
    the infinite variations on the hexagonal
      theme
    that we observe in snowflakes.

HAROLD E. KOHN

Beauty is a fairy; sometimes she hides
herself in a flower cup, or under a leaf,
or creeps into old ivy, and plays hide-
and-seek with the sunbeams, or haunts
some ruined spot, or laughs out of a
bright young face.

Sometimes she takes the form of a
white cloud, and goes dancing over the
green fields or the deep blue sea, where
her misty form, marked out in momentary
darkness, looks like the passing of an
angel's wings.

SALA

Over the winter glaciers
I see the summer glow,
And through the wide-piled snowdrift
The warm rosebuds below.

RALPH WALDO EMERSON

A thing of beauty is a joy forever:
Its loveliness increases; it will never
Pass into nothingness; but still will keep
A bower quiet for us, and a sleep
Full of sweet dreams, and health, and
    quiet breathing.

JOHN KEATS

PIED BEAUTY

Glory be to God for dappled things —
*   For skies of couple-colour as a*
*   brinded cow;*
*   For rose-moles all in stipple upon trout*
*   that swim;*
Fresh-firecoal chestnut-falls; finches'
*   wings;*
*   Landscape plotted and pieced — fold,*
*   fallow, and plough;*
And all trades, their gear and tackle
*   and trim.*

All things counter, original, spare,
*   strange;*
*   Whatever is fickle, freckled (who*
*   knows how?)*
*   With swift, slow; sweet, sour;*
*   adazzle, dim;*
He fathers-forth whose beauty is past
*   change:*
*   Praise him.*

GERARD MANLEY HOPKINS

The fountain of beauty is the heart
And every generous thought illustrates
the walls of your chamber.

QUARLES

I shall walk eager still for what Life holds
Although it seems the hard road will
*   not end —*
One never knows the beauty round the
*   bend!*

ANNA BLAKE MEZQUIDA

WHAT IS BEAUTY TO YOU?

Beauty means this to one person, perhaps, and that to the other. And yet when any one of us has seen or heard or read that which to him is beautiful, he has known an emotion which is in every case the same in kind, if not in degree; an emotion precious and uplifting.

A choir boy's voice, a ship in sail, an opening flower, a town at night, the song of the blackbird, a lovely poem, leaf shadows, a child's grace, the starry skies, a cathedral, apple trees in spring, a thoroughbred horse, sheepbells on a hill, a rippling stream, a butterfly, the crescent moon — the thousand sights or sounds or words that evoke in us the thought of beauty — these are the drops of rain that keep the human spirit from death by drought. They are a soothing and a silent refreshment that we perhaps do not think about but which goes on all the time.

It would surprise any of us if we realized how much store we unconsciously set by beauty, and how little savor there would be left in life if it were withdrawn. It is the smile on the earth's face, open to all, and needs but the eyes to see, the mood to understand.

JOHN GALSWORTHY

Who walks the world with soul awake
*   Finds beauty everywhere;*
Though labor be his portion,
*   Though sorrow be his share,*
He looks beyond obscuring clouds,
*   Sure that the light is there!*

FLORENCE EARLE COATES

A drop of rain caught in the leaf-cup of
a lilac, flashes in the sunlight with an
eternal splendor that outshines the glis-
tening jewels of a monarch.

Let us thank the lavish hand that gives
*   world beauty to our eyes,*
And bless the days that saw us young,
*   and years that made us wise.*

JULIA WARD HOWE

The best part of beauty is that which no picture can express.

FRANCIS BACON

BEAUTIFUL THOUGHTS

The thought that is beautiful is the thought to cherish. The word that is beautiful is worthy to endure. The act that is beautiful is eternally and always true and right. Only beware that your appreciation of beauty is just and true; and to that end, I urge you to live intimately with beauty of the highest type, until it has become a part of you, until you have within you that fineness, that order, that calm, which puts you in tune with the finest things of the universe, and which links you with that spirit that is the enduring life of the world.

BERTHA BAILEY

BEAUTY OF LIFE

*Beauty of life has been given to me
In the patterned leaf of every tree;
In the golden gleam of each ray of light
That comes to me from morn till night;
In the radiant color of every flower,
In fashioned garden or country bower;
In the lilting music of wood bird's call,
In the voice of a dear one, best of all.*

*Beauty for eye and ear and hand,
In voice of sea and voice of land;
Roaring of waves with a rhythmic din,
A low refrain from a violin;
Touch of the hand of a dear old friend,
Words of kindness without end;
Love of man and woman and child
Of all God's creatures tame and wild.*

*Love of the life that was given to me,
Love of the life that is to be;
Love of my work and its stern command,
Love of the strength that is in my hand;
O beauty of life that has come to me,
Let me be grateful enough for thee;
Let me live on and say alway,*

"Thank God for the beauty I've found today."

MARY MILES COLRIN

All the beautiful sentiments in the world weigh less than a single lovely action.

JAMES RUSSELL LOWELL

BEAUTY

Beauty is an all-pervading presence. It unfolds to the numberless flowers of the Spring; it waves in the branches of the trees and in the green blades of the grass; it haunts the depths of the earth and the sea, and gleams out in the hues of the shell and the precious stone. And not only these minute objects, but the ocean, the mountains, the clouds, the heavens, the stars, the rising and the setting sun all overflow with beauty. The universe is its temple; and those men who are alive to it cannot lift their eyes without feeling themselves encompassed with it on every side. Now, this beauty is so precious, the enjoyment it gives so refined and pure, so congenial within tenderest and noblest feelings, and so akin to worship, that it is painful to think of the multitude of men as living in the midst of it, and living almost as blind to it as if, instead of this fair earth and glorious sky, they were tenants of a dungeon. An infinite joy is lost to the world by the want of culture of this spiritual endowment. The greatest truths are wronged if not linked with beauty, and they win their way most surely and deeply into the soul when arrayed in this their natural and fit attire.

WILLIAM ELLERY CHANNING

*Beauty seen is never lost,
God's colors all are fast;*

*The glory of this sunset heaven
Into my soul has passed.*

ALFRED, LORD TENNYSON

**Though we travel the world over
To find the beautiful,
We must carry it with us
Or we will find it not.**

RALPH WALDO EMERSON

The most natural beauty in the world is
honesty
and moral truth. — For all beauty is
truth. —
True features make the beauty of the
face;
true proportions, the beauty of
architecture;
true measures, the beauty of harmony
and music.

LORD SHAFTSBURY

ONE OF GOD'S DAYS

*The blue of the sky and the gold of
  the sun
The call of a bird when day is done
These are all precious in each of their
  ways
So beautiful — so wonderful
  Is one of God's days.*

*The trees as they stretch leafy boughs
  up so high
The fleecy white clouds stealing over
  the sky
The sweet scent of roses, the sun's silent
  rays
So lovely — so marvelous
  Is one of God's days.*

*The falling of rain in all of its wonder
God's lovely rainbow glimpsed through
  the haze*

*Ah, beauty unequaled
  Is one of God's days.*

*The sunset's bright glow as its gold rims
  the sky
The twilight's soft hush as night draws
  nigh
These too are a part of His wonderful
  ways
So precious — so perfect
  Is one of God's days.*

JO KEITH

**A woman deserves no credit for her
beauty at sixteen but beauty at sixty was
her own soul's doing.**

GOD'S WORLD

*O world, I cannot hold thee close enough!
  Thy winds, thy wide gray skies!
  Thy mists, that roll and rise!
Thy woods, this autumn day, that ache
  and sag
And all but cry with color! That gaunt
  crag
To crush! To lift the lean of that black
  bluff!
World, world! I cannot get thee close
  enough!*

*Long have I known a glory in it all
  But never knew I this,
  Here such a passion is
As stretcheth me apart. Lord, I do fear
Thou'st made the world too beautiful
  this year.
My soul is all but out of me — let fall
No burning leaf; prithee, let no bird call.*

EDNA ST. VINCENT MILLAY

The Bible

THE BIBLE

We search the world for truth. We cull
The good, the true, the beautiful,
From graven stone and written scroll,
And all old flower-fields of the soul;
And, weary seekers of the best,
We come back laden from our quest,
To find that all the sages said
Is in the Book our mothers read.

JOHN GREENLEAF WHITTIER

The Bible,
   inerrant in statement,
   infallible in authority,
   immeasurable in influence,
   inexhaustive in its adequacy,
   personal in application,
   regenerative in power,
   inspired in totality,
   is the miracle Book of diversity in unity,
   of harmony in infinite complexity —
     the God-breathed Book that travels
      more highways,
      walks more bypaths,
      knocks at more doors,
      and speaks to more people
       in their mother tongue
        than any book the world
        has ever known,
        can ever know,
        will ever know.

ROBERT G. LEE

The Bible does not need to be rewritten, but reread.

A BIT OF THE BOOK

A bit of the Book in the morning,
   To order my onward way.
A bit of the Book in the evening,
   To hallow the end of the day.

MARGARET E. SANGSTER

Know the Bible in your mind,
Keep it in your heart;
Live it in your life,
Share it with the world.

BIBLE SOCIETY RECORD

THE WHOLE BIBLE CONTAINS

The mind of God.
   The state of man.
      The doom of sinners.
         The happiness of believers.
Its doctrines are holy.
   Its precepts are binding.
      Its histories are true.
         Its decisions are immutable.

The Bible needs less defense and more practice.

To know it is to love it.
To love it is to accept it.
To accept it means life eternal.

JOHN 3:16

God — *the greatest lover.*
So loved — *the greatest degree.*
The world — *the greatest company.*
That He gave — *the greatest act.*
His only begotten Son—*the greatest gift.*
That whosoever — *the greatest
   opportunity.*
Believeth — *the greatest simplicity.*
In Him — *the greatest attraction.*
Should not perish — *the greatest
   promise.*
But — *the greatest difference.*
Have — *the greatest certainty.*
Eternal life — *the greatest possession.*

DAVIES

From MY BOOKS AND I

*And should my soul be torn with grief
   Upon my shelf I find
A little volume, torn and thumbed,
   For comfort just designed.
I take my little Bible down
   And read its pages o'er,
And when I part from it I find
   I'm stronger than before.*

EDGAR A. GUEST

●

To what greater inspiration and counsel can we turn than to the imperishable truth to be found in this treasure house, the Bible?

QUEEN ELIZABETH II

THE WORLD'S BIBLE

*Christ has no hands but our hands
   To do His work today;
He has no feet but our feet
   To lead men in His way;
He has no tongue but our tongues
   To tell men how He died;
He has no help but our help
   To bring them to His side.*

*We are the only Bible
   The careless world will read;
We are the sinner's gospel,
   We are the scoffer's creed;
We are the Lord's last message
   Given in deed and word —
What if the line is crooked?
   What if the type is blurred?*

*What if our hands are busy
   With other work than His?
What if our feet are walking
   Where sin's allurement is?
What if our tongues are speaking
   Of things His lips would spurn?
How can we hope to help Him
   Unless from Him we learn?*

ANNIE JOHNSON FLINT

●

The Bible is a mirror in which man sees himself as he is.

Without the Bible man would be in the midst of a sandy desert, surrounded on all sides by a dark and impenetrable prison.

DANIEL WEBSTER

HOW TO USE THE BIBLE

*Read it through.
Pray it in.
Work it out.
Note it down.
Pass it on.*

THE BOOK MORE PRECIOUS THAN GOLD

Though the cover is worn,
And the pages are torn,
*   And though places bear traces of tears,*
Yet more precious than gold ·
Is the Book worn and old,
*   That can shatter and scatter my fears.*

When I prayerfully look
In the precious old Book,
*   As my eyes scan the pages I see*
Many tokens of love
From the Father above,
*   Who is nearest and dearest to me.*

This old Book is my guide,
'Tis a friend by my side,
*   It will lighten and brighten my way;*
And each promise I find
Soothes and gladdens my mind
*   As I read it and heed it today.*

WHERE TO LOOK IN THE BIBLE

When God seems far away,
   read Psalm 139.
When sorrowful,
   read John 14; Psalm 46.
When men fail you,
   read Psalm 27.
When you have sinned,
   read Psalm 51; I John 1.
When you worry,
   read Matthew 6:19-34; Psalm 43.
When in sickness,
   read Psalm 41.
When in danger,
   read Psalm 91.
When you have the blues,
   read Psalm 34.
When you are discouraged,
   read Isaiah 40.
When you are lonely or fearful,
   read Psalm 23.

When you forget your blessings,
   read Psalm 103.
When you want courage,
   read Joshua 1:1-9.
When the world seems bigger than God,
   read Psalm 90.
When you want rest and peace,
   read Matthew 11:25-30.
When you want assurance,
   read Romans 8.
When looking for joy,
   read Colossians 3.
When you leave home to travel,
   read Psalm 121.
When you grow bitter or critical,
   read I Corinthians 13.
When you think of investments,
   read Mark 10:17-31.
Some rules of conduct?
   read Romans 12.
Why not follow Psalm 119:11?

What you bring away from the Bible depends to some extent on what you carry to it.

OLIVER WENDELL HOLMES

The Bible is a window in this prison of hope, through which we look into eternity.

JOHN SULLIVAN DWIGHT

What is home without a Bible?
*   'Tis a home where daily bread*
For the body is provided,
*   But the soul is never fed.*

C. D. MEIGS

Character

There is not a man living, however poor he may be, but has it in his power to leave as a heritage to those that follow him the grandest thing on earth—character.

Good habits are not made on birthdays, nor Christian character at the new year. The workshop of character is everyday life. The uneventful and commonplace hour is where the battle is lost or won.

MALTBIE D. BABCOCK

Faithfully faithful to every trust,
Honestly honest in every deed,
Righteously righteous and justly just;
This is the whole of the good man's
creed.

Build carefully into your character daily what you want to be like in old age, for you are now becoming what you will some day permanently be.

WILLIAM S. DEAL

Good name in man and woman, dear my
lord,
Is the immediate jewel of their souls:
Who steals my purse steals trash;
'tis something, nothing;
'Twas mine, 'tis his, and has been slave
to thousands;
But he that filches from me my good
name
Robs me of that which not enriches him,
And makes me poor indeed.

WILLIAM SHAKESPEARE

Let us not say: Every man is the architect of his own fortune; but let us say: Every man is the architect of his own character.

G. D. BOARDMAN

Character is like a tree and reputation like its shadow. The shadow is what we think of it; the tree is the real thing.

ABRAHAM LINCOLN

Youth and beauty fade;
Character endures forever.

Sow an act and you reap a habit.
Sow a habit and you reap a character.
Sow a character and you reap a destiny.

A man shows what he is
by what he does
with what he has.

You cannot become a power in your community nor achieve enduring success in any worthy undertaking until you become big enough to blame yourself for your own mistakes and reverses.

If I take care of my character,
my reputation will take care of itself.

DWIGHT L. MOODY

●

LORD, HELP ME TO BE A MAN

As I travel along with my fellows,
  Let me help them all that I can.
And may I not mind when a few are
    unkind . . .
  Lord, help me to be a man.

When my dreams lie all fallen and
    shattered,
  And cloudy horizons I scan,
May my faith not die and my head stay
    high . . .
  Make me, dear Lord, a real man!

When I stand in the heat of the battle,
  Though all of my comrades are gone,
Though my arm is tired and my breath
    comes hard . . .
  Help me then, Lord, to keep on!

In all of life's furious struggles,

Let me win every fight that I can;
But when I must feel the enemy's steel . . .
  Lord, help me to be a man!

LON R. WOODRUM

It matters not what you are thought to be,
but what you are.

SYRUS

Like flakes of snow that fall imperceptibly upon the earth, the seeming unimportant events of life succeed one another. As the snowflakes gather, so our habits are formed. No single flake that is added to the pile produces a sensible change. No single action creates, however it may exhibit, a man's character.

But as the tempest hurls the avalanche down the mountain and overwhelms the inhabitant and his habitation, so passion, acting on the elements of mischief which pernicious habits have brought together, may overthrow the edifice of truth and virtue.

JEREMY BENTHAM

●

Hardship makes character.

●

BE THE BEST OF WHATEVER
YOU ARE

If you can't be a pine on the top of the
    hill,
  Be a scrub in the valley — but be
The best little scrub by the side of the rill;
  Be a bush if you can't be a tree.

If you can't be a bush, be a bit of the
    grass,
  Some highway happier make;

18

*If you can't be a muskie, then just be
    a bass —
    But the liveliest bass in the lake!
We can't all be captains, we've got to be
    crew,
    There's something for all of us here,
There's big work to do, and there's lesser
    to do,
    And the task we must do is the near.*

*If you can't be a highway, then just be
    a trail,
    If you can't be the sun, be a star;
It isn't by size that you win or you fail —
    Be the best of whatever you are!*

DOUGLAS MALLOCH

Labor to keep alive in your heart that little spark of celestial fire called conscience.

GEORGE WASHINGTON

You can no more blame your circumstances for your character than you can the mirror for your looks.

**Character is made by many acts;
It may be lost by a single one.**

Comfort & Consolation

Lose who may — I still can say,
Those who win heaven, blest are they!

ROBERT BROWNING

●

THE SHEPHERD'S PSALM

The Lord is my shepherd;
  I shall not want.
He maketh me to lie down in green
    pastures:
  he leadeth me beside the still waters.
He restoreth my soul:
  he leadeth me in the paths of
    righteousness
  for his name's sake.
Yea, though I walk through the valley
  of the shadow of death,
    I will fear no evil:
      for thou art with me;
        thy rod and thy staff they
        comfort me.
Thou preparest a table before me
  in the presence of mine enemies:
    thou anointest my head with oil;
    my cup runneth over.
Surely goodness and mercy shall follow
  me
  all the days of my life:
    and I will dwell in the house of the
      Lord
    for ever.

PSALM 23

It fortifies my soul to know
That, though I perish, Truth is so:
That, howsoe'er I stray and range,
Whate'er I do, Thou dost not change.
I steadier step when I recall
That, if I slip, Thou dost not fall.

ROBERT BROWNING

●

Life is made up, not of great sacrifices or duties, but of little things, in which smiles and kindnesses and small obligations, given habitually, are what win and preserve the heart and secure comfort.

SIR HUMPHREY DAVY

If I should die and leave you here awhile
Be not like others, sore undone, who keep
Long vigil by the silent dust and weep.
For my sake turn again to life and smile,
Nerving thy heart and trembling hand
* to do*
That which will comfort other souls
* than thine:*
Complete these dear unfinished tasks of
* mine*
And I perchance may therein comfort
* you.*

MARY LEE HALL

20

OUT IN THE FIELDS WITH GOD

The little cares that fretted me,
I lost them yesterday,
Among the fields above the sea,
Among the winds at play,
Among the lowing of the herds,
The rustling of the trees,
Among the singing of the birds,
The humming of the bees.

The foolish fears of what might pass
I cast them all away
Among the clover-scented grass
Among the new-mown hay,
Among the rustling of the corn
Where drowsy poppies nod.
Where ill thoughts die and good are
born —
Out in the fields with God!

ELIZABETH BARRETT BROWNING

●

LITTLE VIRTUES

Do not be troubled because you have not great virtues. God made a million spears of grass where He made one tree. The earth is fringed and carpeted, not with forests, but with grasses. Only have enough of little virtues and common fidelities, and you need not mourn because you are neither a hero or a saint.

HENRY WARD BEECHER

CONSOLATION

There is never a day so dreary
But God can make it bright,
And unto the soul that trusts Him,
He giveth songs in the night.
There is never a path so hidden,
But God can lead the way,
If we seek for the Spirit's guidance
And patiently wait and pray.

There is never a cross so heavy
But the nail-scarred hands are there
Outstretched in tender compassion
The burden to help us bear.
There is never a heart so broken,
But the loving Lord can heal.

The heart that was pierced on Calvary
Doth still for his loved ones feel.

There is never a life so darkened,
So hopeless and unblessed,
But may be filled with the light of God
And enter His promised rest.
There is never a sin or sorrow,
There is never a care or loss,
But that we may bring to Jesus
And leave at the foot of the cross.

●

What I aspired to be,
And was not, comforts me.

ROBERT BROWNING

●

The Lord is the portion of mine
    inheritance
and of my cup:
    thou maintainest my lot.
The lines are fallen unto me in pleasant
    places;
yea, I have a goodly heritage.
I will bless the Lord, who hath given me
    counsel:
my reins also instruct me in the night
    seasons.
Therefore my heart is glad,
and my glory rejoiceth:
my flesh also shall rest in hope.

PSALM 16:5, 6, 7, 9

●

SHUT IN

Shut in? Ah, yes, that's so,
As far as getting out may go,
Shut in away from earthly cares,
But not shut out from Him who cares.

Shut in from many a futile quest,
But Christ can be your daily Guest.
He's not shut out by your four walls,
But hears and answers all your calls.

Shut in with God. Oh that should be
Such a wonderful opportunity.
Then after you have done your best,
In God's hands safely leave the rest.

OUR BURDEN BEARER

The little sharp vexations
  And the briars that cut the feet,
Why not take all to the Helper
  Who has never failed us yet?
Tell Him about the heartache,
  And tell Him the longings too,
Tell Him the baffled purpose
  When we scarce know what to do.
Then, leaving all our weakness
  With the One divinely strong,
Forget that we bore the burden
  And carry away the song.

PHILLIPS BROOKS

Oh, the comfort, the inexpressible comfort of feeling safe with a person; having neither to weigh thoughts nor measure words, but to pour them all out, just as they are, chaff and grain together, knowing that a faithful hand will take and sift them, keep what is worth keeping, and then, with the breath of kindness, blow the rest away.

GEORGE ELIOT

SUSTAINMENT

If wind or wave swept all away
  Those things I now hold dear;
If health should flee
  And sickness come,

Or loved ones leave me here;
  Should fortune change
And hardship come,
  If dreams should fade away:

If tests and trials
  should plague me sore,
And troubles haunt my day;
  When all had gone,

This still I know
  Christ's love will never leave us,
For when all things have passed away
  We still can count on Jesus.

WHEN THE STARS ARE GONE

The stars shine over the mountains,
  the stars shine over the sea,
The stars look up to the mighty God,
  the stars look down on me;
The stars shall last for a million years,
  a million years and a day,
But God and I will live and love
  when the stars have passed away.

ROBERT LOUIS STEVENSON

God often comforts us, not by changing the circumstances of our lives, but by changing our attitude towards them.

IT'S NEVER EASY

It's never easy when one must go
  And one must stay — behind;
It's never easy, I know, I know —
  It sears both heart and mind.

It's never easy, but go one must
  When comes the day, the hour;
It's never easy, but if we trust,
  God will give strength and power.

It's never easy! God knows this, too;
  That's why He stays quite near
To help us as we stumble through
  The vale of grief and fear.

It's never easy, but take God's hand
  And pray till night has passed;
Just trust nor ask to understand —
  And peace will come — at last.

PHYLLIS C. MICHAEL

God is BEFORE Me,
  He will be My Guide;
God is BEHIND Me,
  No Ill can Betide;
God is BESIDE Me
  To Comfort and Cheer;
God is AROUND Me,
  So Why Should I Fear?

Confidence & Trust

All the darkness of the world cannot put out the light of one small candle.

●

THE MYSTERIOUS WAY

God moves in a mysterious way
 His wonders to perform;
He plants his footsteps in the sea
 And rides upon the storm.

Deep in unfathomable mines
 Of never-failing skill,
He treasures up his bright designs
 And works his sovereign will.

Ye fearful saints, fresh courage take:
 The clouds ye so much dread
Are big with mercy, and shall break
 In blessings on your head.

Judge not the Lord by feeble sense,
 But trust him for his grace;
Behind a frowning providence
 He hides a smiling face.

His purposes will ripen fast,
 Unfolding every hour;
The bud may have a bitter taste,
 But sweet will be the flower.

Blind unbelief is sure to err,
 And scan his work in vain;
God is his own interpreter,
 And he will make it plain.

WILLIAM COWPER

Certainty is the mark of the common-sense life: gracious uncertainty is the mark of the spiritual life. To be certain of God means that we are uncertain in all our ways, we do not know what a day may bring forth. This is generally said with a sigh of sadness, it should be rather an expression of breathless expectation. We are uncertain of the next step, but we are certain of God. Immediately we abandon to God, and do the duty that lies nearest, He packs our life with surprises all the time. When we become advocates of a creed, something dies; we do not believe God, we only believe our belief about Him. Jesus said, 'Except ye . . . become as little children.' Spiritual life is the life of a child. We are not uncertain of God, but uncertain of what He is going to do next. If we are only certain in our beliefs, we get dignified and severe and have the ban of finality about our views; but when we are rightly related to God, life is full of spontaneous, joyful uncertainty and expectancy.

OSWALD CHAMBERS

I believe in the hands that work;
in the minds that think;
in the hearts that love.

You have the joy
Of this assurance —
The heavenly Father
Will always answer prayer,
And he knows —
Yes,
He knows —
Just
How much
You can bear.

PHYLLIS HALL

●

I BELIEVE IN . . .

I believe in the stuff I am handing out,
in the firm I am working for,
and in my ability to get results.

I believe that honest stuff can be passed
out to honest men by honest methods.

I believe in working not weeping;
in boosting, not knocking;
and in the pleasure of my job.

I believe that a man gets what he
goes after,
that one deed done today is worth two
deeds tomorrow,
and that no man is down
and out until he has lost faith in himself.

I believe in today and the work I am doing;
in tomorrow and the work I hope to do,
and in the sure reward which the future
holds.

I believe in courtesy, in kindness, in
generosity,
in good cheer, in friendship and in honest
competition.
I believe there is something doing,
somewhere for every man to do it.
I believe I'm ready — *right now!*

Casting the whole of your care — all your
anxieties, all your worries, all your concerns, once and for all — on Him; for He
cares for you affectionately, *and* cares
about you watchfully.

I PETER 5:7
THE AMPLIFIED BIBLE

GOD'S WILL

I know not by what methods rare,
But this I know: God answers prayer.
I know not if the blessing sought
Will come in just the guise I thought.
I leave my prayer to Him alone
Whose will is wiser than my own.

ELIZA M. HICKOK

●

I KNOW NOT WHAT THE FUTURE HOLDS

I know not what the future holds,
Of good or ill for me and mine;
I only know that God enfolds
Me in his loving arms divine.

So I shall walk the earth in trust
That He who notes the sparrow's fall
Will help me bear whate'er I must
And lend an ear whene'er I call.

It matters not if dreams dissolve
Like mists beneath the morning sun,
For swiftly as the worlds revolve
So swiftly will life's race be run.

It matters not if hopes depart,
Or life be pressed with toil and care
If love divine shall fill my heart
And all be sanctified with prayer.

Then let me learn submission sweet
In every thought, in each desire,
And humbly lay at his dear feet
A heart aglow with heavenly fire.

●

ONE DAY AT A TIME

One day at a time, with its failures and
fears,
With its hurts and mistakes, with its
weakness and tears,
With its portion of pain and its burden of
care;
One day at a time we must meet and must
bear.
One day at a time — but the day is so
long.

24

And the heart is not brave, and the soul is
  not strong.
O Thou pitiful Christ, be Thou near all
  the way:
Give courage and patience and strength
  for the day.

Swift cometh His answer, so clear and
  so sweet;
"Yea, I will be with thee, thy troubles
  to meet;
I will not forget thee, nor fail thee, nor
  grieve;
I will not forsake thee; I will never leave."
One day at a time, and the day is His day;
He hath numbered its hours, though they
  haste or delay,
His grace is sufficient; we walk not alone;
As the day, so the strength that He giveth
  His own.

ANNIE JOHNSON FLINT

●

TRUST

Courage, Brother do not stumble,
  though thy path be dark as night;
  there's a star to guide the humble.
Trust in God and do the right.

Let the road be rough and dreary,
  and its end far out of sight,
  foot it bravely, strong or weary;
Trust in God and do the right.

Perish policy and cunning,
  perish all that fears the light;
  whether losing, whether winning
Trust in God and do the right.

Trust no party, sect or faction,
  trust no leaders in the fight;
  but in every word and action
Trust in God and do the right.

Simple rule and safest guiding,
  inward peace and inward might;
  star upon our path abiding,
Trust in God and do the right.

Some will hate thee, some will love thee,
  some will flatter, some will slight;
  cease from man, and look above thee,
Trust in God, and do the right.

NORMAN McCLEOD

Every act of trust increases your capacity
for God. Every time I trust Him I have
more room for Him. He dwells within me
in ever richer fullness, occupying room
after room in my life. That is a glorious
assurance, and one that is filled with infinite comfort. Let me repeat it again,
for it is the very music of the soul;
little acts of trust make larger room for
God. In my trifles I can prepare for emer-
gencies. Along a commonplace road
I can get ready for the hill. In the green
pastures and by the still waters I can prepare myself for the valley of the shadow.
For when I reach the hill, the shadow,
the emergency, I shall be God-pos-
sessed: He will dwell in me. And where
He dwells He controls. If He lives in my
life He will direct my powers. It will not
be I that speak, but my Father that
speaketh in me. He will govern my
speech. He will empower my will. He will
enlighten my mind. He will energize and
vitalize my entire life.

J. H. JOWETT

I NEVER SAW A MOOR

  I never saw a moor,
  I never saw the sea;
  Yet know I how the heather looks,
  And what a wave must be.

  I never spoke with God,
  Nor visited in Heaven;
  Yet certain am I of the spot
  As if the chart were given.

EMILY DICKINSON

●

LEARNED TO TRUST

I have no answer for myself or thee,
Save that I learned beside my mother's
  knee:
"All is of God that is, and is to be;
And God is good." Let this suffice us still,
Resting in childlike trust upon His will
Who moves to His great ends unthwarted
  by the ill.

WILLIAM COWPER

THE WEAVER

My life is but a weaving
Between my Lord and me ...
I may not choose the colors;
He knows what they should be;

For He can view the pattern
Upon the upper side,
While I can see it only
On this, the under side.

Sometimes He weaveth sorrow,
Which seemeth strange to me;
But I will trust His judgment
And work on faithfully.

'Tis He who fills the shuttle;
He knows just what is best;
So I shall weave in earnest
And leave with Him the rest.

Not till the loom is silent
And the shuttles cease to fly,
Shall God unroll the canvas,
And explain the reason why
The dark threads are as needful,
In the weaver's skillful hand,
As the threads of gold and silver
In the pattern He has planned.

**Trust in the Lord with thine heart; and
lean not unto thine own understanding.
In all thy ways acknowledge him, and
he shall direct thy paths.**

PROVERBS 3:5, 6

ONLY TO-DAY

Only to-day is mine,
    And that I owe to Thee;
Help me to make it thine;
    As pure as it may be;
Let it see something done,
Let it see something won,
Then at the setting sun
    I'll give it back to thee.

What if I cannot tell
    The cares the day may bring?
I know that I shall dwell

Beneath Thy sheltering wing;
And there the load is light;
And there the dark is bright,
And weakness turns to might,
    And so I trust and sing.

What shall I ask to-day?
    Naught but Thine own sweet will;
The windings of the way
    Lead to thy holy hill;
And whether here or there
Why should I fear or care?
Thy heavens are everywhere,
    And they are o'er me still.

Give me Thyself to-day,
    I dare not walk alone;
Speak to me by the way,
    And "all things are my own";
The treasures of thy grace,
The secret hiding place,
The vision of thy face,
    The shadow of thy throne!

HENRY BURTON

TO THE FUTURE

The past has its store of joys we
    remember,
The future is ours undefiled ...
Let us carry our weight with courage
    of men,
But proceed with the trust of a child.

KATHLEEN PARTRIDGE

HIS PRESENCE

His presence is wealth,
    His grace is a treasure,
His promise is health
    And joy out of measure.
His Word is my rest,
    His Spirit my guide;
In him I am blest
    Whatever betide,

Since Jesus is mine,
    Adieu to all sorrow;
I ne'er shall repine,
    Nor think of to-morrow;

26

The lily so fair,
   And raven so black,
He nurses with care;
   Then how shall I lack?

Each promise is sure
   That shines in his Word,
And tells me, though poor,
   I'm rich in my Lord.
Hence, sorrow and fear!
   Since Jesus is nigh.
I'll dry up each tear
   And stifle each sigh.

PATRICK BRONTE

●

I ONLY KNOW HE DID

I stood beneath a mighty oak
   And wondered at its size
How from an acorn it could grow
   I never could surmise —
   I only know it did.

How God could make the heavens,
   The water and the land,
The animals and vegetables,
   I cannot understand —
   I only know He did.

I do not know how God could come
   And cleanse my heart from sin
Through Jesus Christ, His blessed Son,
   Whose love abides within —
   I only know He did.

●

I can see how it might be possible
for a man
to look down upon the earth
and be an atheist,
but I cannot conceive how
he could look up into the heavens
and say there is no God.

ABRAHAM LINCOLN

Contemplation

TIME IS

Too Slow for those who Wait,
Too Swift for those who Fear,
Too Long for those who Grieve,
Too Short for those who Rejoice;
  But for those who Love,
  Time is eternity.

HENRY VAN DYKE

It is only in contemplative moments that life is truly vital.

GEORGE SANTAYANA

ANOTHER SPRING

If I might see another Spring
  I'd not plant summer flowers and wait:
I'd have my crocuses at once,
My leafless pink mezereons,
  My chill-veined snowdrops, choicer yet
  My white or azure violet,
Leaf-nested primrose; anything
  To blow at once not late.

If I might see another Spring
I'd listen to the daylight birds
That build their nests and pair and sing,
Nor wait for mateless nightingale;
  I'd listen to the lusty herds,
  The ewes with lambs as white as snow,
I'd find out music in the hail
  And all the winds that blow.

If I might see another Spring —
  O stinging comment on my past
That all my past results in "if" —
  If I might see another Spring
I'd laugh today, today is brief;
  I would not wait for anything:
  I'd use today that cannot last,
  Be glad today and sing.

CHRISTINA ROSSETTI

That I am a man,
  this I share with other men.
That I see and hear and
  that I eat and drink
  is what all animals do likewise.
But that I am I is only mine
  and belongs to me
  and to nobody else;
  to no other man,
  not to an angel, nor to God —
  except inasmuch
  as I am one with Him.

JOHANNES ECKHART

28

I SAW GOD WASH THE WORLD

I saw God wash the world last night
   With His sweet showers on high,
And when morning came, I saw
   Him hang it out to dry.

He washed each tiny blade of grass
   And every trembling tree,
He flung His showers against the hill,
   And swept the billowing sea.

The white rose is a cleaner white,
   The red rose is more red,
Since God washed every fragrant face
   And put them all to bed.

There's not a bird, there's not a bee
   That wings along the way
But is a cleaner bird and bee
   Than it was yesterday.

I saw God wash the world last night.
   Ah, would He had washed me
As clean of all my dust and dirt
   As that old white birch tree.

WILLIAM L. STIDGER

●

I am a part of all that I have met:
Yet all experience is an arch where thro'
Gleams that untravell'd world, whose
   margin fades
For ever and for ever when I move.
How dull it is to pause, to make an end,
To rust unburnish'd, not to shine in use!
As tho' to breathe were life. Life piled
   on life
Were all too little, and of one to me
Little remains: . . . and vile it were
For some three suns to store and hoard
   myself,
And this grey spirit yearning in desire
To follow knowledge like a sinking star,
Beyond the utmost bound of human
   thought.
Tho' much is taken, much abides; and tho'
We are not now that strength which in
   old days
Moved earth and heaven; that which we
   are, we are;
One equal temper of heroic hearts,

Made weak by time and fate, but strong
   in will
To strive, to seek, to find, and not to yield.
ALFRED, LORD TENNYSON

●

AFTERGLOW

The day died in a flood of crimson flame
That bathed the hills in beauty richly
   rare,
All the world bowed down
And I, too, came to stand and wonder in
   worship there.

Then a small voice seemed to question
   me,
When death shall come and I must gladly
   go,
Will there be someone to love my
   memory?
Oh, Lord, shall I, too, leave an afterglow?

●

THE FOUNTAIN

Into the sunshine,
   Full of the light,
Leaping and flashing
   Morning and night.

Into the moonlight,
   Whiter than snow,
Waving so flower-like
   When the winds blow,

Into the starlight
   Rushing in spray,
Happy at midnight
   Happy by day;

Even in motion
   Blithesome and cheery,
Still climbing heavenward,
   Never aweary;

Glorious fountain,
   Let my heart be
Fresh, changeful, constant,
   Upward, like thee!

JAMES RUSSELL LOWELL

No man has a right to lead such a life of contemplation as to forget in his own ease the service due to his neighbor; nor has any man a right to be so immersed in active life as to neglect the contemplation of God.

ST. AUGUSTINE

THE MIND IS AN ENCHANTING THING

is an enchanted thing
   like the glaze on a
katydid-wing
      subdivided by sun
      till the nettings are legion.
Like Gieseking playing Scarlatti;
like the apteryx-awl
   as a beak, or the
kiwi's rain-shawl
      of haired feathers, the mind
      feeling its way as though blind,
walks along with its eyes on the ground.

It has memory's ear
   that can hear without
having to hear.
      Like the gyroscope's fall,
      truly unequivocal
because trued by regnant certainty,

it is a power of
   strong enchantment. It
is like the dove-
      neck animated by
      sun; it is memory's eye;
it's conscientious inconsistency.

It tears off the veil; tears
   the temptation, the
mist the heart wears,
      from its eyes, — if the heart
      has a face; it takes apart
dejection. It's fire in the dove-neck's

iridescence, in the
   inconsistencies
of Scarlatti.
      Unconfusion submits
      its confusion to proof; it's
not a Herod's oath that cannot change.

MARIANNE MOORE

THE SHEPHERD BOY'S SONG

He that is down needs fear no fall,
   He that is low, no pride;
He that is humble ever shall
   Have God to be his guide.

I am content with what I have,
   Little be it, or much:
And, Lord, contentment still I crave,
   Because Thou savest such.

Fulness to such a burden is
   That go on pilgrimage;
Here little, and hereafter bliss,
   Is best from age to age.

JOHN BUNYAN

THE CRAZY WOMAN

I shall not sing a May song.
A May song should be gay.
I'll wait until November
And sing a song of gray.

I'll wait until November.
That is the time for me.
I'll go out in the frosty dark
And sing most terribly.

And all the little people
Will stare at me and say,
"That is the Crazy Woman
Who would not sing in May."

GWENDOLYN BROOKS

TIME

When as a child I laughed and wept,
   Time Crept.
When as a youth I dreamed and talked,
   Time Walked.
When I became a full-grown man,
   Time Ran.
When older still I daily grew,
   Time Flew.
Soon I shall find in traveling on,
   Time Gone.
O, Christ, wilt Thou have saved me then?
   Amen!

HERBERT J. MILES

OF A SMALL DAUGHTER WALKING OUTDOORS

Easy, wind!
Go softly here!
She is small
And very dear.

She is young
And cannot say
Words to chase
The wind away.

She is new
To walking, so
Wind, be kind
And gently blow

On her ruffled head,
On grass and clover.
Easy, wind . . .
She'll tumble over!

FRANCES M. FROST

Leisure is a beautiful garment but it will not do for constant wear.

THE HEART OF A CHILD

The heart of a child is a scroll,
   A page that is lovely and white;
And to it as fleeting years roll,
   Come hands with a story to write.
Be ever so careful, O hand;
   Write thou with a sanctified pen;
Thy story shall live in the land
   For years in the doings of men.
It shall echo in circles of light,
   Or lead to the death of a soul.
Give here but a message of right,
   For the heart of a child is a scroll.

●

LIVING

To live with saints in heaven
   Will be eternal glory;
But to live with them on earth
   Is quite a different story!

A LITTLE FELLOW FOLLOWS ME

A careful man I ought to be,
A little fellow follows me,
I do not dare to go astray
For fear he'll go the selfsame way.

Not once can I escape his eyes;
Whate'er he sees me do he tries.
Like me says he's going to be
That little chap who follows me.

He thinks that I am good and fine;
Believes in every word of mine.
The base in me he must not see
That little chap who follows me.

I must remember as I go,
Thro' summer sun and winter snow,
I'm building for the years to be
That little chap who follows me.

●

My meditation of him shall be sweet:
I will be glad in the Lord.

PSALM 104:34

IF MUSIC BE THE FOOD OF LOVE

If music be the food of love, play on;
Give me excess of it, that, surfeiting,
The appetite may sicken, and so die.
That strain again! it had a dying fall:
O! it came o'er my ear like the sweet
      sound
That breathes upon a bank of violets,
Stealing and giving odour. Enough! no
      more:
'Tis not so sweet now as it was before.
O spirit of love! how quick and fresh art
      thou,
That, notwithstanding thy capacity
Receiveth as the sea, nought enters there,
Of what validity and pitch soe'er,
But falls into abatement and low price,
Even in a minute: so full of shapes is
      fancy.
That it alone is high fantastical.

WILLIAM SHAKESPEARE

31

From CONVERSATION

It happened on a solemn eventide,
Soon after He who was our Surety died;
Two bosom friends, each pensively
    inclined,
The scene of all those sorrows left
    behind;
Sought their own village, busied as they
    went,
In musings worthy of the great event:
They spake of Him they loved, of Him
    whose life
Tho' blameless had incurred perpetual
    strife:
They thought Him, and they justly
    thought Him One
Sent to do more than He appeared to have
    done;
To exalt their nation and to lift them high
Above all else, and wondered He should
    die.
Ere yet they brought their journey to its
    end
A Stranger joined them, courteous as a
    friend,
And asked them, with a kind, engaging
    air,
What their affliction was, and begged a
    share.
Informed, He gathered up the broken
    thread,
And, truth and wisdom gracing all He
    said,
Explained, illustrated, and searched so
    well
The tender theme on which they chose to
    dwell,
That, reaching home, they said, "The
    night is near,
We must not now be parted, sojourn
    here."
The humble Stranger soon became their
    Guest,
And, made so welcome at their simple
    feast,
He blest the bread, but vanished at the
    word,
And left them both exclaiming, " 'Twas
    the Lord!
Did not our hearts feel all He deigned
    to say!
Did not they burn within us by the way?"

WILLIAM COWPER

●

He tried to be somebody.
by trying to be like everybody,
which makes him a nobody.

Death, Heaven, & Immortality

Each departed friend is a magnet that attracts us to the next world.

JEAN PAUL RICHTER

●

THE OTHER SIDE

This isn't death — it's glory!
It is not dark — it's light!
It isn't stumbling, groping,
Or even faith — it's sight!
This isn't grief — it's having
My last tear wiped away;
It's sunrise — it's the morning
Of my eternal day!

This isn't even praying —
It's speaking face to face;
Listening and glimpsing
The wonders of His grace.
This is the end of pleading
For strength to bear my pain;
Not even pain's dark mem'ry
Will ever live again.

How did I bear the earth-life
Before I came up higher,
Before my soul was granted
Its ev'ry deep desire,
Before I knew this rapture
Of meeting face to face
The One who sought me, saved me,
And kept me by His grace!

MARTHA SNELL NICHOLSON

If God hath made this world so fair,
Where sin and death abound,
How beautiful, beyond compare,
Will paradise be found.

JAMES MONTGOMERY

●

THE CHARIOT

Because I could not stop for Death,
He kindly stopped for me;
The carriage held but just ourselves
And Immortality.

We slowly drove, he knew no haste,
And I had put away
My labor, and my leisure too,
For his civility.

We passed the school where children
played,
Their lessons scarcely done;
We passed the fields of grazing grain,
We passed the setting sun.

We paused before a house that seemed
A swelling of the ground;
The roof was scarcely visible,
The cornice but a mound.

Since then 'tis centuries; but each
Feels shorter than the day
I first surmised the horses' heads
Were toward eternity.

EMILY DICKINSON

33

THE HOME-GOING

Let it be light . . .
As the ripe release of an autumn leaf
Tired of clinging . . .
As a bird's swift flight
From the quivering bough
. . . Singing!

HELGA SKOGSBERGH

CROSSING THE BAR

Sunset and evening star,
*   And one clear call for me!*
And may there be no moaning of the bar,
*   When I put out to sea,*

But such a tide as moving seems asleep,
*   Too full for sound and foam,*
When that which drew from out the
*   boundless deep*
*   Turns again home.*

Twilight and evening bell,
*   And after that the dark!*
And may there be no sadness of farewell,
*   When I embark;*

For tho' from out our bourne of Time
*   and Place*
*   The flood may bear me far,*
I hope to see my Pilot face to face
*   When I have crossed the bar.*

ALFRED, LORD TENNYSON

WHAT IS DYING?

I am standing upon the seashore. A ship at my side spreads her white sails to the morning breeze and starts for the blue ocean.

She is an object of beauty and strength, and I stand and watch her until at length she hangs like a speck of white cloud just where the sea and sky come down to mingle with each other. Then, someone at my side says, "There, she's gone."

Gone where? Gone from my sight — that is all. She is just as large in mast and hull and spar as she was when she left my side, and just as able to bear her load of living freight to the place of destination.

Her diminished size is in me, not in her: and just at the moment when someone at my side says, "There, she's gone," there are other eyes watching her coming, and other voices ready to take up the glad shout, "There she comes!"

And that is dying.

HOME AT LAST

To an open house in the evening,
Home shall men come,
To an older place than Eden,
And a taller town than Rome.
To the end of the way of the wandering
*   star,*
To the things that cannot be and are,
To the place where God was homeless,
And all men are at home.

GILBERT KEITH CHESTERTON

Put in the plow
And plant the great hereafter in the now.

ROBERT BROWNING

STEPPING ASHORE

Oh! think to step ashore,
*   And find it Heaven;*
To clasp a hand outstretched,
*   And find it God's hand!*
To breathe new air,
*   And that, celestial air;*
To feel refreshed,
*   And find it immortality;*
Ah, think to step from storm and stress
*   To one unbroken calm:*
To awake and find it Home.

ROBERT E. SELLE

34

How shall I express my thought of it?
It is not mere existence, however
    prolonged
    and free from annoyance.
It is not the pleasures
    of the senses, however vivid.
It is not peace.
It is not happiness.
It is not joy.
But it is all these combined into one
    condition
    of spiritual perfection —
c..e emotion of indescribable rapture —
the peace after the storm has gone by,
the soft repose after the grief is over,
the joy of victory when the conflict is
    ended.

BENJAMIN H. HILL

SONG

When I am dead, my dearest,
    Sing no sad songs for me;
Plant thou no roses at my head,
    Nor shady cypress tree:
Be the green grass above me
    With showers and dewdrops wet;
And if thou wilt, remember,
    And if thou wilt, forget.

I shall not see the shadows,
    I shall not feel the rain;
I shall not hear the nightingale
    Sing on, as if in pain;
And dreaming through the twilight
    That doth not rise nor set,
Haply I may remember,
    And haply may forget.

CHRISTINA ROSSETTI

IN THE MORNING

We shall gather in the morning,
    When the night has passed away;
Gather Home to be with Jesus
    In the Land of fadeless day.

There amid the realms of glory,
    When the trials of life are o'er,

With our blessed Lord and Saviour,
    We shall dwell forever more.

He is waiting to receive us,
    For He died on Calvary,
That with Him in Heaven's glory,
    We may dwell eternally.

And at last when sin's dark traces
    Are forever washed away,
We shall see the dear home faces,
    And rejoice thro' endless day.

They have gone, but not forever —
    'Tis the promise of His love;
We shall see them in the morning
    When we gather Home above.

OSWALD J. SMITH

CARRIED BY ANGELS

"Carried by angels" — it is all we know
Of how they go;
We heard it long ago.
It is enough; they are not lonely there,
Lost nestlings blown about in fields of air.
The angels carry them; the way, they
    know.
Our kind Lord told us so.

AMY CARMICHAEL

INSCRIPTION

**To live in hearts
We leave behind
Is not to die.**

Build thee more stately mansions,
    O my soul!
As the swift seasons roll!
Leave thy low-vaulted past!
Let each temple, nobler than the last,
Shut thee from heaven with a dome more
    vast,
Till thou at length art free,
Leaving thine outworn shell by life's
    unresting sea!

OLIVER WENDELL HOLMES

L'ENVOI

When earth's last picture is painted, and
    the tubes are twisted and dried,
When the oldest colors have faded,
    and the youngest critic has died,
We shall rest, and — faith, we shall
    need it, — lie down for an aeon or two,
Till the Master of all Good Workmen
    shall set us to work anew!

And those that were good shall be happy:
    they shall sit in a golden chair;
They shall splash at a ten-league canvas
    with brushes of comets' hair;
They shall find real saints to draw from—
    Magdalen, Peter, and Paul;
They shall work for an age at a sitting,
    and never be tired at all!

And only the Master shall praise us,
    and only the Master shall blame;
And no one shall work for money,
    and no one shall work for fame;
But each for the joy of the working,
    and each in his separate star
Shall draw the Thing as he sees It
    for the God of the Things as They are!

RUDYARD KIPLING

●

There is a land of pure delight,
    Where saints immortal reign;
Infinite day excludes the night,
    And pleasures banish pain.

ISAAC WATTS

●

THINGS THAT NEVER DIE

The pure, the bright, the beautiful,
    That stirred our hearts in youth,
The impulses to wordless prayer,
    The dreams of love and truth;
The longings after something lost,
    The spirit's yearning cry,
The strivings after better hopes —
    These things can never die.

The timid hand stretched forth to aid
    A brother in his need,
A kindly word in grief's dark hour
    That proves a friend indeed;

The plea for mercy softly breathed,
    When justice threatens nigh,
The sorrow of a contrite heart —
    These things shall never die.

The cruel and bitter word,
    That wounded as it fell;
The chilling want of sympathy
    We feel, but never tell;
The hard repulse that chills the heart,
    Whose hopes were bounding high,
In an unfading record kept —
    These things shall never die.

Let nothing pass, for every hand
    Must find some work to do;
Lose not a chance to waken love —
    Be firm, and just, and true:
So shall a light that cannot fade
    Beam on thee from on high,
And angel voices say to thee —
    These things shall never die.

CHARLES DICKENS

●

IT IS NOT DEATH

It is not death to die —
    To leave this weary road
And midst the brotherhood on high
    To be at home with God.

It is not death to close
    The eye long dimmed with tears
And wake in glorious repose
    To spend eternal years.

It is not death to fling
    Aside this sinful dust
And rise on strong exulting wing
    To live among the just.

Jesus, Thou Prince of Life,
    Thy chosen cannot die;
Like Thee, they conquer in the strife
    To reign with Thee on high.

●

A little girl taking an evening walk with her father looked up at the stars and exclaimed, "Oh, Daddy, if the wrong side of heaven is so beautiful what must the right side be!"

WHEN LIFE'S DAY CLOSES

When on my day the evening shadows
  fall,
  I will go down to where a quiet river
    flows
Into a sea from whence no man returns;
  And there embark for lands where life
    immortal grows.

THOMAS TIPLADY

●

What matter will it be, O mortal man,
  when thou art dying,
Whether upon a throne or on the bare
  earth thou art lying?

THE PERSIAN

●

BEYOND THE REACH OF TIME

I wrote my name upon the sand
And trusted it would stand for aye;
But soon the refluent sea
Had washed my feeble lines away.

I carved my name upon the wood,
And after years, returned again;
I missed the shadow of the tree
That stretched of old upon the plain.

To solid marble next my name
I gave as a perpetual trust;
An earthquake rent it to its base,
And now it lies o'erlaid with dust.

All these have failed. In wiser mood
I turn and ask myself, what then?
If I would have my name endure,
I'll write it on the hearts of men.

In characters of living light,
From kindly words and actions wrought;
And these, beyond the reach of time,
Shall live immortal as my thought.

HORATIO ALGER

●

Our Creator would never have made such
lovely days, and have given us the deep
hearts to enjoy them, above and beyond
all thought, unless we were meant to be
immortal.

NATHANIEL HAWTHORNE

Discovery & Fulfillment

When skill and love work together, expect a masterpiece.

•

LITTLE THINGS

Little drops of water,
  Little grains of sand,
Make the mighty ocean
  And the pleasant land.

So the little moments,
  Humble though they be,
Make the mighty ages
  Of eternity.

So our little errors
  Lead the soul away
From the path of virtue
  Far in sin to stray.

Little deeds of kindness
  Little words of love,
Help make earth happy
  Like the heaven above.

JULIA CARNEY

•

EYES FOR INVISIBLES

I have walked with people whose eyes are full of light but who see nothing in sea or sky, nothing in city streets, nothing in books. It were far better to sail forever in the night of blindness with sense, and feeling, and mind, than to be content with the mere act of seeing. The only lightless dark is the night of darkness in ignorance and insensibility.

HELEN KELLER

I have found . . .
    that those who love a deer, a dog, a bird
        and flowers . . .
    are usually thoughtful of the larger
        needs that may be ours . . .
    . . . Who for God's creatures small will
        plan . . .
    will seldom wrong his fellow man.

•

DISCOVERY

Today a man discovered gold and fame;
Another flew the stormy seas;
Another saw an unnamed world aflame;
One found the germ of a disease.
But what high fates my paths attend:
For I — today I found a friend.

HELEN BAKER PARKER

38

When I want to discover something, I begin by reading up everything that has been done along the line in the past. I see what has been accomplished at great labor and expense in the past. I gather the data of many thousands of experiments as a starting point, and then I make several thousand more.

THOMAS A. EDISON

THE ARROW AND THE SONG

I shot an arrow into the air,
It fell to earth, I knew not where;
For, so swiftly it flew, the sight
Could not follow it in its flight.

I breathed a song into the air,
It fell to earth, I knew not where;
For who has sight so keen and strong,
That it can follow the flight of song?

Long, long afterward, in an oak
I found the arrow, still unbroke;
And the song, from beginning to end,
I found again in the heart of a friend.

HENRY W. LONGFELLOW

AND THEN SOME . . .

A retired business executive was once asked the secret of his success. He replied that it could be summed up in three words: "and then some."

"I discovered at an early age," he said, "that most of the differences between average people and top people could be explained in three words. The top people did what was expected of them — and then some.

"They were thoughtful of others, they were considerate and kind — and then some.

"They were good friends to their friends — and then some.

"They could be counted on in an emergency — and then some.

"And so it is when we put our trust in God's goodness. He returns our love — and then some."

STEP BY STEP

He does not lead me year by year;
Nor even day by day,
But step by step my path unfolds;
My Lord directs my way.
Tomorrow's plans I do not know,
I only know this minute;
But He will say, "This is the way,
By faith now walk ye in it."
And I am glad that this is so,
Today's enough to bear;
And when tomorrow comes, His grace
Shall far exceed its care.
What need to worry then, or fret?
The God who gave His Son
Holds all my moments in His hand
And gives them, one by one.

BARBARA RYBERG

It is not when I am going to meet Him, but when I am just turning away and leaving Him, that I discover that God is.

HENRY DAVID THOREAU

THE CURE

We mutter and sputter,
We fume and we spurt;
We mumble and grumble,
Our feelings get hurt;
We can't understand things,
Our vision grows dim —
When all that we need
Is a moment with Him!

I FOUND GOD

Sophisticated, worldly-wise,
I searched for God and found Him not,
Until one day, the world forgot,
I found Him in my baby's eyes.

MARY AFTON THACKER

I MET THE MASTER

I had walked life's way with an easy
    tread,
Had followed where comforts and
    pleasures led,
Until one day in a quiet place
I met the Master face to face.

With station and rank and wealth for my
    goal,
Much thought for my body but none for
    my soul,
I had entered to win in life's mad race,
When I met the Master face to face.

I met Him and knew Him and blushed
    to see
That His eyes full of sorrow were fixed
    on me,
And I faltered and fell at His feet that day
While my castles melted and vanished
    away.

Melted and vanished, and in their place
Naught else did I see but the Master's
    face;
And I cried aloud, 'Oh, make me meet
To follow the steps of Thy wounded feet.'

My thought is now for the souls of men;
I have lost my life to find it again,
E'er since one day in a quiet place
I met the Master face to face.

Know you what it is to be a child? . . . It is to believe in love, to believe in loveliness, to believe in beliefs; it is to be so little that the elves can reach to whisper in your ear; it is to turn pumpkins into coaches, and mice into horses, lowness into loftiness, and nothing into everything, for each child has its fairy godmother in its own soul.

FRANCIS THOMPSON

LIGHT IN THE CELL

"And a light shined in the cell,"
    And there was not any wall,
    And there was no dark at all,
Only Thou, Immanuel.

Light of Love shined in the cell,
    Turned to gold the iron bars,
    Opened windows to the stars,
Peace stood there as sentinel.

Dearest Lord, how can it be
    That Thou art so kind to me?
    Love is shining in my cell,
Jesus, my Immanuel.

AMY CARMICHAEL

When we find Christ
    We find everything;
When Christ finds us,
    He finds nothing.

Keep thou Thy Dreams! The tissue of all wings is woven first of them. Dreams are such precious and imperishable things.

We must not hope to be mowers,
And to gather the ripe gold ears,
Unless we have first been sowers
And watered the furrows with tears.

It is not just as we take it,
This mystical world of ours,
Life's field will yield as we make it
A harvest of thorns or of flowers.

JOHANN WOLFGANG VON GOETHE

Dreams & Aspirations

MY CREED

I would be true, for there are those who
    trust me;
I would be pure, for there are those who
    care;
I would be strong, for there is much to
    suffer;
I would be brave, for there is much to
    dare.
I would be friend of all — the foe, the
    friendless;
I would be giving, and forget the gift,
I would be humble, for I know my
    weakness,
I would look up, and love, and laugh and
    lift.

HOWARD ARNOLD WALTER

•

SOLITARY DREAMERS

The dreamers are the saviors of the world. As the visible world is sustained by the invisible, so men, through all their trials and sins and sordid vocations, are nourished by the beautiful visions of their solitary dreamers. Humanity cannot forget its dreamers; it cannot let their ideals fade and die; it lives in them; it knows them as the realities which it shall one day see and know.

JAMES ALLEN

I love my humble fireside
Where I can sit and dream.

I see strange pictures in the flames
And memories bring tears;
I live again the yesterdays
And joys of other years.

And then I hear loved voices low,
So happy, cheerful and gay;
These dreams remain so dear to me
When the firelight dies away.

I love my humble fireside
Where I can sit and dream.

GRACE M. WALKER

•

Greatly begin! though thou have time
But for a line, be that sublime —
Not failure, but low aim is crime.

JAMES RUSSELL LOWELL

•

THE DREAM

Ah, great it is to believe the dream
As we stand in youth by the starry
    stream;
But a greater thing is to fight life through,
And say at the end, "The dream is true!"

EDWIN MARKHAM

41

AIM FOR A STAR

Aim for a star!
  Never be satisfied
With a life that is less
  than the best,
Failure lies only
  in not having tried —
In keeping the soul
  suppressed.

Aim for a star!
  Look up and away,
And follow its
  beckoning beam,
Make each Tomorrow
  a better Today —
And don't be afraid
  to dream.

Aim for a star, and keep
  your sights high!
With a heartful of faith
  within,
Your feet on the ground,
  and your eyes on the sky,
Some day you are bound
  to win!

HELEN LOWRIE MARSHALL

●

WINGS

Be like the bird
That, pausing in her flight
Awhile on boughs too slight,
  Feels them give way
Beneath her and yet sings,
Knowing that she hath wings.

VICTOR HUGO

●

EACH DAY

Wouldst shape a noble life? Then cast
No backward glance toward the past,
And though somewhat be lost and gone,
Yet do thou act as one new born;
What each day needs, that shalt thou ask,
Each day will set its proper task.

JOHANN WOLFGANG VON GOETHE

HOLD FAST YOUR DREAMS

Hold fast your dreams!
Within your heart
Keep one, still, secret spot
Where dreams may go,
And sheltered so,
May thrive and grow —
Where doubt and fear are not.
O, keep a place apart,
Within your heart,
For little dreams to go!

LOUISE DRISCOLL

●

Lord, let me not be too content
With life in trifling service spent —
  Make me aspire!
When days with petty cares are filled
Let me with fleeting thoughts be thrilled
  Of something higher!

Help me to long for mental grace
To struggle with the commonplace
  I daily find.
May little deeds not bring to fruit
A crop of little thoughts to suit
  A shriveled mind.

●

Life is too short to waste . . .
  'Twill soon be dark;
Up! mind thine own aim, and
  God speed the mark!

RALPH WALDO EMERSON

●

MY TASK

To love some one more dearly ev'ry day,
To help a wandering child to find his way,
To ponder o'er a noble thought, and pray,
  And smile when evening falls.

To follow truth as blind men long for
  light,
To do my best from dawn of day till night,
To keep my heart fit for His holy sight
  And answer when He calls.

MAUDE LOUISE RAY

BROKEN DREAMS

I do not hold my broken dreams
And cling to them and weep,
Beseeching God to mend them now.
I give them back to Him
From Whom they came, . . .
And a secret joy lightens all my days,
And long sweet nights I dream
Of how it fares with them in Heaven.

I fill my little day
With little tasks,
I give the best I have
To Him who asks.
Years that are full
More quickly pass.

Some day the stars will shine again,
The flowers bloom,
And all the winds blow sweet.
Some day,
In Heaven's golden dawning,
Will tender angels give them back to me,
My broken dreams — unbroken then,
All loveliness,
Complete.

MARTHA SNELL NICHOLSON

•

FOUR THINGS

Four things a man must learn to do
If he would make his record true:
To think without confusion clearly;
To love his fellowmen sincerely;
To act from honest motives purely;
To trust in God and Heaven securely.

HENRY VAN DYKE

•

YOU'RE MY GUEST IN THOUGHT

Once a day, and sometimes more,
You knock upon my daydream door,
And I say warmly, "Come right in,
I'm glad you're here with me again!"
Then we sit down and have a chat,
Recalling this, discussing that,
Until some task that I must do
Forces me away from you —

Reluctantly I say good-bye,
Smiling with a little sigh,
For though my daydreams bring you near
I wish that you were really here —
But what reality can't change
My dreams and wishes can arrange —
And through my wishing you'll be
    brought
To me each day, a guest in thought.

MARY DAWSON HUGHES

**Ah, but a man's reach should exceed his
    grasp,
Or what's heaven for?**

ROBERT BROWNING

One broken dream is not the end of
    dreaming;
One shattered hope is not the end of all—
Beyond the storm and tempests stars are
    gleaming —
Still build your castles, though your
    castles fall.

•

With every rising of the sun
Think of your life as just begun.

•

YE STARS

Ye stars! which are the poetry of heaven!
If in your bright leaves we would read the
    fate
Of men and empires, — 'tis to be forgiven,
That in our aspirations to be great,
Our destinies o'erleap their mortal state,
They claim a kindred with you; for ye are
A beauty and a mystery, and create
In us such love and reverence from afar,
That fortune, fame, power, life, have
    named themselves a star.

LORD BYRON

I dare not ask a kiss;
I dare not beg a smile;
Lest having that, or this,
I might grow proud the while.

No, no, the utmost share
Of my desire, shall be
Only to kiss that air,
That lately kissed thee.

ROBERT HERRICK

●

A dream has the lift of a lever,
A dream has the power to drive,
They who have known no dreaming
Have never been alive.

MARTHA SNELL NICHOLSON

●

GREATNESS

What makes a man great? Is it houses
    and lands?
    Is it argosies dropping their wealth at
        his feet?
    Is it multitudes shouting his name in
        the street?
Is it power of brain? Is it skill of hand?
Is it writing a book? Is it guiding the
    State?
Nay, nay, none of these can make a man
    great.

The crystal burns cold with its beautiful
    fire,
    And is what it is; it can never be more;
    The acorn, with something wrapped
        warm at the core,
In quietness says, "to the oak I aspire."
That something in seed and in tree is the
    same —
What makes a man great is his greatness
    of aim.

What is greatness of aim? Your purpose
    to trim
    For bringing the world to obey your
        behest?
    O no, it is seeking God's perfect and
        best,
Making something the same both in you
    and in him.

Love what he loves, and, child of the sod,
Already you share in the greatness of
    God.

SAMUEL V. COLE

**The supreme desire of my life is to give
myself in reckless abandon to Christ.**

ED McCULLY

BETTER TO CLIMB

Give me a man with an aim,
Whatever that aim may be,
Whether it's wealth, or whether it's fame,
It matters not to me.
Let him walk in the path of right,
And keep his aim in sight,
And work and pray in faith alway,
With his eye on the glittering height.

Give me a man who says,
"I will do something well,
And make the fleeting days
A story of labor tell."
Though the aim he has be small,
It is better than none at all;
With something to do the whole year
    through
He will not stumble or fall.

Give me a man whose heart
Is filled with ambition's fire;
Who sets his mark in the start,
And keeps moving it higher and higher.
Better to die in the strife,
The hands with labor rife,
Than to glide with the stream in an idle
    dream,
And lead a purposeless life.

Better to strive and climb
And never reach the goal,
Than to drift along with time
An aimless, worthless soul.
Aye, better to climb and fall,
Or sow, though the yield be small,
Than to throw away, day after day,
And never to strive at all.

44

Education & Learning

Perhaps the most valuable of all education is the ability to make yourself do the thing you have to do when it ought to be done, whether you like it or not.

BUILDING A TEMPLE

A builder builded a temple,
He wrought it with grace and skill:
Pillars and groins and arches
All fashioned to work his will.
Men said, as they saw its beauty,
"It shall never know decay,
Great is thy skill, O builder,
Thy fame shall endure for aye."

A teacher builded a temple
With loving and infinite care,
Planning each arch with patience,
Laying each stone with prayer.
None praised her unceasing efforts,
None knew of her wondrous plan;
For the temple the teacher builded
Was unseen by the eyes of man.

Gone is the builder's temple,
Crumbled into the dust;
Low lies each stately pillar,
Food for consuming rust.
But the temple the teacher builded
Will last while the ages roll,
For that beautiful unseen temple
Is a child's immortal soul.

THOMAS CURTIS CLARK

Let us learn like a bird for a moment to
   take
Sweet rest on a branch that is ready to
   break;
She feels the branch tremble, yet gaily
   she sings.
What is it to her? She has wings, she has
   wings!

VICTOR HUGO

MARKS OF AN EDUCATED MAN

Has your education made you a friend of all good causes?

Has your education made you a brother to the weak?

Do you see anything to love in a little child?

Would a lost dog follow you in the street?

Do you enjoy being alone?

Do you believe in the dignity of labor?

Can you look into a mud puddle and see the blue sky?

Can you go out in the night, look up in the sky, and see beyond the stars?

Is your life linked with the Infinite?

A LITTLE LEARNING

A little learning is a dangerous thing;
Drink deep, or taste not the Pierian
*   spring:*
There shallow draughts intoxicate the
*   brain,*
And drinking largely sobers us again.

Fired at first sight with what the Muse
*   imparts,*
In fearless youth we tempt the heights of
*   Arts,*
While from the bounded level of our mind
Short views we take, nor see the lengths
*   behind;*
But more advanced, behold with strange
*   surprise*
New distant scenes of endless science
*   rise!*

So pleased at first the towering Alps we
*   try,*
Mount o'er the vales, and seem to tread
*   the sky,*
The eternal snows appear already past,
And the first clouds and mountains seem
*   the last;*
But, those attained, we tremble to survey
The growing labors of the lengthened
*   way,*
The increasing prospects tire our
*   wandering eyes,*
Hills peep o'er the hills, and Alps on Alps
*   arise!*

ALEXANDER POPE

**The best and most important part of
every man's education is that which he
gives himself.**

EDWARD GIBBON

THESE ARE EDUCATED

Whom, then, do I call educated?

First, those who manage well the circumstances which they encounter day by day; and those who possess a judgment which is accurate in meeting occasions as they arise and rarely miss the expedient course of action.

Next, those who are decent and honorable in their dealings with all men, bearing easily and good-naturedly what is unpleasant or offensive in others, and being themselves as agreeable and reasonable to their associates as it is humanly possible to be.

Furthermore, those who hold their pleasures always under control, and are not unduly overcome by their misfortunes, bearing up under them bravely and in a manner worthy of our common nature.

Most important of all, those who are not spoiled by their successes, who do not desert their true selves, but hold their ground steadfastly as wise and soberminded men, rejoicing no more in the good things that have come to them through chance than in those which through their own nature and intelligence are theirs through birth.

Those who have a character which is in accord, not with one of these things, but with all of them—these are educated, possessed of all the virtues.

SOCRATES

**The end and aim of all
education is the development
of character.**

FRANCIS W. PARKER

RECIPE FOR EDUCATION

1 cup of thinking
2 cups of dreams
2 to 4 years of youth
3½ cups of persistence
3 teaspoons of ability
1 cup of co-operation
1 teaspoon of borrowing
1 cup of good books, lectures, and
    teachers

1 cup of health
1 cup of plans made and followed
  through
Cream the thinking and the dreams.
Add the years and beat until creamy.
Sift persistence and ability together and add alternately, with co-operation, to the first mixture.
Add borrowing, books, lectures, teachers, health, and plans.
Fold in the years of youth, beaten stiff.
Bake in any moderately good college or university.
Time in college: 4 or more years, depending on how you like your finished product.
Temperature: plenty hot.
Servings will last for life.

TEACHER'S TREASURY OF STORIES

Virtue and learning, like gold, have their intrinsic value; but if they are not polished, they certainly lose a great deal of their luster; and even polished brass will pass upon more people than rough gold.

LORD CHESTERFIELD

As we acquire more knowledge, things do not become more comprehensible but more mysterious.

ALBERT SCHWEITZER

THE TEACHER'S CREED

I believe in boys and girls, the men and women of tomorrow; that whatsoever the boy soweth the man shall reap.

I believe in the curse of ignorance; in the efficacy of schools; in the dignity of teaching; and in the joy of serving others.

I believe in wisdom as revealed in human lives as well as in the pages of the printed book; in lessons taught, not so much by precept as by example; in ability to work with the hands as well as to think with the head; in everything that makes life large and lovely.

I believe in beauty in the schoolroom, in the home, in daily life and out-of-doors.

I believe in laughter; in love; in faith; in all ideals and distant hopes that lure us on.

I believe that every hour of every day we receive a just reward for all we are and all we do.

I believe in the present and its opportunities; in the future and its promises; and in the divine joy of living.

EDWIN OSGOOD GROVER

TEST OF THE EDUCATED MAN

Can he entertain a new idea?
Can he entertain another person?
Can he entertain himself?

SIDNEY HERBERT WOOD

I am not a teacher, but an awakener.

ROBERT FROST

The highest function of the teacher consists not so much in imparting knowledge as in stimulating the pupil in its love and pursuit.

Knowledge is proud that he has learn'd so much;
Wisdom is humble that he knows no more.

WILLIAM COWPER

A TEACHER'S PRAYER

Lord, speak to me that I may speak
In living echoes of thy tone;
As thou hast sought, so let me seek
Thy erring children lost and lone.

O teach me, Lord, that I may teach
The precious truths thou dost impart,
And wing my words, that they may reach
The hidden depths of many a heart.

O fill me with thy fulness, Lord,
Until my very heart o'erflow
In kindling thought and glowing word
Thy love to tell, thy praise to show.

FRANCES RIDLEY HAVERGAL

Employ your time in improving yourself by other men's writings, so you shall come easily by what others have labored hard for.

SOCRATES

Put it before them briefly so they will read it, clearly so they will appreciate it, picturesquely so they will remember it, and above all, accurately so they will be guided by its light.

JOSEPH PULITZER

No entertainment is so cheap as reading, nor any pleasure so lasting.

●

EDUCATION MEANS . . .

Education does not mean teaching people what they do not know.

It means teaching them to behave as they do not behave.

It is not teaching the youth the shapes of letters and the tricks of numbers, and then leaving them to turn their arithmetic to roguery, and their literature to lust.

It means on the contrary, training them into the perfect exercise and kingly continence of their bodies and souls.

It is a painful, continual, and difficult work to be done by kindness, by watching, by warning, by precept, and by praise, but above all — by example.

JOHN RUSKIN

Next to acquiring good friends, the best acquisition is that of a good book.

CHARLES CALEB COLTON

The man who does not read good books has no advantage over the man who can't read them.

MARK TWAIN

Words are instruments of music: an ignorant man uses them for jargon; but when a master touches them they have unexpected life and soul. Some words sound out like drums; some breathe memories sweet as flutes; some call like a clarionet; some show a charge like trumpets; some are sweet as children's talk; others rich as a mother's answering back.

Seeing much, suffering much, and studying much are the three pillars of learning.

BENJAMIN DISRAELI

●

A good book is the best of friends— the same today and forever.

TUPPER

Encouragement

Every mountain means at least two valleys.

●

DARE TO DO RIGHT

Dare to do right! dare to be true!
You have a work that no other can do,
Do it so bravely, so kindly, so well,
Angels will hasten the story to tell.

Dare to do right! dare to be true!
Other men's failures can never save you;
Stand by your conscience, your honor,
  your faith;
Stand like a hero, and battle till death.

Dare to do right! dare to be true!
God, who created you, cares for you too;
Treasures the tears that his striving ones
  shed,
Counts and protects every hair of your
  head.

Dare to do right! dare to be true!
Keep the great judgment-seat always in
  view;
Look at your work as you'll look at it
  then —
Scanned by Jehovah, and angels, and men.

Dare to do right! dare to be true!
Cannot Omnipotence carry you through?
City, and mansion, and throne all in
  sight —

Can you not dare to be true and do right?

Dare to do right! dare to be true!
Prayerfully, lovingly, firmly pursue
The path by apostles and martyrs once
  trod,
The path of the just to the city of God.

GEORGE LANSING TAYLOR

●

SEVEN THINGS TO DO

1. Be true to yourself. This will insure peace of mind, and you will never betray anyone.
2. Make each day your masterpiece. You cannot change yesterday, and a better tomorrow can only come by improvement today.
3. Help others. This will bring far, far more than you could ever give.
4. Drink deeply from good books. There is none that compares to the Bible, but also read Shakespeare, Tennyson, the philosophers, biographies of great men, and others.
5. Make a friendship a fine art. Be a friend; do not take friendship for granted.
6. Build a shelter against a rainy day.
7. Pray for guidance. Count your blessings and give thanks for them every day.

FATHER OF JOHN WOODEN,
HEAD BASKETBALL COACH, UCLA

**Be noble! and the nobleness that lies
In other men sleeping, but never dead,
Will rise in majesty to meet thine own.**

JAMES RUSSELL LOWELL

●

The stairs of opportunity
  Are sometimes hard to climb;
And that can only be well done
  By one step at a time.
But he who would go to the top
  Ne'er sits down and despairs;
Instead of staring up the steps
  He just steps up the stairs.

●

Good temper, like a sunny day, sheds a brightness over everything. It is the sweetness of toil and the soother of disquietude.

WASHINGTON IRVING

LET US SMILE

The thing that goes the farthest toward
  Making life worthwhile,
That costs the least and does the most,
  Is just a pleasant smile.
The smile that bubbles from a heart
  That loves its fellow men,
Will drive away the clouds of gloom,
  And coax the sun again;
It's full of worth and goodness, too,
  With manly kindness blent,
It's worth a million dollars, and
  It doesn't cost a cent.
There is no room for sadness
  When we see a cheery smile
It always has the same good look —
  It's never out of style;
It nerves us on to try again
  When failure makes us blue,
The dimples of encouragement
  Are good for me and you;
It pays a higher interest
  For it is merely lent,
It's worth a million dollars and
  It doesn't cost a cent.

A good thing to remember
  And a better thing to do
To work with the construction gang
  And not with the wrecking crew.

●

Each time we meet, you always say
  Some word of praise that makes me
    gay.
You see some hidden, struggling trait,
  Encourage it and make it great.
Tight-fisted little buds of good
  Bloom large because you said they
    would.
A glad, mad music in me sings;
  My soul sprouts tiny flaming wings.
My day takes on a brand-new zest.
  Your gift of praising brings my best,
Revives my spirit, flings it high;
  For God loves praise, and so do I.

●

Our mistakes won't irreparably damage our lives unless we let them. It is said that in making Persian rugs the artist stands before the rug while a group of boys stand behind to pull the thread after the artist starts it. If one of the boys makes a mistake, the artist adjusts the pattern accordingly so that when the rug is finished no one can tell where the mistake was made. The same kind of adjustment will take place in our lives if we but let go of the mental thread of each mistake and let God weave it into a successful, orderly pattern.

JAMES E. SWEANEY

IT MIGHT HAVE BEEN

Led by kindlier hand than ours,
  We journey through this earthly scene,
And should not, in our weary hours,
  Turn to regret what might have been.

And yet these hearts, when torn by pain,
  Or wrung by disappointment keen,

Will seek relief from present cares
   In thoughts of joys that might have
     been.

But let us still these wishes vain;
   We know not that of which we dream.
Our lives might have been sadder yet
   God only knows what might have been.

Forgive us, Lord, our little faith;
   And help us all, from morn to e'en,
Still to believe that lot were best
   Which is — not that which might have
     been.

And grant we may so pass the days
   The cradle and the grave between,
That death's dark hour not darker be
   For thought of what life might have
     been.

GEORGE Z. GRAY

●

The glory of love is brightest
When the glory of self is dim,
And they have the most constrained me
Who most have pointed to Him.
They have held me, stirred me, swayed
   me,
I have hung on their very word,
Till I fain would get up and follow
Not them, not them, but my Lord.

●

There is no human being
   With so wholly dark a lot,
But the heart, by turning the picture,
   May find some sunny spot.

●

Got any rivers you think are
   uncrossable?
Got any mountains you can't tunnel
   through?
God specializes in things thought
   impossible,
He does the things others cannot do.

OSCAR C. ELIASON

RECONCILIATION

Ye who have scorned each other,
Or injured friend or brother,
   In the fast fading year;
Ye who by word or deed,
Have made a kind heart bleed,
   Come gather here;
Let sinned against and sinning
Forget their strife's beginning,
   And join in friendship now —
Be links no longer broken;
Be sweet forgiveness spoken
   Under the Holly Bough.

Ye who have loved each other,
Sister and friend and brother,
   In this fast fading year;
Mother and sire and child,
Young man and maiden mild,
   Come gather here;
And let your hearts grow fonder,
As memory shall ponder
   Each past unbroken vow;
Old loves and younger wooing
Are sweet in the renewing,
   Under the Holly Bough.

CHARLES MACKAY

●

AFTER THE WINTER...
GOD SENDS THE SPRING

Springtime is a season
   Of Hope and Joy and Cheer,
There's beauty all around us
   To see and touch and hear...
So, no matter how downhearted
   And discouraged we may be,
New Hope is born when we behold
   Leaves budding on a tree...
Or when we see a timid flower
   Push through the frozen sod
And open wide in glad surprise
   Its petaled eyes to God...
For this is just God saying —
   "lift up your eyes to Me,
And the bleakness of your spirit,
   Like the budding springtime tree,
Will lose its wintry darkness
   And your heavy heart will sing" —
For God never sends The Winter
   Without the Joy of Spring.

HELEN STEINER RICE

BEST THINGS

The Best Law —
   The Golden Rule.
The Best Education —
   Self-Knowledge.
The Best Philosophy —
   A contented mind.
The Best War —
   To war against one's weakness.
The Best Theology —
   A pure and beneficient life.
The Best Medicine —
   Cheerfulness and temperance.
The Best Music —
   The laughter of an innocent child.
The Best Science —
   Extracting Sunshine from a cloudy day.
The Best Art —
   Painting a smile upon the brow of
    childhood.
The Best Journalism —
   Printing the true and beautiful on
    memory's tablet.
The Best Telegraphing —
   Flashing a ray of Sunshine into a
    gloomy heart.

Let us be of good cheer, remembering that the misfortunes hardest to bear are those that never come.

JAMES RUSSELL LOWELL

Be still, sad heart, and cease repining;
Behind the clouds is the sun still shining.

HENRY WADSWORTH LONGFELLOW

Everyday Joys

THE NICEST THINGS

Some nice things come quietly . . .
A russet leaf comes fluttering down,
The sunset beckons without sound,
A tiny sail far out at sea,
Marshmallow snowflakes hovering
Toward the sere earth's covering,
Lamplight flickers happily
From evening firesides
And, love, too, abides . . .
The nicest things come quietly.

MARIE HAND

●

One ought every day at least to hear a
      little song,
   read a good poem,
   see a fine picture,
   and if it were possible,
   to speak a few reasonable words.

JOHANN WOLFGANG VON GOETHE

BARTER

Life has loveliness to sell,
   All beautiful and splendid things,
Blue waves whitened on a cliff,
   Soaring fire that sways and sings,
And children's faces looking up
Holding wonder like a cup.

Life has loveliness to sell,
   Music like a curve of gold,
Scent of pine trees in the rain,
   Eyes that love you, arms that hold,
And for your spirit's still delight,
Holy thoughts that star the night.

Spend all you have for loveliness,
   Buy it and never count the cost;
For one white singing hour of peace
   Count many a year of strife well lost,
And for a breath of ecstasy
Give all you have been, or could be.

SARA TEASDALE

●

LITTLE THINGS

'Tis the little kindly acts you do
   That heartens one along,
And sends the friend away from you
   With glad and happy song.

'Tis the little word you're led to say
   Which touched that other life,
And gave it nerve and strength again
   To conquer in the strife.

'Tis just the secret little talk
   With Jesus by the way.
That keeps you loving, true to Him
   In all you do and say.

MAUD ROSE

53

HUNDREDFOLD

Yesterday,
(After first frost, with maples
Blazing beyond fringes of stubble-hay)
My husband and my sons
Pulled up dead summer's stalks of corn
Laying them flat among the weeds
For ploughing in again, when next
    spring's born.

I'm glad I picked the green tomatoes
Two nights ago
And spread them, newspapered,
To ripen on the basement floor.
Good company for the corn relish, row
And golden row in jars, behind the closet
    door.

Yes, I'm very glad
Something's left, something not dead
After all the hilling and hoeing
Seeding and sprouting, greening and
    growing;
After the blowing
Tassels, high as a woman's hands above
    her head.
  Corn relish for Sunday dinner, grace
  The days when outside snowings
  Whiten winter's face

Let me leave fruit
(But not in someone's basement)
When I grow browned
And old and pulled up by the root
And laid down flat
And ploughed into the ground.

LUCI SHAW

●

THESE JOYS ARE MINE

The joy of a rose with its sweet perfume
  On a lazy summer day.

The blue of the sky as the dawn steals
    through
  To welcome a bright new day.

A little child with a laughing heart . . .
  A hope and a peace supreme.

A hilltop fair with its whispering wind
  And a valley nestled between.

A friendly smile and a handclasp warm
  A gladness to call my own.

A fireside warm and a happy thought
  Whenever I'm alone.

A quiet joy that can fill my mind
  Each night at the long day's end.

A thrill complete and a rich content
  Because I have been a friend.

These joys are mine as I walk life's road
  Wherever the journey might lead.

These are the hope and the faith I know,
  All that my heart can need.

The richest treasures, the brightest
    dreams
  To last throughout all time.

My heart holds a smile and my soul is
    content.
  I'm rich, for these joys are mine!

GARNETT ANN SCHULTZ

●

WANTED . . . TIME

Time to have my close friends in
  to drink a cup of tea;
Time to read the book of verse
  my sister sent to me.
Time to sort my linens out
  and stack them in neat rows;
Time to look my scrapbook o'er
  and work with rhyme and prose.
Time to bake some muffins
  for the boy who mows our lawn;
Time to listen to the lark
  at morning's early dawn.
Time to cut pink roses
  for a neighbor living near;
Time to plan the garden
  I have wanted for a year.
Time to breakfast leisurely
  and scan the paper through . . .
Time, just to do the things
  I really want to do.

GRACE ALLARD MORSE

RECIPE FOR A PICNIC

A basket filled with goodies,
A jug of lemonade,
A lazy summer afternoon,
A cool spot in the shade.

A tablecloth of red and white
Beneath an old oak tree,
And myriad songbirds to produce
A heavenly symphony.

A group of happy people
To laugh and sing and play
Makes any picnic outing
A very joyful day.

CARICE WILLIAMS

●

MY TWELVE LOVELIEST THINGS, PEOPLE NOT COUNTED

By A Little Scotch Girl

1. The scrunch of dry leaves as you walk through them.

2. The feel of clean clothes.

3. Water running into bath.

4. The cold of ice cream.

5. Cool wind on a hot day.

6. Climbing up and looking back.

7. Honey in your mouth.

8. Smell of a drugstore.

9. Hot-water bottle in bed.

10. Babies smiling.

11. The feeling inside when you sing.

12. Baby kittens.

DOUGLAS HORTON

PLEASURES

The dearest pleasures that I know
Are simple things: the fire's glow,
The breath of flowers, whispered words,

The ecstasies of singing birds,
The flash of waters in a brook,
An old tome in a chimney nook,
The sounds of laughter lifting up
From happy hearts, a china cup
Reflecting back the candle gleam
Like figures shifting in a dream;
The murmuring of rustling leaves,
The drip of rain from off the eaves,
The shuffling sounds of weary feet
Along the roadway or the street,
The wonder of a baby's eyes,
An earthly glimpse of paradise,
The stir of life from sun to sun,
And then, with play and labor done,
I love to find at each day's end
The warming handclasp of a friend.

EDGAR DANIEL KRAMER

●

SUNRISE

Though the midnight found us weary,
   The morning brings us cheer;
Thank God for every sunrise
   In the circuit of the year.

MARGARET E. SANGSTER

●

HOME

A little house — a cozy house,
   Paint-scarred, low-eaved, and humble;

Bright morning glories round the door —
   Their hues a gorgeous jumble;

A small red wagon — one wheel gone;
   A tree with blossoms swinging;

A kettle humming on the fire;
   A cheerful mother singing;

A place where loved ones gather round
   When evening prayers are given —

The dearest spot we'll ever know
   Till we go home to heaven!

KATHRYN BLACKBURN PECK

Faith & Hope

All I have seen teaches me to trust the Creator for all I have not seen.

RALPH WALDO EMERSON

●

FAITH

Faith has neither
Wall nor roof,
No concrete offering
Of proof.

Its substance frail
As winds that pass,
As image seen
In mirrored glass.

Yet mountains move
And valleys fill
When faith is linked
To wish and will.

KATHERINE EDELMAN

●

The preaching of the Gospel requires faith: not faith in believing, nor faith in wishful thinking, but faith in Jesus Christ as Lord of history and Savior of the world.

The saving power of Jesus Christ is the one inexhaustible resource God has given to men, but it requires the instru-mentality of faith to make it real. "According to your faith be it unto you."

BILLY GRAHAM

ENCOURAGED

Because you love me I have much
    achieved,
Had you despised me then I must have
    failed,
But since I knew you trusted and
    believed,
I could not disappoint you and so
    prevailed.

PAUL LAURENCE DUNBAR

●

SYMBOL

My faith is all a doubtful thing,
    Wove on a doubtful loom, —
Until there comes, each showery spring,
    A cheery tree in bloom;

And Christ who died upon a tree
    That death had stricken bare,
Comes beautifully back to me,
    In blossoms, everywhere.

DAVID MORTON

The earth is the Lord's,
And the fulness thereof;
The world, and they that dwell therein.
For He hath founded it upon the seas,
And established it upon the floods.
Who shall ascend into the hill
    of the Lord?
Or who shall stand in His holy place?
He that hath clean hands,
    and a pure heart;
Who hath not lifted up his soul
    unto vanity,
Nor sworn deceitfully.
He shall receive the blessing
    from the Lord,
And righteousness from the God
    of his salvation.

PSALM 24:1-5

THE WASHER-WOMAN'S SONG

In a very humble cot, in a rather quiet
    spot,
    In the suds and in the soap, worked a
    woman full of hope;
Working, singing, all alone — in a sort
    of undertone:
        "With the Saviour for a Friend,
        He will keep me to the end."

Sometime happening along, I have heard
    the semi-song,
    And I often used to smile, more in
    sympathy than guile;
But I never said a word, in regard to what
    I heard,
        As she sang about her Friend
        Who would keep her to the end.

Not in sorrow, nor in glee, working all
    day long was she,
    As her children, three or four, played
    around her on the floor;
But in monotones the song, she was
    humming all day long:
        "With the Saviour for a Friend,
        He will keep me to the end."

It's a song I do not sing, for I scarce
    believe a thing,
    Of the stories that are told, of the
    miracles of old;

But I know that her belief is the anodyne
    of grief,
        And will always be a Friend
        That will keep her to the end.

Just a trifle lonesome she, just as poor as
    poor could be;
    But her spirits always rose, like the
    bubbles in the clothes;
And the widowed and alone, cheered her
    with the monotone
        Of a Saviour and a Friend
        Who would keep her to the end.

I have seen her rub and scrub on the
    washboard in the tub,
    While the baby, sopped in suds, rolled
    and tumbled in the duds;
Or was paddling in the pools, with old
    scissors stuck in spools —
        She still humming of her Friend,
        Who could keep her to the end.

Human hopes and human creeds have
    their root in human needs,
    And I should not wish to strip from
    that washer-woman's lip
Any song that she can sing, any hope that
    songs can bring,
        For the woman has a Friend
        Who will keep her to the end.

EUGENE F. WARE

FAITH

Faith came singing into my room,
    And other guests took flight;
Fear and anxiety, grief and gloom
    Sped out into the night.
I wondered that such peace could be,
    But Faith said gently, "Don't you see?
They really cannot live with me."

Let us have faith that right makes might,
and in that faith let us dare to do our
duty as we understand it.

ABRAHAM LINCOLN

FAITH AND DOUBT

Doubt sees the obstacles,
　Faith sees the way;
Doubt sees the blackest night,
　Faith sees the day;
Doubt dreads to take a step,
　Faith soars on high;
Doubt questions, "Who believes?"
　Faith answers, "I!"

●

WIND IN THE PINE

Oh, I can hear you, God, above the cry
　Of the tossing trees —
Rolling your windy tides across the sky,
　And splashing your silver seas
　　Over the pine,
To the water-line
　of the moon.
Oh, I can hear you, God,
Above the wail of the lonely loon —
When the pine-tops pitch and nod —
　Chanting your melodies
Of ghostly waterfalls and avalanches,
Swashing your wind among the branches
　To make them pure and white.
Wash over me, God, with your piney
　　breeze,
　And your moon's wet-silver pool;
Wash me, God, with your wind and night,
　And leave me clean and cool.

LEW SARETT

●

Now faith is the substance of things
　　hoped for,
　the evidence of things not seen.

HEBREWS 11:1

MY LIFE IS LIKE A RIVER

From where I sit my eyes can scan
　A picture rare to mortal man.
It is of mountains tall and high,
　Of rivers deep and cloud filled sky.

Its voice is mute, no word is said;
　I only see its white topped head.
And hear its voice as rapids roar
　And spread its life along the shore.

The reason why this river flows,
　Is all because of winter snows.
And locked within that whitened shroud
　Is life and power and voices loud.

And when the heat of spring and sun
　Began to make the riv'letts run,
'Twas then its voice was heard aloud
　From deepest vale to highest cloud.

And as the river turned and flowed,
　Upon its crest it bore a load
To every town and every mart
　And gave its life and left its heart.

I am that stream that now is free;
　That winds its way out toward the sea.
And you my God, were warmth and love
　That brought the melting from above.

I love you more than I can say,
　And if I live another day
To heal a heart of bitter woe,
　And leave some sunshine where I go.

'Twas you who warmed a weary me,
　And fanned a flame for those to see;
And gave me hope that made me new —
　You came, just when I needed you.

IRA STANPHILL

●

Patience walks with steady tread,
　Faith, with uplifted eyes,
But Hope, tiptoeing on ahead,
　Sees first the sun arise.

ISLA PASCHAL RICHARDSON

●

Fair is the soul, rare is the soul
　Who has kept, after youth is past,
All the art of the child, all the heart of the
　　child,
　Holding his faith at last.

FRANK GELETT BURGESS

58

POSSESSION

Heaven above is softer blue
Earth beneath is sweeter green.
Something lives in every hue,
Christless eyes have never seen.
Birds with gladder songs o'erflow,
Flowers with deeper beauty shine
Since I know as now I know
I am His and He is mine.

●

A little bit of hope
Makes a rainy day look gay;
A little bit of charity
Makes glad a weary way!

●

THE INCOMPARABLE CHRIST

More than 1900 years ago there was a man born contrary to the laws of life . . . This man lived in poverty and was reared in obscurity. He did not travel extensively. Only once did He cross the boundary of the country in which He lived; that was during His exile in childhood. He possessed neither wealth nor influence. His relatives were inconspicuous, and had neither training nor formal education.

In infancy He startled a king: in childhood He puzzled doctors; in manhood He ruled the course of nature, walked upon the billows as if pavements and hushed the sea to sleep. He healed the multitudes without medicine and made no charge for His service. He never wrote a song and yet He has furnished the theme for more songs than all the songwriters combined. He never founded a college but all the schools put together cannot boast of having as many students.

He never marshaled an army nor drafted soldiers nor fired a gun; and yet no leader ever had more volunteers who have, under His orders, made more rebels stack arms and surrender without a shot fired.

He never practiced psychiatry and yet He has healed more broken hearts than all the doctors far and near. Once each week the wheels of commerce cease their turning and the multitudes wend their way to worshiping assemblies to pay homage and respect to Him. The names of the past proud statesmen of Greece and Rome have come and gone. The names of the past scientists, philosophers and theologians have come and gone; but the name of this man abounds more and more.

Though time has spread nineteen hundred years between the people of this generation and the scene of His crucifixion, yet He lives. Herod could not destroy Him and the grave could not hold Him!

He stands forth upon the highest pinnacle of heavenly glory proclaimed of God, acknowledged by Angels, adored by saints and feared by devils, as a living, personal Christ, our Lord and Saviour.

We are either going to be forever with Him or forever without Him . . .

●

All that is, at all,
Lasts ever, past recall;
Earth changes, but thy soul and God
stand sure.

ROBERT BROWNING

●

Oh! for a closer walk with God,
A calm and heav'nly frame;
A light to shine upon the road
That leads me to the Lamb!

WILLIAM COWPER

59

Favorites

OUTLOOK

Forget each kindness that you do
As soon as you have done it,
Forget the praise that falls on you
The moment you have won it;
Forget the slander that you hear
Before you can repeat it;
Forget each slight, each spite, each sneer,
Wherever you may meet it.

Remember every kindness done
To you, whate'er its measure;
Remember praise by others won
And pass it on with pleasure;
Remember those who lend you aid
And be a grateful debtor;
Remember every promise made
And keep it to the letter.

Remember all the happiness
That comes your way in living.
Forget each worry and distress;
Be hopeful and forgiving.
Remember good, remember truth,
Remember heaven's above you,
And you will find, through age and youth,
True joys and hearts to love you!

PRISCILLA LEONARD

I'll not willingly offend,
Nor be easily offended:
What's amiss I'll strive to mend,
And endure what can't be mended.

ISAAC WATTS

MAY YOU HAVE

Enough happiness to keep you sweet,
Enough trials to keep you strong,
Enough sorrow to keep you human,
Enough hope to keep you happy;
Enough failure to keep you humble,
Enough success to keep you eager,
Enough friends to give you comfort,
Enough wealth to meet your needs;
Enough enthusiasm to look forward,
Enough faith to banish depression,
Enough determination to make each day
    better than yesterday.

A PRAYER

Give me a good digestion, Lord
And also something to digest.
Give me a healthy body, Lord
And sense enough to keep it at its best.
Give me a healthy mind, O Lord
To keep the good and pure in sight,
Which seeing sin is not appalled
But finds a way to set it right.
Give me a mind that is not bound
That does not whimper, whine or sigh.
Don't let me worry overmuch
About this funny thing called I.
Give me a sense of humor, Lord,
And sense enough to see a joke,
To get more happiness out of life
And pass it on to other folk.

LITTLE THINGS

A crumpled bunch of violets
   in a chubby little fist,
A tired mother gladdened
   with a sticky little kiss.

A golden batch of cookies
   and a steaming loaf of bread,
A little note, a "get-well" card
   brought sunshine to a bed.

A cheery song, a sunny smile,
   a friendly word or nod . . .
A prayer for someone who's lost
   in a talk with them of God.

Perhaps a friendly greeting
   to the stranger on the street,
A helping hand for handicapped
   or elders we may meet.

Perhaps you think your talents
   are little and are few,
But God looks down in tenderness
   at the "little things" you do.

DOLORES HENDERSON NASH

●

TO A WATERFOWL

Whither, midst falling dew,
While glow the heavens with the last
   steps of day,
Far through their rosy depths dost thou
   pursue
   Thy solitary way?

Vainly the fowler's eye
Might mark thy distant flight to do thee
   wrong,
As, darkly seen against the crimson sky,
   Thy figure floats along.

Seek'st thou the plashy brink
Of weedy lake or marge of river wide,
Or where the rocking billows rise and
   sink
On the chafed ocean-side?

There is a Power whose care
Teaches thy way along that pathless
   coast —
The desert and illimitable air, —
   Lone wandering, but not lost.

All the day thy wings have fanned,
At that far height, the cold thin
   atmosphere,
Yet stoop not, weary, to the welcome
   land,
   Though the dark night is near.

And soon that toil shall end:
Soon shalt thou find a summer home, and
   rest,
And scream among thy fellows; reeds
   shall bend,
   Soon, o'er thy sheltered nest.

Thou'rt gone, the abyss of heaven
Hath swallowed up thy form; yet, on my
   heart
Deeply has sunk the lesson thou hast
   given,
   And shall not soon depart.

He who, from zone to zone,
Guides through the boundless sky thy
   certain flight,
In the long way that I must tread alone,
   Will lead my steps aright.

WILLIAM CULLEN BRYANT

●

"ONE LITTLE ROSE . . ."

I would rather have one little rose
   From the garden of a friend,
Than to have the choicest flowers
   When my stay on earth must end.
I would rather have a pleasant word
   In kindness said to me
Than flattery when my heart is still
   And this life has ceased to be.
I would rather have a loving smile
   From friends I know are true
Than tears shed around my casket
   When this world I bid adieu.
Bring me all the flowers today,
   Whether pink or white, or red.
I'd rather have one blossom now
   Than a truck load when I'm dead.

●

**We never test the resources of God until
we attempt the impossible.**

F. B. MEYER

61

ARISTOCRACY

The pedigree of honey
Does not concern the bee;
A clover, any time, to him
Is aristocracy.

EMILY DICKINSON

●

He prayeth best, who loveth best
All things both great and small;
For the dear God who loveth us,
He made and loveth all.

SAMUEL T. COLERIDGE

●

UNDERSTANDING

If I knew you and you knew me,
If both of us could clearly see,
And with an inner sight divine
The meaning of your heart and mine,
I'm sure that we would differ less,
And clasp our hands in friendliness;
Our thoughts would pleasantly agree
If I knew you and you knew me.

NIXON WATERMAN

●

THE EVERLASTING MERCY

O Christ who holds the open gate,
O Christ who drives the furrow straight,
O Christ, the plough, O Christ, the
    laughter
Of holy white birds flying after,
Lo, all my heart's field red and torn,
And Thou wilt bring young green corn,
The young green corn divinely springing,
The young green corn forever singing;
And when the field is fresh and fair
Thy blessed feet shall glitter there.
And we will walk the weeded field,
And tell the golden harvest's yield,
The corn that makes the holy bread
By which the soul of man is fed,
The holy bread, the food unpriced,
Thy everlasting mercy, Christ.

JOHN MASEFIELD

THE TOUCH OF THE MASTER'S HAND

'Twas battered and scarred, and the
    auctioneer
Thought it scarcely worth his while
To waste much time on the old violin,
But he held it up with a smile.
"What am I bidden, good folks," he cried,
"Who'll start the bidding for me?"
"A dollar, a dollar"; then, "Two!
    Only two?
Two dollars, and who'll make it three?
Three dollars, once; three dollars, twice;
Going for three —" But no,
From the room, far back, a gray-haired
    man
Came forward and picked up the bow;
Then wiping the dust from the old violin,
And tightening the loose strings,
He played a melody pure and sweet
As a caroling angel sings.

The music ceased, and the auctioneer,
With a voice that was quiet and low,
Said: "What am I bid for the old violin?"
And he held it up with the bow.
"A thousand dollars, and who'll make
    it two?
Two thousand! And who'll make it three?
Three thousand, once; three thousand,
    twice,
And going, and gone," said he.
The people cheered, but some of them
    cried,
"We do not quite understand
What changed its worth." Swift came the
    reply:
"The touch of a master's hand."

And many a man with life out of tune,
And battered and scarred with sin,
Is auctioned cheap to the thoughtless
    crowd,
Much like the old violin.
A "mess of pottage," a glass of wine;
A game — and he travels on.
He is "going" once, and "going" twice,
He's "going" and almost "gone."
But the Master comes, and the foolish
    crowd
Never can quite understand
The worth of a soul and the change that's
    wrought
By the touch of the Master's hand.

MYRA BROOKS WELCH

ABUNDANT LIVING

Think deeply,
Speak gently,
Laugh often,
Work hard,
Give freely,
Pay promptly,
Pray earnestly,
Be kind.

Some have much, and some have more,
Some are rich, and some are poor,
Some have little, some have less,
Some have not a cent to bless
Their empty pockets, yet possess
True riches in true happiness.

JOHN OXENHAM

DARE TO BE HAPPY

Dare to be happy —
    don't shy away,
Reach out and capture
    the joy of Today!

Life is for living!
    Give it a try;
Open your heart to that
    sun in the sky.

Dare to be loving, and
    trusting, and true;
Treasure the hours with
    those dear to you.

Dare to be kind — it's
    more fun than you know;
Give joy to others, and
    watch your own grow.

Dare to admit all your
    blessings, and then
Every day count them
    all over again.

Dare to be happy,
    don't be afraid —
This is the day which
    the Lord hath made!

HELEN LOWRIE MARSHALL

ONLY ONE MOTHER

Hundreds of stars in the pretty sky,
Hundreds of shells on the seashore
    together,
Hundreds of birds that go singing by,
Hundreds of lambs in the sunny weather.
Hundreds of dewdrops to greet the dawn,
Hundreds of bees in the purple clover,
Hundreds of butterflies on the lawn,
But only one mother the wide world over.

GEORGE COOPER

LESSONS IN LIVING

Learn to laugh. A good laugh is better
than medicine.

Learn to attend to your own business.
Few men can handle their own well.

Learn to tell a story. A well-told story is
like a sunbeam in a sick room.

Learn to say kind things. Nobody ever
resents them.

Learn to avoid sarcastic remarks. They
give neither the hearer nor the speaker
any lasting satisfaction.

Learn to stop grumbling. If you can't see
any good in the world, keep the bad to
yourself.

Learn to hide aches with a smile. Nobody
else is interested anyway.

Learn to keep troubles to yourself. Nobody wants to take them from you.

Above all, learn to smile. It pays!

If any little thought of ours
Can make one life the stronger;
If any cheery smile of ours
Can make its brightness longer;
Then let us speak that thought today,
With tender eyes aglowing,
So God may grant some weary one
Shall reap from our glad sowing.

GOD'S GIFT

God sought to give the sweetest thing
    In His almighty power
To earth; and deeply pondering
    What it should be, one hour
In fondest joy and love of heart
    Outweighing every other,
He moved the gates of heaven apart
    And gave to earth a mother.

●

THE RECESSIONAL

God of our fathers, known of old —
    Lord of our far-flung battle-line —
Beneath whose awful Hand we hold
    Dominion over palm and pine —
Lord God of Hosts, be with us yet,
Lest we forget, lest we forget!

The tumult and the shouting dies —
    The captains and the kings depart —
Still stands Thine ancient sacrifice,
    An humble and a contrite heart.
Lord God of Hosts, be with us yet,
Lest we forget, lest we forget!

Far-call'd our navies melt away —
    On dune and headland sinks the fire —
Lo, all our pomp of yesterday
    Is one with Nineveh and Tyre!
Judge of the Nations, spare us yet,
Lest we forget, lest we forget!

If, drunk with sight of power, we loose
    Wild tongues that have not Thee in
    awe —
Such boasting as the Gentiles use
    Or lesser breeds without the Law —
Lord God of Hosts, be with us yet,
Lest we forget, lest we forget!

For heathen heart that puts her trust
    In reeking tube and iron shard —
All valiant dust that builds on dust,
    And guarding calls not Thee to guard—
For frantic boast and foolish word,
Thy Mercy on Thy People, Lord!

RUDYARD KIPLING

FAITH

I will not doubt, though all my ships at
        sea
    Come drifting home with broken masts
        and sails;
    I shall believe the Hand which never
        fails,
From seeming evil worketh good to me;
    And, though I weep because those sails
        are battered,
    Still will I cry, while my best hopes lie
        shattered,
            "I trust in Thee."

I will not doubt, though all my prayers
        return
    Unanswered from the still, white realm
        above;
    I shall believe it is an all-wise Love
Which has refused those things for which
        I yearn;
    And though, at times, I cannot keep
        from grieving,
    Yet the pure ardor of my fixed believing
            Undimmed shall burn.

I will not doubt, though sorrows fall like
        rain,
    And troubles swarm like bees about
        a hive;
    I shall believe the heights for which I
        strive,
Are only reached by anguish and by pain;
    And, though I groan and tremble with
        my crosses,
    I yet shall see, through my severest
        losses,
            The greater gain.

I will not doubt, well anchored in the
        faith,
    Like some stanch ship, my soul braves
        every gale,
    So strong its courage that it will not fail
To breast the mighty, unknown sea of
        death.
    Oh, may I cry when body parts with
        spirit,
    "I do not doubt," so listening worlds
        may hear it
            With my last breath.

ELLA WHEELER WILCOX

Freedom & Patriotism

The God who gave us life, gave us liberty at the same time.

THOMAS JEFFERSON

HERITAGE

Let us not forget the religious character of our origin. Our fathers were brought here by their high veneration for the Christian religion. They journeyed by its light, and labored in its hope. They sought to incorporate its principles with the elements of their society, and to diffuse its influence through all their institutions —civil, political and literary. Let us cherish these sentiments, and extend this influence still more widely, in the full conviction that this is the happiest society, which partakes in the highest degree of the mild and peaceable spirit of Christianity.

DANIEL WEBSTER

Give me your tired, your poor,
Your huddled masses yearning to breathe
free,
The wretched refuse of your teeming
shore.

Send these, the homeless, tempest-tost
to me,
I lift my lamp beside the golden door.

WRITTEN BY EMMA LAZARUS
AND INSCRIBED ON THE STATUE OF LIBERTY

I only regret that I have but one life to lose for my country.

NATHAN HALE

Here is J. Edgar Hoover's answer to the question, "Where do you believe freedom has its beginnings?"

"In religion. Christ championed the sanctity of the individual. There is respect for human dignity only where Christ and the Bible are a way of life. The philosophy of Christ has meant freedom from despair and tyranny throughout history."

Where liberty dwells, there is my country.

BENJAMIN FRANKLIN

OUR HERITAGE

Would that each true American, however
*   great or small,*
Might journey to that shrine of shrines,
*   old Independence Hall.*
And there within those sacred walls
*   where those immortals met,*
Renew our pledge to keep the faith,
*   "Lest we forget — lest we forget."*
Lest we forget that we must be
*   The keepers of our liberty.*

JAMES WILLIARD PARKS

THE GETTYSBURG ADDRESS

Fourscore and seven years ago
our fathers brought forth on this
    continent a new nation,
conceived in liberty,
and dedicated to the proposition
that all men are created equal.
    Now we are engaged in a great civil
        war,
testing whether that nation,
or any nation so conceived and so
    dedicated,
can long endure.
We are met on a great battlefield of that
    war.
We have come to dedicate a portion of
    that field
as a final resting place
for those who here gave their lives
that that nation might live.
It is altogether fitting and proper that we
    should do this.
    But in a larger sense,
we cannot dedicate —
we cannot consecrate —
we cannot hallow this ground.
The brave men, living and dead, who
    struggled here,
have consecrated it far above our poor
    power to add or detract.
The world will little note nor long
    remember
what we say here,
but it can never forget what they did here.
It is for us, the living,
rather, to be dedicated here to the
    unfinished work
which they who fought here have thus far
    so nobly advanced.

It is rather for us to be here dedicated
to the great task remaining before us —
that from these honored dead we take
    increased devotion
to that cause for which they gave the last
    full measure of devotion;
that we here highly resolve that these
    dead shall not have died in vain;
that this nation, under God, shall have a
    new birth of freedom;
and that government of the people,
by the people,
for the people,
shall not perish from the earth.

ABRAHAM LINCOLN

God grants liberty only to those who
**   love it,**
and are always ready to guard and
**   defend it.**

DANIEL WEBSTER

FREEDOM

Freedom is a breath of air,
pine-scented, or salty like the sea;
Freedom is a field new-plowed . . .
Furrows of democracy!

Freedom is a forest,
Trees tall and straight as men!
Freedom is a printing press . . .
The power of the pen!

Freedom is a country church,
A cathedral's stately spire;
Freedom is a spirit
That can set the soul on fire!

Freedom is a man's birthright,
A sacred, living rampart;
The pulsebeat of humanity . . .
The throb of a nation's heart!

CLARA SMITH REBER

I do not agree with a word that you say,
but I will defend to the death your
**   right to say it.**

VOLTAIRE

MY COUNTRY

God grant that not only
   the love of liberty
But a thorough knowledge
   of the rights of man
May pervade all nations
   of the earth, so that
A philosopher may set
   his foot anywhere
On its surface, and say,
   "This is my country."

BENJAMIN FRANKLIN

Is life so dear, or peace so sweet, as to be purchased at the price of chains and slavery? Forbid it, Almighty God! I know not what course others may take, but as for me, give me liberty, or give me death!

PATRICK HENRY

No one can be free who does not work for the freedom of others.

Let our object be our country, our whole country, and nothing but our country. And, by the blessing of God, may that country itself become a vast and splendid monument, not of oppression and terror, but of wisdom, of peace and of liberty, upon which the world may gaze with admiration forever.

DANIEL WEBSTER

You have freedom of choice but not freedom from choice.

WENDELL JONES

The greatest glory of a free-born people is to transmit that freedom to their children.

WILLIAM HARVARD

One who is a patriot is as willing to live sacrificially for his country as he is to die for it.

AMERICA'S GOSPEL

Our country hath a gospel of her own
To preach and practice before all the
   world —
The freedom and divinity of man,
The glorious claims of human
   brotherhood,
And the soul's fealty to none but God.

JAMES RUSSELL LOWELL

THE STRIFE IS O'ER

The strife is o'er, the battle done;
The victory of life is won;
The song of triumph has begun.
Alleluia!

The powers of death have done their
   worst,
But Christ their legions hath dispersed:
Let shouts of holy joy outburst.
Alleluia!

The three sad days have quickly sped;
He rises glorious from the dead:
All glory to our risen Head!
Alleluia!

He closed the yawning gates of hell;
The bars from heaven's high portals fell:
Let hymns of praise His triumphs tell.
Alleluia!

Lord, by the stripes which wounded Thee,
From death's dread sting Thy servants
   free,
That we may live and sing to Thee.
Alleluia!

LATIN HYMN
TRANSLATED BY FRANCIS POTT

False freedom leaves a man free to do
   what he likes;
True freedom, to do what he ought.

Friendship

**Friendship is like two clocks
keeping time.**

●

NO FRIENDS LIKE OLD ONES

There are no friends like old friends,
　And none so good and true;
We greet them when we meet them
　As roses greet the dew;
No other friends are dearer,
　Though born of kindred mold;
And while we prize the new ones,
　We treasure more the old.

There are no friends like old friends.
　Where'er we dwell or roam:
In lands beyond the ocean,
　Or near the bounds of home;
And when they smile to gladden,
　Or sometimes frown to guide,
We fondly wish those old friends
　Were always by our side.

There are no friends like old friends
　To help us with the load
That all must bear who journey
　O'er life's uneven road;
And when unconquered sorrows
　The weary hours invest,
The kindly words of old friends
　Are always found the best.

There are no friends like old friends
　To calm our frequent fears,

When shadows fall and deepen
　Through life's declining years;
And when our faltering footsteps
　Approach the Great Divide
We'll long to meet the old friends
　Who wait on the other side.

DAVID BANKS SICKLES

●

So long as we love we serve; so long as
we are loved by others, I would almost
say that we are indispensable; and no
man is useless while he has a friend.

ROBERT LOUIS STEVENSON

●

FRIENDSHIP IS ETERNAL

Friendship is like a song . . .
A beautiful melody that lingers on.

Friendship is like a ray of light . . .
Its radiance is pure and bright.

Friendship is like a flower . . .
Its beauty has infinite power.

Friendship is like a star . . .
That guides the way, near and far.

Friendship is like a prayer . . .
Its benediction is always there.

CATHERINE PLUMB

What wealth it is to have such friends that we cannot think of them without elevation.

HENRY DAVID THOREAU

●

WHAT IS A FRIEND?

*A friend is a person of great
    understanding
Who shares all our hopes and our
    schemes,
A companion who listens with infinite
    patience
To all of our plans and our dreams,
A true friend can make all our cares melt
    away
With the touch of a hand or a smile,
And with calm reassurance make
    everything brighter,
And life always seem more worth
    while —
A friend shares so many bright moments
    of laughter
At even the tiniest thing —
What memorable hours of light-hearted
    gladness
And pleasure this sharing can bring!
A friend is a cherished and precious
    possession
Who knows all our hopes and our fears,
And someone to treasure deep down in
    our hearts
With a closeness that grows through the
    years!*

KATHERINE DAVIS

●

THERE IS NO FRIEND LIKE
AN OLD FRIEND

*There is no friend like an old friend
    Who has shared our morning days.
No greeting like his welcome,
    No homage like his praise.*

OLIVER WENDELL HOLMES

●

A friend is one who walks in when the rest of the world walks out.

*Friendship is the sunshine
That turns the sky to gold.
Friendship is the fragrance
A thousand blessings hold.*

*Friendship is the pathway that
Leads to dreams come true . . .
For friendship is the blessing
Of knowing someone like you.*

●

A DESCRIPTION OF TRUE FRIENDSHIP

I love you not only for what you are, but for what I am, when I am with you.

I love you not only for what you are making of yourself, but for what you are making of me.

I love you for that part of me that you bring out.

I love you for putting your hand into my heaped-up heart, and passing over all the foolish, and frivolous, and weak things that you cannot help dimly seeing there, for drawing out into the light all the beautiful and radiant qualities that no one else has looked quite deep enough to find.

I love you for ignoring the possibility of the fool in me, and laying hold of the possibility of good.

I love you for closing your ears to the discords in me, and for adding to the harmony in me by reverent listening.

I love you because you are helping me to make the structure of my life, not a tavern but a temple; and the words of my every day not a reproach but a song . . . Perhaps this is what being a friend means after all.

*True friendship's laws are by this rule
    expressed,
Welcome the coming, speed the parting
    guest.*

HOMER

69

A FRIEND...
WHO STANDS BY

When troubles come your soul to try,
You love the friend who just stands by,
Perhaps there's nothing he can do,
The thing is strictly up to you,
For there are troubles all your own,
And paths the soul must tread alone,
Times when love can't smooth the road,
Nor friendship lift the heavy load.
But just to feel you have a friend
Who will stand by until the end.
Whose sympathy through all endures,
Whose warm handclasp is always yours,
It helps somehow to pull you through,
Although there's nothing he can do;
And so with fervent heart we cry,
"God bless the friend who just stands by."

●

True friendship is a plant of slow growth,
and must undergo and withstand the
shocks of adversity, before it is entitled
to the appellation.

GEORGE WASHINGTON

**Laughter is not at all a bad beginning for
a friendship, and it is far the best ending
for one.**

OSCAR WILDE

GROWING FRIENDSHIP

Friendship is like a garden
  of flowers, fine and rare,

It cannot reach perfection
  except through loving care;

Then, new and lovely blossoms
  with each new day appear...

For Friendship, like a garden,
  grows in beauty year by year.

**Do good to thy friend to keep him,
to thy enemy to gain him.**

BENJAMIN FRANKLIN

●

Friends, like all good things in this life,
can be had by any one who wants them.
There is only one simple rule to follow;
it is this: to have a friend, be one yourself.

THE GIFT OF FRIENDS

God knew we needed something more
Than budding earth and sunlit sky,
And so He sent us friends to love,
To lift our hearts and spirits high;
God chose to teach Love's wondrous art,
Of comfort, cheer that never ends
By giving to the thankful heart
The dear, good gift of faithful friends.

●

WHAT MAKES US FRIENDS?

What makes us friends throughout the
  years
Regardless what we share,
The shadowed days that we must face,
Or when the skies are fair.

What makes us friends when
  circumstance
Decides that we must part;
Although our roads must separate
We're ever close in heart.

What makes us friends... God only
  knows
The answer to our quest...
So humbly we accept this gift
And know we're truly blessed.

HILDA BUTLER FARR

●

A friend is a present you give yourself.

ROBERT LOUIS STEVENSON

SPEAK OUT

If you have a friend worth loving,
  Love him. Yes, and let him know
That you love him, ere life's evening
  Tinge his brow with sunset glow.
Why should good words ne'er be said
Of a friend — till he is dead?

If you hear a song that thrills you,
  Sung by any child of song,
Praise it. Do not let the singer
  Wait deserved praises long.
Why should one who thrills your heart
Lack the joy you may impart?

If you hear a prayer that moves you
  By its humble, pleading tone.
Join it. Do not let the seeker
  Bow before his God alone.
Why should not thy brother share
The strength of "two or three" in prayer?

If your work is made more easy
  By a friendly, helping hand,
Say so. Speak out brave and truly.
  Ere the darkness veil the land.
Should a brother workman dear
Falter for a word of cheer?

Scatter thus your seeds of kindness
  All enriching as you go —
Leave them. Trust the Harvest-Giver;
  He will make each seed to grow.
So, until the happy end,
Your life shall never lack a friend.

●

Greater love hath no man than this,
that a man lay down his life for his
  friends.
Ye are my friends,
  if ye do whatsoever I command you.

JOHN 15:13, 14

Actions, not words, are the true char-
acteristic mark of the attachment of
friends.

GEORGE WASHINGTON

The value of true friends
  Cannot be measured on a chart.
No scale on earth can weigh their worth
  Except the human heart.

●

We cannot tell the precise moment when
friendship is formed. As in filling a vessel
drop by drop, there is at last a drop which
makes it run over. So in a series of kindnesses . . . there is at last one which
makes the heart run over.

JAMES BOSWELL

**What language shall I borrow
To thank Thee, dearest Friend?**

BERNARD OF CLAIRVAUX

●

If I were to covet any honour of author-
ship, it would be this: That some letters
of mine might be found in the desks of
my friends when their life struggle is
ended.

SIR W. ROBERTSON NICOLL

**Of all the things which wisdom provides
to make life entirely happy, much the
greatest is the possession of friendship.**

EPICURUS

99

I want someone to laugh with me, someone to be grave with me, someone to
please me and help my discrimination
with his or her own remark, and at times,
no doubt, to admire my acuteness and
penetration.

ROBERT BURNS

BECAUSE OF THOSE

It's because of those who love us,
Those we know do really care,
That this life is worth the living
With the sorrows we must share.

It's because of those who know us,
Those who always understand,
That we find the going easy
When we need a helping hand.

They are true friends who can take us,
When we are not up to par,
And can still appreciate us
Just exactly as we are.

VIRGINIA K. OLIVER

If you forgive people enough you belong to them, and they to you, whether either person likes it or not — squatter's rights of the heart.

JAMES HILTON

Talk not of wasted affection,
affection never was wasted.

HENRY WADSWORTH LONGFELLOW

"What is the secret of your life?" asked Mrs. Browning of Charles Kingsley. "Tell me, that I may make mine beautiful, too." He replied: "I had a friend."

RELATED BY WILLIAM CHANNING GANNETT

FRIENDSHIP IS A GARDEN

Scatter seeds of friendship, thoughts and words and deeds . . . Though the soil looks stony, scatter wide your seeds. Every kindly action, every word sincere . . . Every good intention meant to help and cheer is a seed of friendship . . . And somewhere, someday, it will bud and blossom in its own sweet way.

Time must bring its changes as the years roll by . . . Flowers of love must perish, friendships fade and die. But if you have scattered all along the track, seeds of true affection . . . You will never lack. Always there'll be someone who will understand . . . Someone who is ready with a helping hand. Do not dread the future, full of doubts and fears . . . Sow the seeds of friendship for the coming years.

PATIENCE STRONG

Gifts & Giving

God's gifts put man's best dreams to shame.

ELIZABETH BARRETT BROWNING

•

MAGIC

It costs so little, I wonder why
We give it so little thought;
A smile, kind words, a glance, a touch —
What magic by them is wrought.

•

GIFT

Let us ask ourselves as we arise each morning, What is my work today? We do not know where the influence of today will end. Our lives may outgrow all our present thoughts and outdazzle all our dreams. God puts each fresh morning, each new chance of life, into our hands as a gift, to see what we will do with it.

ANNA R. BROWN LINDSAY

What I kept I lost,
What I spent I had,
What I gave I have.

PERSIAN PROVERB

GIFTS

The best thing to give:
  to your enemy, forgiveness;
  to an opponent, tolerance;
  to a friend, your heart;
  to a child, a good example:
  to a father, deference;
  to your mother, conduct that will make
    her proud of you;
  to yourself, respect;
  to all men, charity.

ARTHUR JAMES BALFOUR

A SONG OF SERVICE

If all my pain and all my tears,
And all that I have learned throughout
* the years*
Could make one perfect song
To lift some fallen head
To light some darkened mind,
I should feel that not in vain
I served mankind.

MARGUERITE FEW

•

If you want to be rich, give;
If you want to be poor, grasp;
If you want abundance, scatter;
If you want to be needy, hoard!

DAILY CHALLENGE

I cannot add the number,
The list is much too long,
Of gifts that God has given
To make of life a song.

So this remains my motto
To still my heart's unrest;
Remembering I'm lucky,
And so divinely blessed.

The road has not been easy,
I've had my share of tears,
A load of disappointments
And pain throughout the years.

But every day's a challenge
To try and meet the test;
And always to remember
I'm so divinely blessed.

HILDA BUTLER FARR

Never be afraid of giving up your best,
And God will give you His better.

HINTON

What can I give Him
Poor as I am?
If I were a shepherd,
I would give Him a lamb,
If I were a Wise Man,
I would do my part, —
But what I can I give Him,
Give my heart.

CHRISTINA ROSSETTI

●

Give all to love;
Obey thy heart;
Friends, kindred, days,
Estate, good fame,
Plans, credit and muse —
Nothing refuse.

RALPH WALDO EMERSON

I have held many things in my hands and lost them all; but whatever I have placed in God's hands, that I still possess.

MARTIN LUTHER

LET ME GIVE

I do not know how long I'll live,
But while I live, Lord, let me give,
Some comfort to someone in need,
By smile or nod, kind word or deed.
And let me do whate'er I can
To ease things for my fellow man.
I want naught but to do my part
To lift a tired or weary heart,
To change folks' frowns to smiles again.
Then I will not have lived in vain.
And I'll not care how long I'll live
If I can give — and give — and give.

●

Every good gift and every perfect gift is from above.

JAMES 1:17

●

THESE ARE THE GIFTS I ASK

These are the gifts I ask
Of thee, Spirit serene:
Strength for the daily task,
Courage to face the road,
Good cheer to help me bear the traveller's
load,
And, for the hours of rest that come
between,
An inward joy in all things heard and
seen.
These are the sins I fain
Would have thee take away:
Malice, and cold disdain,
Hot anger, sullen hate,
Scorn of the lowly, envy of the great,
And discontent that casts a shadow gray
On all the brightness of a common day.

HENRY VAN DYKE

There's not a joy the world can give like that it takes away.

LORD BYRON

THE GIFT
*A wise lover
  values not so much
  the gift of the lover
  as the love of the giver.*

THOMAS A KEMPIS

●

Give what you have. To some one, it may be better than you dare to think.

HENRY WADSWORTH LONGFELLOW

GIVING

*It is strange, but very true — giving
  just enriches you.
If you give a kindly deed, if you plant
  a friendship seed,
If you share a laugh or song, if your
  giving rights a wrong,
Then joy you feel and share makes
  more goodness everywhere.
It is strange, but very true — giving
  just enriches you!*

●

*Not what we give, but what we share, —
For the gift without the giver is bare;
Who gives himself with his alms feeds
  three, —
Himself, his hungering neighbor, and me.*

JAMES RUSSELL LOWELL

God & Jesus Christ

THE EXTRAVAGANCE OF GOD

More sky than man can see,
More seas than he can sail,
More sun than he can bear to watch,
More stars than he can scale.

More breath than he can breathe,
More yield than he can sow,
More grace than he can comprehend,
More love than he can know.

RALPH W. SEAGER

•

HE WHO OWNS A GARDEN

He who owns a garden,
    However small it be,
Whose hands have planted in it
    Flower or bush or tree;
He who watches patiently
    The growth from nurtured sod,
Who thrills at newly-opened bloom
    Is very close to God.

KATHERINE EDELMAN

•

**In the Kingdom of God no one can see so
long as he remains merely a spectator.**

NATHAN SODERBLOM

O depth of wealth, wisdom, and
    knowledge in God!
How unsearchable his judgements, how
    untraceable his ways!
Who knows the mind of the Lord?
Who has been his counsellor?
Who has ever made a gift to him, to
    receive a gift in return?
Source, Guide, and Goal of all that is —
    to him be glory for ever! Amen.

ROMANS 11:33-36
THE NEW ENGLISH BIBLE

God is so high you can't get above Him.
God is so low you can't get beneath Him.
God is so wide you can't get around Him.
You'd better come in by the gate.

NEGRO SPIRITUAL

•

GOD CARES!

When His eye is on the sparrow
    And each budding leaf that grows;
When He sends the dew each morning
    And the sunshine to the rose;
You may know beyond all doubting,
    In this trial you're passing through,
God cares . . . and every moment
    He is watching over you!

KEITH BENNETT

DEVOUTLY LOVED

No one else holds or has held the place in the heart of the world which Jesus holds. Other gods have been as devoutly worshiped; no other man has been so devoutly loved.

JOHN KNOX

As the hart panteth after the water
brooks,
so panteth my soul after thee, O God.
My soul thirsteth for God, for the living
God:
when shall I come and appear before
God?
My tears have been my meat day and
night,
while they continually say unto me,
Where is thy God?
When I remember these things,
I pour out my soul in me:
for I had gone with the multitude,
I went with them to the house of
God,
with the voice of joy and praise,
with a multitude that kept holy day.
Why art thou cast down, O my soul?
and why art thou disquieted in me?
hope thou in God . . .
Deep calleth unto deep at the noise of thy
waterspouts:
all thy waves and thy billows are gone
over me.
Yet the Lord will command his loving-
kindness in the daytime,
and in the night his song shall be
with me,
and my prayer unto the God of
my life.

PSALM 42:1-8

Not in our working hours alone
His constancy and care are known,
But locked in slumber fast and deep
He giveth to us while we sleep.

FREDERICK LUCIAN HOSMER

MY LORD AND I

I have a Friend so precious,
So very dear to me,
He loves me with such tender love,
He loves so faithfully;
I could not live apart from Him,
I love to feel Him nigh
And so we dwell together,
My Lord and I.

Sometimes I'm faint and weary,
He knows that I am weak,
And as He bids me lean on Him,
His help I gladly seek;
He leads me in the paths of light
Beneath a sunny sky,
And so we walk together,
My Lord and I.

He knows how much I love Him,
O that I loved Him well;
But with what love He loveth me,
My tongue can never tell;
It is an everlasting love,
In ever rich supply,
And so we love each other,
My Lord and I.

**Love is the verb of which God is
the object.**

LYCURGUS M. STARKEY, JR.

GOD'S CARE

God watches over the birds that fly;
He sets the stars in the evening sky;
He paints the flower and He sends the rain
That patters against the window pane.

The round, red sun in the eastern sky
He bids ascend to its place on high;
And keeps it there till it sinks to rest,
A ball of fire in the glowing west.

His loving care is around us all —
We rise each day at His gentle call;
We go to sleep at His wise command;
We are led each step by His guiding hand.

For the Lord is a great God,
    and a great King above all gods.
In His hand are the deep places
    of the earth: the strength
    of the hills is His also.
The sea is His, and He made it:
    and His hands formed the dry land.

PSALM 95:3-5

There is a living God; He has spoken in the Bible. He means all He says, and will do all He has promised.

J. HUDSON TAYLOR

Let one more attest:
I have seen God's hand through a lifetime
And all was for best.

ROBERT BROWNING

I know not where His islands lift
Their fronded palms in air;
I only know I cannot drift
Beyond His love and care.

JOHN GREENLEAF WHITTIER

Jesus is
    heaven's bread for earth's hunger,
    heaven's clothing for earth's
        nakedness,
    heaven's riches for earth's poverty,
    heaven's water for earth's thirst,
    heaven's light for earth's darkness,
    heaven's grace for earth's guilt,
    heaven's gladness for earth's grief,
    heaven's glory for earth's shame,
    heaven's gain for earth's loss,
    heaven's love for earth's hate,
    heaven's wisdom for earth's follies,
    heaven's peace for earth's strife,
    heaven's hope for earth's despair,

    heaven's prompting for earth's
        perplexity,
    heaven's justification for earth's
        condemnation,
    heaven's comfort for earth's sorrows,
    heaven's cleansing for earth's dirt,
    heaven's salvation for earth's
        damnation,
    heaven's life for earth's death.
This One had no sin *in* Him but all sin
    on Him.

ROBERT G. LEE

OVERHEARD IN AN ORCHARD

Said the Robin to the Sparrow:
    "I should really like to know
Why these anxious human beings
    Rush about and worry so."

Said the Sparrow to the Robin:
    "Friend, I think that it must be
That they have no heavenly Father
    Such as cares for you and me."

ELIZABETH CHENEY

Therefore the Lord himself shall give you
    a sign;
Behold, a virgin shall conceive,
and bear a son,
and shall call his name Immanuel.

ISAIAH 7:14

Jesus Christ, the condescension of divinity, and the exaltation of humanity.

PHILLIPS BROOKS

A man should be ashamed to run his own life the minute he finds out there is a God.

For unto us a child is born,
unto us a son is given:
and the government shall be upon his
    shoulder:
and his name shall be called
    Wonderful,
    Counsellor, The mighty God,
    The everlasting Father,
    The Prince of Peace.

ISAIAH 9:6

THE LAMB

Little lamb, who made thee?
Dost thou know who made thee,
Gave thee life, and bade thee feed
By the stream and o'er the mead;
Gave thee clothing of delight,
Softest clothing, woolly, bright;
Gave thee such a tender voice,
Making all the vales rejoice?
    Little lamb, who made thee?
    Dost thou know who made thee?

Little lamb, I'll tell thee;
Little lamb, I'll tell thee;
He is called by thy name,
For He calls Himself a Lamb,
He is meek, and He is mild,
He became a little child,
I a child, and thou a lamb,
We are called by His name.

Little Lamb, God bless thee!
Little Lamb, God bless thee!

WILLIAM BLAKE

JESUS SAID "I AM"

"I am the bread of life" (John 6:35).
"I am the light of the world" (John 8:12).
"I am the door" (John 10:9).
"I am the good shepherd" (John 10:11).
"I am the way, the truth, and the life"
    (John 14:6).

**The one thing we need is to know
God better.**

J. HUDSON TAYLOR

The life of Christ is concerning Him
who, being the holiest among the mighty,
and the mightiest among the holy, lifted
with His pierced hand empires off their
hinges, and turned the stream of centuries out of its channel, and still governs
the ages.

JEAN PAUL RICHTER

Goodness & Greatness

No man or woman can really be strong, gentle, pure, and good without the world being better for it.

PHILLIPS BROOKS

●

Do all the good you can,
By all the means you can,
In all the ways you can,
In all the places you can,
At all the times you can,
To all the people you can,
As long as ever you can.

JOHN WESLEY

●

Did it ever strike you that goodness is not merely a beautiful thing, but by far the most beautiful thing in the whole world? So that nothing is to be compared for value with goodness; that riches, honor, power, pleasure, learning, the whole world and all in it, are not worth having in comparison with being good; and the utterly best thing for a man is to be good, even though he were never to be rewarded for it.

CHARLES KINGSLEY

In men whom men condemn as ill
I find so much of goodness still,
In men whom men pronounce divine
I find so much of sin and blot,
I do not dare to draw a line
Between the two, where God has not.

JOAQUIN MILLER

●

SIMPLE GOODNESS

Goodness is richer than greatness. It lifts us nearer to God. It is manifested according to our abilities, within our sphere. Every day I bless God that the great necessary work of the world is so faithfully carried on by humble men in narrow spaces and by faithful women in narrow circles, performing works of simple goodness.

EDWIN HUBBELL CHAPIN

GREAT THINGS

Great things are only done by men
Who, having failed, will try again:
Who risk their all to venture out,
And having ventured, never doubt:
Whose confidence in self is strong,
And dare defy the doubting throng.

80

Goodness and love mold the form into their own image, and cause the joy and beauty of love to shine forth from every part of the face. When this form of love is seen, it appears ineffably beautiful, and effects with delight the inmost life of the soul.

EMANUEL SWEDENBORG

MEASURE OF A MAN

Not, how did he die?
But, how did he live?
Not, what did he gain?
But, what did he give?

These are the merits
To measure the worth
Of a man as a man
Regardless of birth.

Not, what was his station?
But, had he a heart?
And how did he play
His God-given part?

Was he ever ready
With a word of good cheer
To bring a smile,
To banish a tear?

Not, what was his church?
Nor, what was his creed?
But had he befriended
Those really in need?

Not, what did the sketch
In the newspaper say?
But, how many were sorry
When he passed away?

●

The steadfast love of the Lord never ceases, his mercies never come to an end;
they are new every morning;
great is thy faithfulness.
"The Lord is my portion," says my soul,
"therefore I will hope in him."
The Lord is good to those who
wait for him, to the soul that seeks him.

LAMENTATIONS 3:22-25

You can only make others better by being good yourself.

HUGH R. HAWEIS

●

Withdraw into yourself and look. And if you do not find yourself beautiful yet, do as does the creator of a statue that is to be made beautiful; he cuts away here, he smooths there, he makes this line lighter, this other purer, until he has shown a beautiful face upon his statue. So do you also; cut away all that is excessive, straighten all that is crooked, bring light to all that is shadowed, labor to make all glow with beauty, and do not cease chiselling your statue until there shall shine out on you the godlike splendor of virtue, until you shall see the final goodness surely established in the stainless shrine.

PLOTINUS

Goodness is the only investment that never fails.

HENRY DAVID THOREAU

Difficulty is the nurse of greatness — a harsh nurse, who roughly rocks her foster children into strength and athletic proportion. The mind, grappling with great aims and wrestling with mighty impediments, grows by a certain necessity to their stature.

WILLIAM CULLEN BRYANT

Good, better, best; never let it rest
Till your good is better,
And your better, best.

OLD MAXIM

SIGNS OF TRUE GREATNESS

The ability to apologize;
   to forgive and forget;
To avoid arguments;
To avoid being self-conscious;
To take snubs and reproof well;
To have mastery over the flesh;
To stoop to help others.

TRUE GREATNESS

A man is as great as the dreams he
   dreams,
   As great as the love he bears;
As great as the values he redeems,
   And the happiness he shares.
A man is as great as the thoughts he
   thinks,
   As the worth he has attained;
As the fountains at which his spirit drinks
   And the insight he has gained.
A man is as great as the truth he speaks,
   As great as the help he gives,
As great as the destiny he seeks,
   As great as the life he lives.

C. E. FLYNN

The greatest pleasure I know is to do a
good action by stealth and have it found
out by accident.

CHARLES LAMB

The greatest men are the simplest.

A retentive memory is a good thing,
but the ability to forget is the true token
of greatness.

ELBERT HUBBARD

From THE ETERNAL GOODNESS

Who fathoms the Eternal Thought?
   Who talks of scheme and plan?
The Lord is God! He needeth not
   The poor device of man.

I see the wrong that round me lies,
   I feel the guilt within;
I hear, with groan and travail-cries,
   The world confess its sin.

Yet, in the maddening maze of things,
   And tossed by storm and flood,
To one fixed trust my spirit clings;
   I know that God is good!

I long for household voices gone,
   For vanished smiles I long,
But God hath led my dear ones on,
   And He can do no wrong.

I know not what the future hath
   Of marvel or surprise,
Assured alone that life and death
   His mercy underlies.

JOHN GREENLEAF WHITTIER

The price of greatness is responsibility.

SIR WINSTON CHURCHILL

RECIPE FOR GREATNESS

To bear up under loss;
To fight the bitterness of defeat and the
   weakness of grief;
To be victor over anger;
To smile when tears are close;
To resist disease and evil men and base
   instincts;
To hate hate and to love love;
To go on when it would seem good to die;
To look up with unquenchable faith in
   something ever more about to be.
That is what any man can do, and be
   great.

ZANE GREY

Gratitude

THANK GOD FOR LITTLE THINGS

*Thank you, God, for little things
  that often come our way,
The things we take for granted
  but don't mention when we pray,
The unexpected courtesy,
  the thoughtful, kindly deed,
A hand reached out to help us
  in the time of sudden need —
Oh make us more aware, dear God,
  of little daily graces
That come to us with "sweet surprise"
  from never-dreamed-of places.*

HELEN STEINER RICE

●

GRATITUDE

As flowers carry dewdrops,
  trembling on the edges
  of the petals,
  and ready to fall
  at the first waft
  of the wind
  or brush of bird,
so the heart should carry
  its beaded words
  of thanksgiving.
At the first breath
  of heavenly flavor,
  let down the shower,
  perfumed with
  the heart's gratitude.

HENRY WARD BEECHER

PRAYER FOR APPRECIATION

*Oh teach me, Lord, to treasure much
The simple things of life — the touch
Of wind and snow, of rain and sun;
And when the hours of work are done,
The quietness of rest, the fair
And healing sustenance of prayer.
And, Lord of living, help me keep
A shining, singing gladness deep
Within for blessings yet to be
Through all eternity.*

●

---

*Gratitude takes three forms:
  a feeling in the heart,
  an expression in words,
  and a giving in return.*

●

Thank God every morning when you get up that you have something to do that day which must be done, whether you like it or not. Being forced to work and forced to do your best will breed in you temperance and self-control, diligence and strength of will, cheerfulness and content, and a hundred virtues which the idle never know.

CHARLES KINGSLEY

83

When thou hast thanked thy God for
  every blessing sent,
What time will then remain for
  murmurs or lament?

●

Praise ye the Lord.
Praise God in His sanctuary:
  praise Him in the firmament of His
    power.
Praise Him for His mighty acts:
  praise Him according to His excellent
    greatness.
Praise Him with the sound of the trumpet:
  praise Him with the psaltery and harp.
Praise Him with the timbrel and dance:
  praise Him with stringed instruments
    and organs.
Praise Him upon the loud cymbals:
  praise Him upon the high sounding
    cymbals.
Let every thing that hath breath praise
  the Lord.
Praise ye the Lord.

PSALM 150

SAY SO

Does a neighbor help a little,
  As along the way you go —
Help to make your burden lighter?
  Then why not tell him so!

Does a handclasp seem to lift you
  From the depth of grief and woe,
When an old friend shares your sorrow?
  Then why not tell him so!

Does your Heavenly Father give you
  Many blessings here below?
Then on bended knee before Him
  Frankly, gladly, tell Him so!

GERALDINE SEARFOSS

●

**Gratitude is a duty which ought to be
paid, but which none have a right to
expect.**

A HEART TO PRAISE THEE

Thou hast given so much to me,
Give one thing more — a grateful heart:
Not thankful when it pleaseth me,
As if thy blessings had spare days,
But such a heart whose Pulse may be
Thy Praise.

GEORGE HERBERT

●

WE THANK THEE

For flowers that bloom about our feet,
  Father, we thank Thee,
For tender grass so fresh and sweet,
  Father, we thank Thee,
For song of bird and hum of bee,
For all things fair we hear or see,
  Father in heaven, we thank Thee.

For blue of stream and blue of sky,
  Father, we thank Thee,
For pleasant shade of branches high,
  Father, we thank Thee,
For fragrant air and cooling breeze,
For beauty of the blooming trees
  Father in heaven, we thank Thee.

For this new morning with its light,
  Father, we thank Thee,
For rest and shelter of the night,
  Father, we thank Thee,
For health and food, for love and friends,
For everything Thy goodness sends,
  Father in heaven, we thank Thee.

●

MY HEART LEAPS UP

My heart leaps up when I behold
  A rainbow in the sky;
So was it when my life began;
So is it now I am a man;
So be it when I shall grow old.
  Or let me die!
The Child is father of the Man;
And I could wish my days to be
Bound each to each by natural piety.

WILLIAM WORDSWORTH

**The thought of our past years in me
   doth breed
   Perpetual benediction.**

WILLIAM WORDSWORTH

●

THANK GOD THAT I'M ME

When my luck seems all out, and I'm
   down in the mouth,
When I'm stuck in the North and I want
   to go South:
When the world seems a blank and
   there's no one I love,
And it seems even God's not in Heaven
   above,
I've a cure for my grouch and it works
   like a shot —
I just think of the things I am glad I am
   not:
         A bird in a cage.
            A fish in a bowl.
         A pig in a pen,
            A fox in a hole.
         A bear in a pit.
            A wolf in a trap.
         A fowl on a spit.
            A rug on a lap.
         A horse in a stable.
            A cow in a shed.
         A plate on a table.
            The sheet on a bed.
         The case on a pillow.
            A bell on a door.
         A branch on a willow.
            A mat on the floor.
When I think of the hundreds of things I
   might be,
I get down on my knees and thank God
   that I'm me.
Then my blues disappear, when I think
   what I've got,
And quite soon I've forgotten the things I
   have not.

ELSIE JANIS

●

A MOTHER SPEAKS

It is not gratitude, my child, I ask,
   Nor do I seek to make my will your
      own;

The memory of your babyhood, though
   you are grown
   Enchants me still; nor ever was a task
Performed for you save lovingly; I do
   Indeed thank you that you have
      brought me days
Of bright felicity in all your ways,
   And hours of grieving and of tears,
      so few!

No, do not thank me now, but think upon
   Your childhood tenderly when I have
      gone,
And if in sudden sweet remembering,
   You, too, find deepening joy in each
      small thing
Done for your child, or in your ministry
To one beloved, you will be thanking me.

●

HYMN OF THANKSGIVING

The roar of the world is in my ears;
Thank God for the roar of the world!
Thank God for the mighty tide of fears
Against me always hurled!
Thank God for the bitter and ceaseless
   strife
And the sting of His chastening rod!
Thank God for the stress and the pains
   of life
And oh! Thank God for God!

JOYCE KILMER

●

FATHER, WE THANK THEE

Father, we thank thee:
For peace within our favored land,
For plenty from thy bounteous hand,
For means to give to those in need,
For grace to help in thought and deed,
For faith to walk, our hands in thine,
For truth to know thy law divine,
For strength to work with voice and pen,
For love to serve our fellow men,
For light the goal ahead to see,
For life to use alone for thee,
Father, we thank thee.

GRENVILLE KLEISER

85

Happiness

There is no cosmetic for beauty like happiness.

●

If I have faltered more or less
In my great task of happiness;
If I have moved among my race
And shown no glorious morning face;
If beams from happy human eyes
Have moved me not; if morning skies,
Books, and my food, and summer rain
Knocked on my sullen heart in vain —
Lord, Thy most pointed pleasure take
And stab my spirit broad awake;

Or, Lord, if too obdurate I,
Choose Thou, before that spirit die,
A piercing pain, a killing sin,
And to my dead heart run them in!

ROBERT LOUIS STEVENSON

●

The happiness of life is made up of minute fractions — the little soon-forgotten
charities of a kiss or smile, a kind look, a
heartfelt compliment, and the countless
infinitesimals of pleasurable and genial
feeling.

SAMUEL T. COLERIDGE

A RECIPE FOR HAPPINESS

Take a heaping cup of PATIENCE and a
    big heartful of LOVE;
Add two handsful of GENEROSITY to all
    of the above.
Then blend in a dash of LAUGHTER and
    some UNDERSTANDING, too;
Sprinkle generously with KINDNESS and
    MEMORIES, old and new;
Add a lot of FAITH and mix well to make
    it rich and sweet,
And enjoy a heaping portion with
    everyone you meet!

JON GILBERT

●

THE HAPPY MAN

If you observe a really happy man you
will find him building a boat, writing a
symphony, educating his son, growing
double dahlias in his garden, or looking
for dinosaur eggs in the Gobi desert. He
will not be searching for happiness as if it
were a collar button that has rolled under
the radiator. He will not be striving for it
among the nebulous wastes of meta-
physics.

To find happiness we must seek for it
in a focus outside ourselves.

W. BERAN WOLFE

There's happiness in little things,
  There's joy in passing pleasure,
But friendships are, from year to year,
  The best of all life's treasure.

**To love and be loved is the greatest
happiness of existence.**

HAPPINESS

A deep chair by the fireside.
A chair just right for two;
The dim soft light of candles . . .
Love's old sweet song and you.

NETTIE E. CONROW

•

From THE FAMILY REUNION

I feel quite happy, as if happiness
Did not consist in getting what one
  wanted
Or in getting rid of what can't be got rid of
But in a different vision.

T. S. ELIOT

Talk happiness each chance you get —
  and talk it good and strong!
Look for it in the byways as you grimly
  pass along;
Perhaps it is a stranger now whose visit
  never comes,
But talk it! Soon you'll find that you and
  happiness are chums.

•

HAPPINESS

Happiness is like a crystal,
  Fair and exquisite and clear,
Broken in a million pieces,
  Scattered far and near.
Now and then along life's pathway,

Lo, some shining fragments fall,
But there are so many pieces,
  No one ever finds them all.

You may find a bit of beauty,
  Or an honest share of wealth,
While another just beside you
  Gathers honor, love or health.
Vain to choose or grasp unduly,
  Broken is the perfect ball,
And there are so many pieces,
  No one ever finds them all.

Yet the wise, as on they journey,
  Treasure every fragment clear;
Fit them as they may together,
  Imagining the shattered sphere,
Learning ever to be thankful,
  Though their share of it be small,
For it has so many pieces,
  No one ever finds them all.

•

BLIND BUT HAPPY

O what a happy soul am I!
  Although I cannot see,
I am resolved that in this world
  Contented I will be;
How many blessings I enjoy
  That other people don't!
To weep and sigh because I'm blind,
  I cannot, and I won't.

FANNY CROSBY

**Happiness consists of three things:
  someone to love,
    work to do,
      and a clear conscience.**

HAPPINESS

The sweetest bird builds near the ground,
  The loveliest flower springs low;
And we must stoop for happiness
  If we its worth would know.

CHARLES SWAIN

There are two ways of being happy; we may either diminish our wants or augment our means. Either will do, the result is the same. And it is for each man to decide for himself, and do that which happens to be the easiest.

But if you are wise, you will do both at the same time. And if you are very wise, you will do both in such a way as to augment the general happiness of society.

BENJAMIN FRANKLIN

Be happy with what you have and are, be generous with both, and you won't have to hunt for happiness.

WILLIAM E. GLADSTONE

Who is the happiest of men? He who values the merits of others, and in their pleasure takes joy, even as though 'twere his own.

I am not fully dressed until I adorn myself with a smile of joy.

The collected pleasures of everyday life fade quickly away unless there is at the heart of them the gladness of having done something that has made someone happier.

All people smile in the same language.

You cannot purchase happiness,
It's something you must earn;
Give happiness to other folks,
And get joy in return.

HAROLD G. HOPPER

It isn't your position that makes you happy or unhappy. It's your disposition.

The greatest happiness in life is the conviction that we are loved, loved for ourselves, or rather loved in spite of ourselves.

VICTOR HUGO

Helpfulness & Sharing

No one is useless in this world who lightens the burden of it to anyone else.

CHARLES DICKENS

●

If I can stop one heart from breaking,
I shall not live in vain;
If I can ease one life the aching,
Or cool one pain,
Or help one fainting robin
Unto his nest again,
I shall not live in vain.

EMILY DICKINSON

●

HELPFULNESS

I will lift up mine eyes unto the hills,
  from whence cometh my help.
My help cometh from the Lord,
  which made heaven and earth.
He will not suffer thy foot to be moved:
  he that keepeth thee will not slumber.
Behold, he that keepeth Israel
  shall neither slumber nor sleep.
The Lord is thy keeper:
  the Lord is thy shade,
    upon thy right hand.
The sun shall not smite thee by day,
  nor the moon by night.
The Lord shall preserve thee from all evil:
  he shall preserve thy soul.

The Lord shall preserve thy going out
  and thy coming in
    from this time forth and even for
    evermore.

PSALM 121

●

A GOOD CREED

If any little word of ours
  Can make one life the brighter;
If any little song of ours
  Can make one heart the lighter;
God help us speak that little word,
  And take our bit of singing
And drop it in some lonely vale
  To set the echoes ringing.

If any little love of ours
  Can make one life the sweeter;
If any little care of ours
  Can make one step the fleeter;
If any little help may ease
  The burden of another;
God give us love and care and strength
  To help along each other.

●

**If you ever need a helping hand,
look at the end of your arm.**

89

Cast thy bread upon the waters of this
   troubled human sea;
Never turn away from giving all that may
   be asked of thee,
— The gift, the lift, the toil, the tears —
   thy bread — shall not be lost.
After many days it shall return, just when
   you need it most.

LORIE C. GOODING

SOME THOUGHT LINES

If I might share
A brother's load along the dusty way,
And I should turn and walk alone that
   day,
   How could I dare —
When in the evening watch I kneel to
   pray —
To ask for help to bear my pain and
   loss,
If I had heeded not my brother's
   cross?

I SHALL BE GLAD

If I can put new hope within the heart
Of one who has lost hope,
If I can help a brother up
Some difficult long slope
That seems too steep for tired feet to go,
If I can help him climb
Into the light upon the hill's far crest,
I shall begrudge no time
Or strength that I can spend, for well I
   know
How great may be his need.
If I can help through any darkened hour,
I shall be glad indeed.

For I recall how often I have been
Distressed, distraught, dismayed,
And hands have reached to help, and
   voices called
That kept me unafraid.
If I can share this help that I have had,
God knows I shall be glad.

GRACE NOLL CROWELL

He who helps a child helps humanity with
an immediateness which no other help
given to human creature in any other
stage of human life can possibly be given.

PHILLIPS BROOKS

True worth is in being, not seeming, —
   In doing, each day that goes by,
Some little good — not in dreaming
   Of great things to do by and by.

ALICE CARY

PAUSE AWHILE

Do you take the time to pause
To share a friendly smile
With some wayfaring stranger as
He walks life's lonely mile?

Or do you ever stop to stroke
A small child's tousled head?
Or take the time to but admire
A lovely flower bed?

When was the last time you looked up
To watch the clouds go by,
Or stopped to watch a bird in flight
Across the azure sky?

This world is brighter when we stop
To share a book, a smile,
When we appreciate little things,
When we just pause a while.

GEORGIA B. ADAMS

**Whoever makes home seem to the young
dearer and more happy, is a public bene-
factor.**

HENRY WARD BEECHER

The bread that bringeth strength I want
   to give;
The water pure that bids the thirsty live;
I want to help the fainting day by day;
I'm sure I shall not pass again this way.

A cheerful heart
And a smiling face
Put sunshine
In the darkest place.

I shall pass through this world but once. Any good therefore that I can do or any kindness that I can show to any human being, let me do it now. Let me not deter or neglect it, for I shall not pass this way again.

STEPHEN GRELLETT

Not in having or receiving,
But in giving, there is bliss;
He who has no other pleasure
Ever may rejoice in this.

THE TIDES OF PROVIDENCE

It's not what you gather but what you sow
That gives the heart a warming glow.
It's not what you get but what you give
Decides the kind of life you live.

It's not what you hoard but what you
spare.
It's not what you take but what you
share —
That pays the greater dividend
And makes you richer in the end.

It's not what you spend upon yourself
Or hide away upon a shelf,
That brings a blessing for the day.
It's what you scatter by the way.

A wasted effort it may seem,
But what you cast upon the stream,
Comes back to you in recompense
Upon the tides of Providence.

PATIENCE STRONG

He has the right to criticize who has the heart to help.

ABRAHAM LINCOLN

PASS IT ON

Have you had a kindness shown?
Pass it on.
It was not given to you alone,
Pass it on.
Let it travel through the years;
Let it wipe another's tears;
Till in heaven the deed appears,
Pass it on.
Have you found the heavenly light?
Pass it on.
Souls are groping in the night,
Daylight gone.
Lift your lighted lamp on high,
Be a star in someone's sky,
He may live who else would die.
Pass it on.

HENRY BURTON

Home & Family

CHARACTER OF A HAPPY HOME

Economically sound
Physically healthful
Morally wholesome
Mentally stimulating
Spiritually inspiring
Artistically satisfying
Socially responsible
Center of unselfish love.

BLESS THIS HOUSE

Bless this house, O Lord, we pray,
　Make it safe by night and day;
Bless these walls, so firm and stout,
　Keeping want and trouble out;
Bless the roof and chimney tall,
　Let thy peace be over all;
Bless this door, that it may prove
　Ever open to joy and love.

HELEN TAYLOR

●

Except the Lord build the house,
　they labour in vain that build it:
　　except the Lord keep the city,
　　　the watchman waketh but in vain.
It is vain for you to rise up early,
　to sit up late,
　　to eat the bread of sorrows:

for so he giveth his beloved sleep.
Lo, children are an heritage of the Lord:
　and the fruit of the womb is his reward.
As arrows are in the hand of a mighty
　　man;
　so are children of the youth.
Happy is the man that hath his quiver full
　　of them:
　they shall not be ashamed,
　　but they shall speak with the
　　　enemies
　　　in the gate.

PSALM 127

●

The lights of home . . . they bring us
　A sense of warmth and peace.
　They promise untold loveliness,
　Rest, laughter and release.

They are like hands that beckon us,
　Like arms that draw us near . . .
The lights of home! They whisper words
　Of comfort and good cheer.

●

Home is the place where character is
built, where sacrifices to contribute to the
happiness of others are made, and where
love has taken up its abode.

ELIJAH KELLOGG

THE HOUSE YOU CALL HOME

May the house you call home
Have sturdy walls,
And windows that face
the sun;
With doors that swing wide
With a welcome inside
To warm you when day
is done.

May the echo of laughter
Resound from each rafter,
And peace and contentment
dwell there.
May the house you call home
Be a haven of rest,
Secure 'neath a roof
of prayer.

HELEN LOWRIE MARSHALL

THE HOUSE BEAUTIFUL

The Crown of the house is Godliness.
The Beauty of the house is Order.
The Glory of the house is Hospitality.
The Blessing of the house is Contentment.

OLD INSCRIPTION

AN ADORED MOTHER

She mended a doll
and the washing waited.
The dust lay thick
while a fish hook was baited.

When Injuns attacked
her dinner burned up.
She provided a bed
for a straying pup.

A two-year-old helped
with the cookie dough,
The ironing dried out
while she romped in the snow.

Her neighbors whispered
to one another,
But the children laughed
and adored their mother.

CAROLYN BEAUCAMP

HOME VIRTUES

The beauty of a house is harmony.
The security of a house is loyalty.
The joy of a house is love.
The plenty of a house is in children.
The rule of a house is service.
The comfort of a house is in contented
spirits.
The maker of a house, of a real human
house,
is God himself, the same who made the
stars and built the world.

FRANK CRANE

**Mother is the name for God in the lips
and hearts of little children.**

WILLIAM MAKEPEACE THACKERAY

SONG

Stay, stay at home, my heart and rest;
Home-keeping hearts are happiest,
For those that wander they know not
where
Are full of trouble and full of care;
To stay at home is best.

Weary and homesick and distressed,
They wander east, they wander west,
And are baffled and beaten and blown
about
By the winds of the wilderness of doubt;
To stay at home is best.

Then stay at home, my heart, and rest;
The bird is safest in its nest,
Over all that flutter their wings and fly
A hawk is hovering in the sky;
To stay at home is best.

HENRY WADSWORTH LONGFELLOW

A house is built of logs and stone,
Of tiles and posts and piers;
A home is built of loving deeds
That stand a thousand years.

VICTOR HUGO

Most of our homes are having this painful contemplation: A child is born in the home and for twenty years makes so much noise we think we can hardly stand it, and then he departs leaving the home so silent that we think we'll go mad.

MOTHERS

What a wonderful thing
Is a mother!
Other folks can love you,
But only your mother understands;
She works for you —
Looks after you —
Loves you, forgives you —
Anything you may do;
And then the only thing
Bad she ever does do —
Is to die and leave you.

BARONESS VON HUTTON

THE HOUSEWIFE

Jesus, teach me how to be
Proud of my simplicity.

Sweep the floors, wash the clothes,
Gather for each vase a rose.

Iron and tend a tiny frock,
Keeping one eye on the clock.

Always having time kept free
For childish questions asked of me.

Grant me wisdom Mary had
When she taught her little Lad.

CATHERINE CATE COBLENTZ

The family is a storehouse in which the world's finest treasures are kept. Yet the only gold you'll find is golden laughter. The only silver is in the hair of Dad and Mom. The family's only real diamond is on Mother's left hand. Yet can it sparkle like children's eyes at Christmas or shine half as bright as the candles on a birthday cake?

ALAN BECK

WHEN FATHER ASKED THE BLESSING

When Father asked the blessing
And in reverence bowed his head,
Our hearts were filled with gladness
And our spirits too, were fed.

The table spread before us
Was one of modest fare,
The food was always wholesome
And served with love and care.

The sharing of our problems
While at the noonday meal
Lightened our burdens somehow,
And joy seemed more real.

In telling to our family
Our future plans and schemes,
We furthered worthwhile ventures
And helped realize our dreams.

A home is such a happy place
Where loved ones share together
The brightness of the fireside
In times of chilly weather.

When Father asked the blessing
And in reverence bowed his head,
We thanked the Lord in unison
For this, our daily bread.

INEZ LEMKE

A house is built by human hands, but a home is built by human hearts.

Peace and rest at length have come,
All the day's long toil is past,
And each heart is whispering,
"Home, home at last."

THOMAS HOOD

The real empire is at the fireside.

CICERO

●

THESE ARE THE THINGS

These are the things men seek at dusk:
Firelight across a room,
Cool rain splashing against dim roofs,
Gardens where flowers bloom.

Light-lighted gold of a windowpane,
Trees with high stars above,
Women who watch a darkening street
For somebody whom they love.

Faith of a small child's rhyming prayer,
Candleshine . . . tables spread
With a blossom or two in a gay blue bowl,
Fragrance of crusted bread.

For men may dream of a clipper ship,
A wharf, or a gypsy camp,
But their footsteps pattern a homing way
To a mother, a child, a lamp.

HELEN WELSHIMER

●

A WEDDING PRAYER

May the God of love abide
  With you, whatso'er betide,
  As you journey side by side;
Guiding onward day by day,
  Keeping sin's dark stain away,
  Leading safely thro' life's fray.

OSWALD J. SMITH

Ideals & Goals

GOD'S PURPOSE

Each day we all get twenty-four hours. There is democracy in God's bestowal of time. There is real aristocracy in the way we use it, however, for some waste it by not using it or by spending it on their own ambitions while others enrich it by making everything subservient to God's purpose for life: to learn to know, use, and enjoy life, the very center of which is made up of personal relations.

NELS F. S. FERRE

FOUR THINGS

Four things in any land must dwell,
If it endures and prospers well:
One is manhood true and good;
One is noble womanhood;
One is child life, clean and bright;
And one an altar kept alight.

BEGIN GREATLY

A life without a purpose is a languid, drifting thing.

Every day we ought to renew our purpose, saying to ourselves: This day let us make a sound beginning, for what we have hitherto done is nought.

Our improvement is in proportion to our purpose.

We hardly ever manage to get completely rid even of one fault, and do not set our hearts on daily improvement.

Always place a definite purpose before thee.

THOMAS A KEMPIS

It is high time that the ideal of success should be replaced by the ideal of service.

ALBERT EINSTEIN

He who floats with the current, who does not guide himself according to higher principles, who has no ideal, no convictions—such a man is a mere article of the world's furniture—a thing moved, instead of a living and moving being — an echo, not a voice. The man who has no inner life is the slave of his surroundings, as the barometer is the obedient servant of the air at rest and the weathercock the humble servant of the air in motion.

MY TASK

To be honest, to be kind;
To earn a little and to spend a little less;
To make upon the whole a family happier
    for his presence;
To renounce when that shall be
     necessary
    and not to be embittered;
To keep a few friends, but those without
    capitulation;
Above all, on the same grim conditions,
    to keep friends with himself —
Here is a task for all that man has of
    fortitude and delicacy.

ROBERT LOUIS STEVENSON

THE GOAL

Each life converges to some center
Expressed or still;
Exists in every human nature
A goal . . .

EMILY DICKINSON

Far away there in the sunshine are my
highest aspirations. I may not reach them,
but I can look up and see their beauty,
believe in them, and try to follow where
they lead.

LOUISA MAY ALCOTT

With malice toward none;
   with charity for all;
     with firmness in the right as God
      gives us to see the right,
let us strive on to finish the work we are in.

ABRAHAM LINCOLN

WHAT THE HEART CHERISHES

No vision, and you perish;
No ideals, and you're lost;

The heart must ever cherish
Some faith at any cost —
Some dream, some hope to cling to,
Some rainbow in the sky;
Some melody to sing to,
Some service that is high.

BE SUCH A MAN

Be such a man, and live such a life,
That if every man were such as you,
And every life a life like yours,
This earth would be God's Paradise.

PHILLIPS BROOKS

**We are haunted by an ideal life, and it is
because we have within us the beginning
and the possibility of it.**

PHILLIPS BROOKS

THOMAS JEFFERSON'S DECALOGUE

    I. Never put off till tomorrow what you
       can do today.
   II. Never trouble another for what you
       can do yourself.
  III. Never spend your money before you
       have it.
  IV. Never buy what you do not want,
       because it is cheap; it will be dear
       to you.
   V. Pride costs us more than hunger,
       thirst, and cold.
  VI. We never repent of having eaten
       too little.
 VII. Nothing is troublesome that we do
       willingly.
VIII. How much pain have cost us the
       evils which have never happened.
  IX. Take things always by their smooth
       handle.
   X. When angry, count ten, before you
       speak; if very angry, an hundred.

THE WINDS OF FATE

One ship drives east and another drives
    west
  With the selfsame winds that blow.
     'Tis the set of the sails
     And not the gales
  Which tells us the way to go.

Like the winds of the sea are the ways of
    fate,
  As we voyage along through life:
     'Tis the set of a soul
     That decides its goal,
  And not the calm or the strife.

ELLA WHEELER WILCOX

I have four things to learn in life:
  To think clearly without hurry or
    confusion;
  To love everybody sincerely;
  To act in everything with the highest
    motives;
  To trust in God unhesitatingly.

HELEN KELLER

Thank God! there is always a Land of
  Beyond
  For us who are true to the trail;
A vision to seek, a beckoning peak,
  A farness that never will fail;
A pride in our soul that mocks at a goal,
  A manhood that irks at a bond,
And try how we will, unattainable still,
  Behold it, our Land of Beyond!

ROBERT W. SERVICE

THOROUGHBRED CODE

I believe in work. For discontent and
labor are not often companions.
I believe in thrift. For to store up a little
regularly is to store up character as
well.
I believe in simple living. For simplicity means health and health means
happiness.

I believe in loyalty. For if I am not true to
others, I can not be true to myself.
I believe in a cheerful countenance. For a
sour face is the sign of a grouch.
I believe in holding up my chin. For self-
respect commands respect from others.
I believe in keeping up courage. For
troubles flee before a brave front.
I believe in bracing up my brother. For an
encouraging word may save the day for
him.
I believe in living up to the best that is in
me. For to lower the standard is to give
up the fight.

CALVIN COOLIDGE

**The ideals which have always shone be-
fore me and filled me with the joy of
living are goodness, beauty, and truth.**

ALBERT EINSTEIN

STAR GAZERS

Ideals are like stars, you will not succeed
in touching them with your hands, but
like the seafaring man on the desert of
waters, you choose them as your guides,
and, following them, you reach your
destiny.

CARL SCHURZ

**I find the great thing in this world is, not
so much where we stand, as in what direction we are moving.**

JOHANN WOLFGANG VON GOETHE

To become Christlike is the only thing in
the whole world worth caring for, the
thing before which every ambition of man
is folly and all lower achievement vain.

HENRY DRUMMOND

Influence & Example

Let no man imagine that he has no influence.

HENRY GEORGE

●

SERMONS WE SEE

I'd rather see a sermon than hear one,
*   any day;*
I'd rather one would walk with me than
*   merely tell the way;*
The eye's a better pupil and more willing
*   than the ear.*
Fine counsel is confusing, but example's
*   always clear,*
And the best of all the preachers are the
*   men who live their creeds,*
For to see good put in action is what
*   everybody needs.*

I soon can learn to do it if you'll let me
*   see it done;*
I can watch your hands in action, but
*   your tongue too fast may run.*
And the lecture you deliver may be very
*   wise and true,*
But I'd rather get my lessons by observing
*   what you do.*
For I might misunderstand you and the
*   high advice you give,*
But there's no misunderstanding how you
*   act and how you live.*

EDGAR A. GUEST

TO MAKE THIS LIFE WORTH WHILE

May every soul that touches mine —
Be it the slightest contact —
Get therefrom some good;
Some little grace; one kindly thought;
One aspiration yet unfelt;
One bit of courage
For the darkening sky;
One gleam of faith
To brave the thickening ills of life;
One glimpse of brighter skies
Beyond the gathering mists —
To make this life worth while . . .

GEORGE ELIOT

GENEROSITY

A song we sing. We cannot know
How far the sound of it will go.
How long its echo will be heard.
We can but pray that every word,
Each note in this, the song we sing,
Will find its resting place and bring
Some little measure of repose,
Some strength, some happiness to those
Who hear our song. If just one smiles
To hear its echo down the miles,
Then we should be content and know
Our song was meant — God willed it so.

HELEN LOWRIE MARSALL

A sunbeam does not deserve any credit for shining,
because it is the business of a sunbeam to shine.
I am sure if it could talk, it would never say, "I did it" but "I am so grateful to be a ray of light and reflect the sun." We do not deserve any credit for being sunbeams of our heavenly Father, for He has created us in His own likeness, to reflect the light of His Presence to all His children, and when we do this in our daily lives, naturally and joyously, God is glorified and all those around us are blest.

MARY W. STRAIN

EXAMPLE

Like the star
Shining afar
Slowly now
And without rest,
Let each man turn, with steady sway,
Round the task that rules the day
And do his best.

JOHANN WOLFGANG VON GOETHE

●

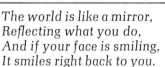

The world is like a mirror,
Reflecting what you do,
And if your face is smiling,
It smiles right back to you.

●

If the whole world followed you,
Followed to the letter,
Tell me — if it followed you,
Would the world be better?

●

YOUR OWN VERSION

You are writing a Gospel,
A chapter each day,

By deeds that you do,
By words that you say.

Men read what you write,
Whether faithless or true;
Say, what is the Gospel
According to You?

PAUL GILBERT

●

Let not him who is houseless pull down the house of another, but let him labor diligently and build one for himself, thus, by example, assuring that his own shall be safe from violence when built.

ABRAHAM LINCOLN

THE SOUL OF A CHILD

The soul of a child is the loveliest flower
That grows in the garden of God.
Its climb is from weakness to knowledge
and power,
To the sky from the clay and the clod.
To beauty and sweetness it grows under
care,
Neglected, 'tis ragged and wild.
'Tis a plant that is tender, but wondrously
rare,
The sweet, wistful soul of a child.

Be tender, O gardener, and give it its
share
Of moisture, of warmth, and of light,
And let it not lack for the painstaking
care,
To protect it from frost and from blight.
A glad day will come when its bloom
shall unfold,
It will seem that an angel has smiled,
Reflecting a beauty and sweetness untold
In the sensitive soul of a child.

●

A kind heart is a fountain of gladness, making everything in its vicinity freshen into smiles.

WASHINGTON IRVING

CAUSE AND EFFECT

Once, someone said something
   nice about me,
And, all undeserved though
   I knew it to be,
I treasured it there on
   my heart's deepest shelf,
Till one day I quite
   surprised even myself
By honestly making
   an effort to be
That nice thing that
   somebody said about me!

HELEN LOWRIE MARSHALL

**That mercy I to others show
That mercy show to me.**

ALEXANDER POPE

THOSE EVENING BELLS

Those evening bells! those evening bells!
How many a tale their music tells
Of youth, and home, and that sweet time
When last I heard their soothing chime!

And so 'twill be when I am gone —
That tuneful peal will still ring on,
While other bards shall walk these dells
And sing your praise, sweet evening bells.

THOMAS MOORE

**If Jesus Christ be God and died for me,
then no sacrifice is too great to be made
for him.**

C. T. STUDD

UPON THE HEARTS OF MEN

There are three lessons I would write,
Three words, as with a burning pen,

In tracings of eternal light,
Upon the hearts of men.

. . . Have Hope.
Though clouds environ 'round,
And gladness hides her face in scorn,
Put off the shadow from thy brow;
No night but hath its morn.

. . . Have Faith.
Where'er thy barque is driven . . .
The calm's disport, the tempest's mirth . . .
Know this: God rules the hosts of heaven,
The inhabitants of earth.

. . . Have Love.
Not love alone for one,
But man, as man, thy brother call;
And scatter, like a circling sun,
Thy charities on all.

FRIEDRICH VON SCHILLER

**Whatever makes men good Christians,
makes them good citizens.**

DANIEL WEBSTER

FORTY THOUSAND ROSES

To make one ounce of attar of roses requires forty thousand roses. For each drop eight full-blown roses are needed. What a tremendous amount of concentrated goodness an ounce of exquisite perfume contains! It fills the air with its magic!

Creating a fine personality is much like making an ounce of attar of roses. It calls for concentrating in our lives the essence of the best that life has to offer. Forty thousand beautiful thoughts! Forty thousand acts of kindness! Forty thousand smiles!

Such personalities fill their spheres of influence with a radiance that makes this a happier world in which to live.

Inspiration

Nobody can inspire who does not have
  deep convictions,
They are the results, but also the feeders
  of the spirit.

ROBERT ULICH

•

FOR INSPIRATION

The prayers I make will then be sweet
  indeed,
  If Thou the spirit give by which I pray;
  My unassisted heart is barren clay,
Which of its native self can nothing feed;
Of good and pious works Thou art the
  seed
  Which quickens where Thou say'st it
  may;
  Unless Thou show us then Thine own
  true way,
No man can find it! Father, Thou must
  lead!
Do Thou, then, breathe those thoughts
  into my mind
  By which such virtue may in me be bred
  That in Thy holy footsteps I may tread:
The fetters of my tongue do Thou unbind,
  That I may have the power to sing of
  Thee
  And sound Thy praises everlastingly.

MICHELANGELO
TRANSLATED BY WILLIAM WORDSWORTH

INDUSTRY

The glory of the star,
the glory of the sun —
we must not lose either
in the other.
We must not be so full
of the hope of heaven
that we cannot do
our work on the earth;
we must not be so lost
in the work of the earth
that we shall not
be inspired by
the hope of heaven.

PHILLIPS BROOKS

Love the beautiful,
Seek out the true,
Wish for the good,
And the best do.

MOSES MENDELSSOHN

•

A glance of heaven to see,
  To none on earth is given;
And yet a happy family
  Is but an earlier heaven.

SIR JOHN BOWRING

INSPIRATION

Inspiration is such a fragile thing . . . just a fragile thing. Just a breeze, touching the green foliage of a city park. Just a whisper from the soul of a friend. Just a line of verse, clipped from some forgotten magazine . . . or a paragraph standing out from among the matter-of-fact chapters of a learned book.

Inspiration . . . who can say where it is born, and why it leaves us? Who can tell of its reasons for being . . . or for not being?

Only this . . . I think that inspiration comes from the Heart of Heaven to give the lift of wings, and the breath of divine music to those of us who are earth-bound.

MARGARET E. SANGSTER

**I know the Bible
is inspired
because
it inspires me.**

DWIGHT L. MOODY

●

LIGHT AFTER DARKNESS

Light after darkness,
  Gain after loss,
Strength after weakness,
  Crown after cross,
Sweet after bitter,
  Song after fears,
Home after wandering,
  Praise after tears.

Sheaves after sowing,
  Sun after rain,
Light after mystery,
  Peace after pain,
Joy after sorrow,
  Calm after blast,
Rest after weariness,
  Sweet rest at last.

Near after distant,
  Gleam after gloom,
Love after loneliness,
  Life after tomb;
After long agony,
  Rapture of bliss;
Right was the pathway
  Leading to this!

●

WEDDING PRAYER

Thou God, whose high, eternal Love
  Is the only blue sky of our life,
Clear all the Heaven that bends above
  The life-road of this man and wife.

May these two lives be but one note
  In the world's strange-sounding
    harmony,
Whose sacred music e'er shall float
  Through every discord up to Thee.

As when from separate stars two beams
  Unite to form one tender ray:
As when two sweet but shadowy dreams
  Explain each other in the day:

So may these two dear hearts one light
  Emit, and each interpret each.
Let an angel come and dwell to-night
  In this dear double-heart, and teach!

SIDNEY LANIER

●

INSPIRATION

It is said that hope goes with youth; but I fancy that hope is the last gift given to man, and the only gift not given to youth. For youth the end of every episode is the end of the world. But the power of hoping through everything, the knowledge that the soul survives its adventures — that great inspiration comes to the middle-aged.

GILBERT KEITH CHESTERTON

OPPORTUNITY

This I beheld, or dreamed it in a dream:—
There spread a cloud of dust along a
   plain;
And underneath the cloud, or in it, raged
A furious battle, and men yelled, and
   swords
Shocked upon swords and shields. A
   prince's banner
Wavered, then staggered backward,
   hemmed by foes.
A craven hung along the battle's edge,
And thought, "Had I a sword of keener
   steel —
That blue blade that the king's son
   bears, — but this
Blunt thing — !" he snapped and flung it
   from his hand,
And lowering crept away and left the
   field.
Then came the king's son, wounded, sore
   bestead,
And weaponless, and saw the broken
   sword,
Hilt-buried in the dry and trodden sand,
And ran and snatched it, and with battle
   shout
Lifted afresh he hewed his enemy down,
And saved a great cause that heroic day.

EDWARD ROWLAND SILL

The year's at the spring
And day's at the morn;
Morning's at seven:
The hillside's dew-pearled;
The lark's on the wing;
The snail's on the thorn;
God's in his heaven —
All's right with the world!

ROBERT BROWNING

●

PUT FORTH BY THE MOON

Morning to morning speaketh in light,
And in the darkness night unto night,
Never a dark but somewhere a song
Singeth the whole night long.

Precious the things put forth by the moon;
Let not the heat and hurry of noon
Silence the silver song that I heard,
Stifle the whispered word.

AMY CARMICHAEL

●

BUT ONLY ONE MOTHER

Most of all the other beautiful things in
life come by twos and threes, by dozens
and hundreds. Plenty of roses, stars,
sunsets, rainbows, brothers and sisters,
aunts and cousins, but only one *mother*
in the whole world.

KATE DOUGLAS WIGGIN

THE BUSINESS OF THE DAY

It's just the way we carry through
The business of the day
That makes and molds the character —
The things we do and say;
The way we act when we are vexed;
The attitude we take;
The sort of pleasures we enjoy;
The kind of friends we make.
It's not the big events alone
That make us what we are;
And not the dizzy moments when
We're swinging on a star.
It's just the things that happen as
Along the road we plod.
The little things determine what
We're really worth to God.

PATIENCE STRONG

●

We ought to hear at least one little song
every day, read a good poem, see a first-
rate painting, and if possible speak a few
sensible words.

JOHANN WOLFGANG VON GOETHE

THE HOUND OF HEAVEN

I fled Him, down the nights and down the
　　　days;
　　I fled Him, down the arches of the
　　　years;
I fled Him, down the labyrinthine ways
　　Of my own mind; and in the mist of
　　　tears
I hid from Him, and under running
　　laughter.
　　　Up vistaed hopes, I sped;
　　　And shot, precipitated,
Adown Titanic glooms of chasmed fears,
　　From those strong Feet that followed,
　　　followed after.
　　　But with unhurrying chase,
　　　And unperturbed pace,
　　Deliberate speed, majestic instancy,
　　　They beat — and a Voice beat
　　　More instant than the Feet —
　　"All things betray thee, who
　　　betrayest Me."

　　　I pleaded, outlaw-wise,
By many a hearted casement, curtained
　　red,
　　Trellised with intertwining charities;
(For, though I knew His love Who
　　followèd,
　　　Yet was I sore adread
Lest, having Him, I must have naught
　　beside.)
But, if one little casement parted wide,
　　The gust of His approach would clash
　　　it to.
　　Fear wist not to evade as Love wist to
　　　pursue.
Across the margent of the world I fled,
　　And troubled the gold gateways of the
　　　stars,
　　Smiting for shelter on their clangèd
　　　bars;
　　　Fretted to dulcet jars
And silvern chatter the pale ports o' the
　　moon.
I said to dawn: Be sudden; to eve: Be
　　soon —
　　With thy young skyey blossoms heap
　　　me over
　　From this tremendous Lover!
Float thy vague veil about me, lest He see!
　　I tempted all His servitors, but to find

My own betrayal in their constancy,
In faith to Him their fickleness to me,
　　Their traitorous trueness, and their
　　　loyal deceit.
To all swift things for swiftness did I sue;
　　Clung to the whistling mane of every
　　　wind.
　　　But whether they swept, smoothly
　　　fleet,
　　The long savannahs of the blue;
　　Or whether, Thunder-driven,
　　They clanged His chariot thwart a
　　　heaven,
Plashy with flying lightnings round the
　　spurn o' their feet: —
　　Fear wist not to evade as Love wist to
　　　pursue.
　　　Still with unhurrying chase,
　　　And unperturbèd pace,
　　Deliberate speed, majestic constancy,
　　　Came on the following Feet,
　　　And a Voice above their beat —
　　"Naught shelters thee, who wilt not
　　　shelter Me."

I sought no more that after which I
　　strayed
　　In the face of man or maid;
But still within the little children's eyes
　　Seems something, something that
　　　replies,
They at least are for me, surely for me!
I turned me to them very wistfully;
But just as their young eyes grew sudden
　　fair
　　With dawning answers there,
Their angel plucked them from me by the
　　hair.
"Come then, ye other children, Nature's
　　— share
With me" (said I) "your delicate
　　fellowship;
　　Let me greet you lip to lip,
Let me twine with you caresses,
　　　Wantoning
　　With our Lady-Mother's vagrant
　　　tresses.
　　　Banqueting
　　With her in her wind-walled palace,
　　Underneath her azured dais,
　　Quaffing, as your taintless way is,
　　　From a chalice
Lucent-weeping out of the dayspring."

So it was done:
I in their delicate fellowship was one —
Drew the bolt of Nature's secrecies;
    I knew all the swift importings
    On the wilful face of skies;
    I knew how the clouds arise,
    Spumèd of the wild sea-snortings;
    All that's born or dies
    Rose and drooped with; made them
        shapers
Of mine own moods, or wailful or
        divine —
    With them joyed and was bereaven.
    I was heavy with the even,
    When she lit her glimmering tapers
    Round the day's dead sanctities
    I laughed in the morning's eyes.
I triumphed and I saddened with all
        weather,
    Heaven and I wept together,
And its sweet tears were salt with mortal
        mine;
Against the red throb of its sunset-heart
    I laid my own to beat
    And share commingling heat;
But not by that, by that, was eased my
        human smart.
In vain my tears were wet on Heaven's
        gray cheek.
For ah! we know not what each other
        says,
    These things and I; in sound I
        speak —
Their sound is but their stir, they speak
        by silences.
Nature, poor stepdame, cannot slake my
        drouth;
    Let her, if she would owe me,
Drop yon blue bosom-veil of sky, and
        show me
    The breasts o' her tenderness:
Never did any milk of hers once bless
        My thirsting mouth.
    Nigh and nigh draws the chase,
    With unperturbèd pace,
    Deliberate speed, majestic instancy,
    And past those noisèd Feet
    A Voice comes yet more fleet —
"Lo! naught contents thee, who content'st
    not Me."

Naked I wait Thy love's uplifted stroke!
My harness piece by piece Thou hast
        hewn from me,

    And smitten me to my knee;
    I am defenseless utterly.
    I slept, methinks, and woke,
And, slowly gazing, find me stripped in
        sleep.
In the rash lustihead of my young powers,
    I shook the pillaring hours
And pulled my life upon me; grimed with
        smears,
I stand amid the dust o' the mounded
        years —
My mangled youth lies dead beneath the
        heap.
My days have crackled and gone up in
        smoke,
Have puffed and burst as sun-starts on a
        stream.
        Yea, faileth now even dream
The dreamer, and the lute the lutanist;
Even the linked fantasies, in whose
        blossomy twist
I swung the earth a trinket at my wrist,
Are yielding; cords of all too weak
        account
For earth, with heavy griefs so
        overplussed,
        Ah! is Thy love indeed
A weed, albeit an amaranthine weed,
Suffering no flowers except its own to
        mount?
        Ah! must —
        Designer infinite! —
Ah! must Thou char the wood ere Thou
        canst limn with it?
My freshness spent its wavering shower
        i' the dust;
And now my heart is as a broken fount,
Wherein tear-dripping stagnate, split
        down ever
    From the dank thoughts that shiver
Upon the sightful branches of my mind.
    Such is; what is to be?
The pulp so bitter, how shall taste the
        rind?
I dimly guess what Time in mists
        confounds;
Yet ever and anon a trumpet sounds
From the hid battlements of Eternity:
Those shaken mists a space unsettle, then
Round the half-glimpsèd turrets slowly
        wash again;
    But not ere him who summoneth
    I first have seen, enwound

With glooming robes purpureal, cypress-
    crowned;
His name I know, and what his trumpet
    saith.
Whether man's heart or life it be which
    yields
    Thee harvest, must Thy harvest fields
    Be dunged with rotten death?

    Now of that long pursuit
    Comes on at hand the bruit;
That Voice is round me like a bursting
    sea:
    "And is thy earth so marred
    Shattered in shard on shard?
Lo, all things fly thee, for thou fliest Me!
    Strange, piteous, futile thing!
Wherefore should any set thee love
    apart?
Seeing none but I makes much of naught"
    (He said),
"And human love needs human meriting:
    How hast thou merited —
Of all man's clotted clay the dingiest clot?
    Alack, thou knowest not
How little worthy of any love thou art!
Whom wilt thou find to love ignoble thee,
    Save Me, save only Me?
All which I took from thee I did but take,
    Not for thy harms,
But just thou might'st seek it in My arms,
    All which thy child's mistake
Fancies as lost, I have stored for thee
    at home:
    Rise, clasp My hand, and come!"
    Halts by me that footfall:
    Is my gloom, after all
Shade of His hand, outstretched
    caressingly?
    "Ah, fondest, blindest, weakest,
    I am He Whom thou seekest!
Thou dravest love from thee, who dravest
    Me."

FRANCIS THOMPSON

●

Whatsoever things are true,
whatsoever things are honest,
whatsoever things are just,
whatsoever things are pure,
whatsoever things are lovely,
whatsoever things are of good

report; if there be any virtue,
and if there be any praise,
think on these things.

PHILIPPIANS 4:8

WHEN WE SEE ...

When we see the lilies
    Spinning in distress,
Taking thought to
    Manufacture loveliness;
When we see the birds all
    Building barns for store,
'Twill be time for us to worry —
    Not before!

●

O, blessed is that man of whom some soul
    can say,
"He was an inspiration along life's
    toilsome way,
A well of sparkling water, a fountain
    flowing free,
Forever like his Master, in tenderest
    sympathy."

●

BOUNDLESS

They talk about a woman's sphere
As though it had a limit;
There's not a place in earth or Heaven,
There's not a task to mankind given,
There's not a blessing or a woe,
There's not a whispered yes or no,
There's not a life, or death, or birth,
That has a feather's weight of worth —
    Without a woman in it.

Integrity & Truth

The truth is always the strongest argument.

SOPHOCLES

●

BE TRUE

Thou must be true thyself
   If thou the truth wouldst teach;
Thy soul must overflow if thou
   Another's soul wouldst reach!
It needs the overflow of heart
   To give the lips full speech.

Think truly, and thy thoughts
   Shall the world's famine feed;
Speak truly, and each word of thine
   Shall be a fruitful seed;
Live truly, and thy life shall be
   A great and noble creed.

HORATIUS BONAR

●

If truth be not diffused, error will be; if God and His Word are not known and received, the devil and his works will gain the ascendancy; if the evangelical volume does not reach every hamlet, the pages of a corrupt and licentious literature will; if the power of the Gospel is not felt through the length and breadth of the land, anarchy and misrule, degradation and misery, corruption and darkness will reign without mitigation or end.

DANIEL WEBSTER

For whatsoever men say in their
   blindness,
   And spite of the fancies of youth,
There's nothing so kingly as kindness,
   And nothing so royal as truth.

ALICE CARY

●

Time to me this truth has taught
   — 'Tis a treasure worth revealing —
More offend from want of thought
   Than from any want of feeling.

CHARLES SWAIN

●

One truth stands firm. All that happens in world history rests on something spiritual. If the spiritual is strong, it creates world history. If it is weak, it suffers world history.

ALBERT SCHWEITZER

Truth never hurts the teller.

ROBERT BROWNING

God is more interested in making you what He wants you to be than He is in giving you what you would like to have.

Justice and truth are the common ties of society.

JOHN LOCKE

In vain we call old nations fudge,
*   And bend our conscience to our*
*   dealing;*
The Ten Commandments will not budge,
*   And stealing will continue stealing.*

JAMES RUSSELL LOWELL

To make your children capable of honesty is the beginning of education.

JOHN RUSKIN

I AM NOT BOUND TO WIN

I am not bound to win,
But I am bound to be true,
I am not bound to succeed,
But I am bound to live up to what light I
    have.
I must stand with anybody that stands
    right;
Stand with him while he is right,
And part with him when he goes wrong.

ABRAHAM LINCOLN

The truer we become, the more unerringly we know the ring of truth.

F. W. ROBERTSON

If any man seeks for greatness, let him
    forget greatness and ask for truth,
        and he will find both.

HORACE MANN

Trust men and they will be true to you; treat them greatly, and they will show themselves great.

RALPH WALDO EMERSON

Though the mills of God grind slowly,
*   yet they grind exceeding small;*
Though with patience he stands waiting
*   with exactness grinds he all.*

HENRY WADSWORTH LONGFELLOW

Great truths are portions of the soul of
**   man;**
Great souls are portions of Eternity

JAMES RUSSELL LOWELL

Truth is love —
Bright as sunlight,
Clear as living water,
Soft as moonlight,
Old as time,
Sure as eternity.

CLYTA SHAW

Jewels of Thought

All that is necessary for evil to triumph is for good people to do nothing.

EDMUND BURKE

●

Of all the thoughts of God that are
Borne inward into souls afar,
Along the Psalmist's music deep,
Now tell me if that any is,
For gift or grace, surpassing this,
"He giveth His beloved sleep."

ELIZABETH BARRETT BROWNING

●

You can never tell what your thoughts
  can do,
In bringing you hate or love;
For thoughts are things,
And their airy wings
Are swifter than carrier dove.
They follow the law of the universe —
Each thing must create its kind;
They speed over the track,
To bring you back
Whatever went out of your mind.

●

The horizon is not the boundary
of the world.

HIDDEN THOUGHTS

The thoughts which you hide are the most precious. The shells which the sea rolls out on shore are not its best. The pearls have to be dived for.

HENRY WARD BEECHER

I KNOW SOMETHING GOOD ABOUT YOU

Wouldn't this old world be better
If the folks we met would say,
"I know something good about you!"
And then treat us just that way?

Wouldn't it be fine and dandy,
If each handclasp, warm and true,
Carried with it this assurance
"I know something good about you?"

Wouldn't life be lots more happy,
If the good that's in us all
Were the only thing about us
That folks bothered to recall?

Wouldn't life be lots more happy,
If we praised the good we see?
For there's such a lot of goodness
In the worst of you and me.

Wouldn't it be nice to practice
That fine way of thinking, too;
You know something good about me;
I know something good about you?

However high your thoughts of God may be yet they will still be mean and poor; for He is so great that He far transcends all that a merely human mind can fathom or imagine.

MOTHER BASILEA

The mind is a garden where thought flowers grow,

The thoughts that we think are seeds that we sow.

A NOBLE THOUGHT

A man might frame and let loose a star to roll in its orbit, and yet not have done so memorable a thing before God as he who lets go a golden-orbed thought to roll through the generations of time.

HENRY WARD BEECHER

The most important thought that ever occupied my mind is that of my individual responsibility to God.

DANIEL WEBSTER

The mountains are God's thoughts piled up.
The oceans are God's thoughts spread out.
The flowers are God's thoughts in bloom.
The dewdrops are God's thoughts in pearls.

They are never alone that are accompanied with noble thoughts.

SIDNEY

TAKE BACK THESE THOUGHTS

Beloved, thou hast brought me many flowers
Plucked in the garden, all the summer through
And winter, and it seemed as if they grew
In this close room, nor missed the sun and showers,
So, in the like name of that love of ours,
Take back these thoughts which here unfolded too,
And which on warm and cold days I withdrew
From my heart's ground. Indeed, those beds and bowers
Be overgrown with bitter weeds and rue,
And wait thy weeding; yet here's eglantine,
Here's ivy! — take them, as I used to do
Thy flowers, and keep them where they shall not pine.
Instruct thine eyes to keep their colours true,
And tell thy soul their roots are left in mine.

ELIZABETH BARRETT BROWNING

What we put into the thought stream of our children will appear in the life stream of tomorrow.

Don't let the world around you squeeze you into its own mold, but let God remold your minds from within, so that you may prove in practice that the plan of God for you is good, meets all his demands and moves toward the goal of true maturity.

ROMANS 12:2
PHILLIPS TRANSLATION

A thought once awakened does not slumber.

THOMAS CARLYLE

111

If instead of a gem, or even a flower, we should cast the gift of a loving thought into the heart of a friend, that would be giving as the angels give.

GEORGE MACDONALD

GOSSIP

Gossip is like a snowball —
So the saying goes;
The more you roll it over,
The more it grows and grows.

MABEL H. NANCE

You may glean knowledge by reading, but you must separate the chaff from the wheat by thinking.

Keep your knees down, and your chin up.

V. RAYMOND EDMAN

My life has been filled with terrible misfortunes—most of which never happened.

MICHEL DE MONTAIGNE

Kindness

KINDNESS

A little word in kindness spoken,
  A motion, or a tear,
Has often healed the heart that's broken
  And made a friend sincere.

A word, a look, has crushed to earth
  Full many a budding flower,
Which, had a smile but owned its birth,
  Would bless life's darkest hour.

Then deem it not an idle thing
  A pleasant word to speak;
The face you wear, the thought you bring,
  A heart may heal or break.

JOHN GREENLEAF WHITTIER

**Kindness is the golden chain by which
society is bound together.**

JOHANN WOLFGANG VON GOETHE

WHAT IS GOOD?

"What is the real good?"
 I asked in musing mood,
"Order," said the law court;
"Knowledge," said the school;
"Truth," said the wise man;
"Pleasure," said the fool;
"Love," said the maiden;

"Beauty," said the page;
"Freedom," said the dreamer;
"Home," said the sage;
"Fame," said the soldier;
"Equity," the seer.
 Spake my heart full sadly
"The answer is not here."
 Then within my bosom
 Softly this I heard:
"Each heart holds the secret,
 Kindness is the word."

JOHN BOYLE O'REILLY

THE COST IS SMALL

Kindness has been described in many ways.

It is the poetry of the heart, the music of the world. It is a golden chain which binds society together. It is a fountain of gladness.

Kind hearts are more than coronets.

Kind words produce their own beautiful image in man's soul.

Everyone knows the pleasure of receiving a kind look, a warm greeting, a hand held out in time of need. And such gestures can be made at so little expense, yet they bring such dividends to the investor.

THE WAR CRY

113

I have wept in the night for the shortness
of sight
That to somebody's need made me
blind;
But I never have yet felt a twinge of regret
For being a little too kind.

Kind hearts are the gardens
Kind thoughts are the roots,
Kind words are the flowers,
Kind deeds are the fruits.

Take care of the gardens,
And keep them from weeds.
Fill, fill them with flowers,
Kind words and kind deeds.

HENRY WADSWORTH LONGFELLOW

Kind words are jewels that live in the heart and soul and remain as blessed memories years after they have been spoken.

MARVEA JOHNSON

He who does a kindness to an ungrateful person, sets his seal to a flint and sows his seed upon sand; on the former he makes no impression, and from the latter finds no product.

ROBERT SOUTH

The greatness of a man can nearly always be measured by his willingness to be kind.

G. YOUNG
THE IRISH DIGEST

KIND WORDS CAN NEVER DIE

Kind words can never die;
Cherished and blest,
God knows how deep they lie
Lodged in the breast.
Like childhood's simple rhymes,
Said o'er a thousand times,
Through all the years and climes,
The heart they cheer.

Sweet thoughts can never die,
Though, like the flowers,
Their brightest hues may fly
In wintry hours.
But when the gentle dew
Gives them their charms anew,
With many an added hue,
They bloom again.

**That best portion of a good man's life,—
His little, nameless, unremembered acts
Of kindness and of love.**

WILLIAM WORDSWORTH

When life seems just a dreary grind,
And things seem fated to annoy,
Say something nice to someone else —
And watch the world light up with joy.

A part of kindness consists in loving people more than they deserve.

JOSEPH JOUBERT

Kindness is a language which the deaf man can hear and the blind man read.

MARK TWAIN

Laughter

Those who bring sunshine to the lives of others cannot keep it from themselves.

JAMES M. BARRIE

If you hold your nose to the grindstone rough,
And hold it there long enough,
You'll soon forget there are such things
As brooks that babble and birds that sing!
These three things will your world compose,
Just you, and a stone, and your darned old nose!

Laughter is the best medicine for a long and happy life. He who laughs—lasts.

WILFRED A. PETERSON

99

THE HEART HELD HIGH

God made me a gift of laughter
And a heart held high,
Knowing what life would bring me
By and by,

Seeing my roses wither
One by one,

Hearing my life-song falter,
Scarce begun,

Watching me walk with Sorrow . . .
That is why
He made me this gift of laughter —
This heart held high!

MARTHA SNELL NICHOLSON

Man is the only creature endowed with the gift of laughter; is he not also the only one that deserves to be laughed at?

FULKE GRENVILLE

66

Humor is the harmony of the heart.
DOUGLAS JERROLD

GOD'S MEDICINE

Mirth is God's medicine. Everybody ought to bathe in it. Grim care, moroseness, anxiety — all this rust of life ought to be scoured off by the oil of mirth. It is better than emery. Every man ought to rub himself with it. A man without mirth is like a wagon without springs, in which everyone is caused disagreeably to jolt by every pebble over which it runs.

HENRY WARD BEECHER

115

PESSIMIST AND OPTIMIST

This one sits shivering in Fortune's smile,
Taking his joy with bated, doubtful
breath.
This one, gnawed by hunger, all the while
Laughs in the teeth of death.

THOMAS BAILEY ALDRICH

●

LAUGHTERTOWN

Would ye learn the road to Laughtertown,
O ye, who have lost the way?
Would ye have young heart though your
hair be gray?
Go learn from a little child each day,
Go serve his wants and play his play,
And catch the lilt of his laughter gay,
And follow his dancing feet as they stray;
For he knows the road to Laughtertown,
O ye who have lost the way!

KATHERINE DUER BLAKE

Real joy comes not from ease or riches or from the praise of men, but from doing something worthwhile.

WILFRED T. GRENFELL

SYMBOL

Laughter is a beautiful symbol of humanity. No creature but man can laugh. Beauty there is and power and survival in the vegetable and the animal and the mineral kingdoms, but laughter can be heard in the forest only if children play there or lovers stroll beneath its high colonnades. Upon the ability to laugh, to perceive the humorous, to sense perspectives, to catch proportions, to see oneself as ridiculous on occasion, depends the achievement of much of one's relationship to God. For to be able to laugh presupposes personality and humanity, moral nature and outlook.

WINNIFRED WYGAL

A laugh is worth one hundred groans in any market.

CHARLES LAMB

●

THE LAND OF BEGINNING AGAIN

I wish that there were some wonderful
place
In the Land of Beginning Again;
Where all our mistakes and all our
heartaches
And all of our poor selfish grief
Could be dropped like a shabby old coat
at the door
And never put on again.

We would find all the things we intended
to do
But forgot, and remembered too late,
Little praises unspoken, little promises
broken,
And all of the thousand and one
Little duties neglected that might have
perfected
The day for one less fortunate.

It wouldn't be possible not to be kind
In the Land of Beginning Again,
And the ones we misjudged and the ones
whom we grudged
Their moments of victory here,
Would find in the grasp of our loving
hand-clasp
More than penitent lips could explain.

For what had been hardest we'd know
had been best,
And what had seemed loss would be
gain;
For there isn't a sting that will not take
wing
When we've faced it and laughed it
away
And I think that the laughter is most what
we're after
In the Land of Beginning Again.

LOUISE FLETCHER TARKINGTON

●

A good laugh is sunshine in a house.

WILLIAM MAKEPEACE THACKERAY

116

In good truth, we know what a man is like by the things he finds laughable, we gauge both his understanding and his culture by his sense of the becoming and the absurd. If the capacity for laughter be one of the things which separates men from brutes, the quality of laughter draws a sharp dividing line between the trained intelligence and the vacant mind.

AGNES REPPLIER

Learn to laugh at yourself and you'll always be amused.

A light heart lives long.

WILLIAM SHAKESPEARE

Laughter — while it lasts, slackens and unbraces the mind, weakens the faculties, and causes a kind of remissness and dissolution in all the powers of the soul; and thus far it may be looked upon as weakness in the composition of human nature. But if we consider the frequent reliefs we receive from it, and how often it breaks the gloom which is apt to depress the mind and dampen our spirit, with transient, unexpected gleams of joy, one would take care not to grow too wise for so great a pleasure of life.

JOSEPH ADDISON

No one feels like laughing when he bumps his funny bone.

MARY WILSON LITTLE

PRAYER

Give me a sense of humor, Lord;
Give me the grace to see a joke,
To get some happiness from life,
And pass it on to other folk.

CHESTER CATHEDRAL

There are amusing people who do not interest and interesting people who do not amuse.

BENJAMIN DISRAELI

Life

Life is a continuous experience; but God gives it to us in stages — one day at a time. Anyone who chooses to do so can live one day victoriously. To live each day in this manner is to experience a victorious life.

J. H. CHITWOOD

O, life! how pleasant is thy morning,
Young Fancy's rays the hills adorning!
Cold pausing Caution's lesson scorning,
  We frisk away,
Like schoolboys at the expected warning,
To joy and play.

ROBERT BURNS

The secret of life is not to do what you like, but to like what you do.

ONE LIFE

One life and one alone we have to live upon this little earth. One life in which to learn so much . . . to seek and find and prove our worth. So many dreams there are to dream . . . so many things to know and do. So many rosy peaks to climb . . . so many pathways to pursue.

So waste no time on fruitless quests that get you nowhere in the end. The gold of Time is yours to squander or with care to use and spend. It's folly to postpone good deeds. To-morrow never comes they say. The future times belong to God. Your only chance is now . . . To-day.

PATIENCE STRONG

'Tis life whereof our nerves are scant,
O life, not death, for which we pant;
More life and fuller that I want.

ALFRED, LORD TENNYSON

Life is not made up of great
  sacrifices and duties,
But of little things; in
  which smiles
And kindness and small
  obligations,
Given habitually, are
  what win and
Preserve the heart and
  secure comfort.

SIR HUMPHREY DAVY

OH, THE WILD JOYS OF LIVING!

Oh, the wild joys of living!
  the leaping from rock up to rock,
The strong rending of boughs from the
    fir-tree,
  the cool silver shock
Of the plunge in the pool's living water,
  the hunt of the bear,
And the sultriness showing the lion
  is couched in his lair.
And the meal, the rich dates yellowed
  over the gold dust divine,
And the locust-flesh stuped in the pitcher,
  the full draft of wine,
And the sleep in the dried river-channel
  where bulrushes tell
That the water was wont to go warbling
  so softly and well.
How good is man's life, the mere living!
  How fit to employ
All the heart and the soul and the senses
  forever in joy!

ROBERT BROWNING

●

MAKE HASTE, O MAN! TO LIVE

Make haste, O man! to live,
  For thou so soon must die;
Time hurries past thee like the breeze;
  How swift its moments fly.
    Make haste, O man! to live.

Make haste, O man! to do
  Whatever must be done,
Thou hast no time to lose in sloth,
  Thy day will soon be gone,
    Make haste, O man! to live.

To breathe, and wake, and sleep,
  To smile, to sigh, to grieve,
To move in idleness through earth,
  This, this is not to live.
    Make haste, O man! to live.

The useful, not the great;
  The thing that never dies,
The silent toil that is not lost,
  Set these before thine eyes.
    Make haste, O man! to live.

Make haste, O man! to live.
  Thy time is almost o'er;

Oh! sleep not dream not, but arise,
  The Judge is at the door.
    Make haste, O man! to live.

HORATIUS BONAR

●

ALPHABET OF LIFE

Act promptly
Be courteous
Cut worry out
Deal squarely
Eat what is wholesome
Forgive and forget
Get religion
Hope always
Imitate the best
Judge generously
Knock nobody
Love somebody
Make friends
Never despair
Owe nobody
Play occasionally
Quote your mother
Read good books
Save something
Touch no liquor
Use discretion
Vote independently
Watch your step
X-ray yourself
Yield to superiors
Zealously live

Life is always flowing on like a river, sometimes with murmurs, sometimes without bending this way and that, we do not exactly see why; now in beautiful picturesque places, now through barren and uninteresting scenes, but always flowing with a look of treachery about it; it is so swift, so voiceless, yet so continuous.

FREDERICK WILLIAM FABER

119

JUST ONE DAY

If I could live to God for just one day
  One blessed day, from rosy dawn of
      light
  Till purple twilight deepened into night,
  A day of faith unfaltering, trust
      complete,
Of love unfeigned and perfect charity,
Of hope undimmed, of courage past
      dismay,
  Of heavenly peace, patient humility —
  No hint of duty to constrain my feet,
  No dream of ease to lull to listlessness,
  Within my heart no root of bitterness,
No yielding to temptation's subtle sway,
  Methinks, in that one day would so
      expand
  My soul to meet such holy, high
      demand
  That never, never more could hold me
      bound
  This shriveling husk of self that wraps
      me round.
So might I henceforth live to God alway.

SUSAN E. GAMMONS

●

LIFE

A little sunshine,
A little rain,
A little loss,
A little gain;
A little happiness,
A little pain,
Not all sweet,
Not all sour;
Now a weed,
Now a flower;
A goodly average
Of sunshine and shower.

FRANK B. JENNINGS

●

**What do we live for, is it not to make
life less difficult for each other?**

GEORGE ELIOT

LIVING

O wondrous Life that lets me see
A sky of blue, a golden tree!
A small child's happy little face,
Bright flowers in a lovely vase;
That lets me hear a song so sweet
Gay people, laughing, down the street;
That lets me feel a tiny hand
Nestled in mine — and understand
The thrill of fun, the ache of pain,
The warmth of sun, the wet of rain.
That bestows Love, and lets me give,
And then say: "Thank you, God, I live!"

THELMA WILLIAMSON

●

I TAKE HANDS OFF MY LIFE

I take hands off my life
It is no longer mine
I take hands off my life
Let it be forever Thine.
Help me to walk each day
Close to Thee
Every part of me
All the heart of me
Just for Thee.

SYBIL LEONARD ARMES

●

Anyone can carry his burden,
  however hard, until nightfall.

Anyone can do his work,
  however hard, for one day.

Anyone can live sweetly, patiently,
  lovingly, purely, till the sun
    goes down . . .

And this is all that life really means.

ROBERT LOUIS STEVENSON

120

JOYFUL EXPECTATION

I do not fear death. Often I wake in the night and think of it. I look forward to it with a thrill of joyful expectation and anticipation, which would become impatience were it not that Jesus is my Master, as well as my Savior. I feel I have work to do for Him that I would not shirk, and also that His time to call me home will be the best and right time, and therefore I am content to wait.

I could not do without Jesus. I cannot and I do not live without Him. It is a new and different life, and this life which takes away all fear of death is what I want others to have and enjoy.

FRANCES RIDLEY HAVERGAL

Every man must live with the man he makes of himself.

JAMES M. LAWSON

Be it health or be it leisure,
    Be it skill we have to give,
Still in spending it for others
    Christians only really live.

THE LAST ROSE OF SUMMER

'Tis the last rose of summer,
Left blooming alone;
All her lovely companions
Are faded and gone;
No flower of her kindred,
No rosebud is nigh,
To reflect back her blushes,
Or give sigh for sigh!

I'll not leave thee, thou lone one,
To pine on the stem;
Since the lovely are sleeping,
Go to sleep thou with them.

Thus kindly I scatter
Thy leaves o'er the bed
Where thy mates of the garden
Lie scentless and dead.

So soon may I follow,
When friendships decay,
And from Love's shining circle
The gems drop away!
When true hearts lie withered,
And fond ones are flown,
Oh! who would inhabit
This bleak world alone?

So live that when thy summons comes to
    join
The innumerable caravan which moves
To that mysterious realm where each
    shall take
His chamber in the silent halls of death,
Thou go not like the quarry slave at night
Scourged to his dungeon, but, sustained
    and soothed
By an unfaltering trust, approach thy
    grave
Like one who wraps the drapery of his
    couch
About him and lies down to pleasant
    dreams.

WILLIAM CULLEN BRYANT

THE CLOCK OF LIFE

The clock of life is wound but once,
    And no man has the power —
To tell just when the hands will stop,
    At late or early hour.
Now is the only time you own —
    So live, love, toil with a will.
Place no faith in tomorrow,
    For the clock may then be still.

The whole secret of life is to be interested in one thing profoundly, and in a thousand things well.

HUGH WALPOLE

To awaken each morning with a smile brightening my face; to greet the day with reverence for the opportunities it contains; to approach my work with a clean mind; to meet men and women with laughter on my lips and love in my heart; to be gentle, kind, and courteous through all the hours; to approach the night with weariness that ever woos sleep and the joy that comes from work well done—this is how I desire to waste wisely my days.

THOMAS DEKKER

TO NIGHT

I have loved wind and light,
  And the bright sea,

But, holy and most secret Night,
  Not as I love and have loved thee.

God, like all highest things,
  Hides light in shade,
And in the night his visitings
  To sleep and dreams are clearliest
      made.

Love, that knows all things well,
  Loves the night best;
Joys whereof daylight dares not tell
  Are his, and the diviner rest.

And Life, whom day shows plain
  Its prison-bars,
Feels the close wall and the hard chain
  Fade when the darkness brings the
      stars.

ARTHUR SYMONS

Love & Devotion

Love Is . . .

Slow to suspect — quick to trust,
Slow to condemn — quick to justify,
Slow to offend — quick to defend,
Slow to expose — quick to shield,
Slow to reprimand — quick to forbear,
Slow to belittle — quick to appreciate,
Slow to demand — quick to give,
Slow to provoke — quick to help,
Slow to resent — quick to forgive.

GOD BLESS YOU, DEAR

God bless you, dear, for happiness;
For loving me;
For things of beauty in this life
You help me to see;

For sharing burdens that are mine;
For gentleness;
For tears you've dried, for words you've
*   said*
That live to bless;

For laughter, fun, the little things
Of every day;
For teaching me the way to turn
Work into play;

For qualities of mind and heart
Nobly expressed;
For courage, honor, kindness, faith
That meet each test;

For changing drab days into gold
And shining hours;
For facing storms as calmly as
The summer showers.

Your tender smile and warmth of love
Are always near;
For everything you are to me,
God bless you, dear.

ISLA PASCHAL RICHARDSON

Do not keep the alabaster boxes of your love and tenderness sealed up until your friends are dead. Fill their lives with sweetness. Speak approving, cheering words while their ears can hear them, and while their hearts can be thrilled and made happier by them.

GEORGE WILLIAM CHILDS

From THE SONG OF HIAWATHA

As the bow unto the cord is
So unto the man is woman.
Though she bends him, she obeys him,
Though she draws him, yet she follows,
Useless each without the other.

HENRY WADSWORTH LONGFELLOW

123

Love has power to give in a moment what toil can scarcely reach in an age.

JOHANN WOLFGANG VON GOETHE

●

WHAT IS LOVE?

To love very much is to love inadequately; we love — that is all.

Love cannot be modified without being nullified. Love is a short word but it contains everything.

Love means the body, the soul, the life, the entire being.

We feel love as we feel the warmth of our blood, we breathe love as we breathe the air, we hold it in ourselves as we hold our thoughts. Nothing more exists for us.

Love is not a word; it is a wordless state indicated by four letters . . .

GUY DE MAUPASSANT

Love ever gives,
Forgives, outlives,
And ever stands with open hands,
And while it lives it gives,
For this is Love's prerogative
To give — and give — and give.

●

Love knows no limit to its endurance,
  no end to its trust,
  no fading of its hope;
  it can outlast anything.
Love still stands when all else has fallen.

I CORINTHIANS 13:7-8
PHILLIPS TRANSLATION

●

LOVE

Love has a language of its own to reach . . .
From heart to heart, more positive than
  speech . . .
And more enduring than the written
  word . . .
What love says with a gesture can be
  heard . . .
As music, without need of mortal ears . . .
What love says with a gentle touch
  appears . . .
More beautiful than a sunrise fair . . .
To one who is, for all appearances,
  unaware . . .
Love is the praise even a flower can
  understand . . .
The strength a child can grasp with eager
  hand . . .
The immemorial and sacred tongue . . .
In which the loveliest of songs are sung.

R. H. GRENVILLE

●

Love is a good above all others, which
  alone maketh every burden light.
Love is watchful, and whilst sleeping still
  keeps watch; though fatigued is not
  weary; though pressed is not forced.
Love is sincere, gentle, strong, patient,
  faithful, prudent, long-suffering, manly.
Love is circumspect, humble, upright; not
  weary, not fickle, nor intent on vain
  things; sober, chaste, steadfast, quiet,
  and guarded in all the senses.

THOMAS A KEMPIS

IF

If I can make each day a poem
From each dew-sprinkled dawn;
If I can hold within my heart
Each golden moment when it is gone;

If I can hold within my palm
Your hand, then I'll be strong;
If I can hold this love of mine,
My heart will always sing a song.

If one small star will shed its light
Across my path, I'll have no fear . . .
And I shall live, and love, and laugh,
If I have you, my dear!

CLARA SMITH REBER

THE WAY OF LOVE

Love vaunteth not itself, is not puffed up,
Doth not behave itself unseemly,
Seeketh not its own,
Is not easily provoked,
Thinketh no evil;
Rejoiceth not in iniquity, but rejoiceth in
    the truth;
Beareth all things,
Believeth all things,
Hopeth all things,
Endureth all things.
Love never faileth:
But whether there be prophecies, they
    shall fail;
Whether there be tongues, they shall
    cease;
Whether there be knowledge, it shall
    vanish away.
For we know in part, and we prophesy
    in part.
But when that which is perfect is come,
That which is in part shall be done away.
When I was a child, I spake as a child,
I understood as a child, I thought as a
    child:
But when I became a man, I put away
    childish things.
For now we see through a glass, darkly;
But then face to face:
Now I know in part;
But then shall I know even as also I am
    known.
    And now abideth faith, hope, love,
        these three;
But the greatest of these is love.

I CORINTHIANS 13:4-13

HOW DO I LOVE THEE?

How do I love thee? Let me count the
    ways.
I love thee to the depth and breadth and
    height
My soul can reach, when feeling out of
    sight
For the ends of Being and ideal Grace.
I love thee to the level of everyday's
Most quiet need, by sun and candlelight.
I love thee freely, as men strive for Right;
I love thee purely, as they turn from
    Praise.

I love thee with the passion put to use
In my old griefs, and with my childhood's
    faith.
I love thee with a love I seemed to lose
With my lost saints, — I love thee with
    the breath,
Smiles, tears, of all my life! — and, if God
    choose,
I shall but love thee better after death.

ELIZABETH BARRETT BROWNING

**The test of our love to God
Is the love we have one for another.**

The kindest and the happiest pair
Will find occasion to forbear;
And something, every day they live,
To pity, and perhaps forgive.

WILLIAM COWPER

For God so loved the world, that He gave
    His only begotten Son,
    that whosoever believeth in Him
    should not perish,
but have everlasting life.

JOHN 3:16

OUTWITTED

He drew a circle that shut me out,
Heretic, rebel, a thing to flout.
But love and I had the wit to win;
We drew a circle that took him in.

EDWIN MARKHAM

**This tear which you caused me to shed
is yours. I place it at your feet.**

VICTOR HUGO

The quarrels of lovers are like summer storms.
Everything is more beautiful when they have passed.

SONNET ON LOVE

Let me not to the marriage of true minds
Admit impediments. Love is not love
Which alters when it alteration finds,
Or bends with the remover to remove:
Oh, no! it is an ever-fixed mark,
That looks on tempests, and is never
        shaken;
It is the star to every wandering bark,
Whose worth's unknown, although his
        height be taken.
Love's not Time's fool, though rosy lips
        and cheeks
Within his bending sickle's compass
        come:
Love alters not with his brief hours and
        weeks,
But bears it out even to the edge of doom:
    If this be error and upon me proved,
    I never writ, nor no man ever loved.

WILLIAM SHAKESPEARE

●

NO EAST OR WEST

In Christ there is no East or West,
    In Him no South or North,
But one great Fellowship of Love
    Throughout the whole wide earth.

In Him shall true hearts everywhere
    Their high communion find.
His service is the golden cord
    Close-binding all mankind.

Join hands then, Brothers of the Faith,
    Whate'er your race may be! —
Who serves my Father as a son
    Is surely kin to me.

In Christ now meet both East and West,
    In Him meet South and North,
All Christly souls are one in Him,
    Throughout the whole wide earth.

JOHN OXENHAM

If there is anything better than to be loved, it is loving.

●

FIRST LOVE

Her hair was gold, her eyes were blue,
Her lips were ruby red;
To me she seemed a fairy queen
Some mighty king might wed.

I told my love, she pledged her troth,
And vowed she would be true,
Then for awhile she looked askance
When others came to woo.

But she was false! She changed her mind,
And took another mate,
She broke my heart — when she was
    seven,
And I was nearly eight.

L. M. BECK

●

Has some resentment
    wrought strife and ill-will?
Love and forgiveness
    work miracles still.

●

WALKING WITH GOD

O for a closer walk with God,
    A calm and heavenly frame,
A light to shine upon the road
    That leads me to the Lamb!

Where is the blessedness I knew
    When first I saw the Lord?
Where is the soul-refreshing view
    Of Jesus and His word?

What peaceful hours I once enjoy'd!
    How sweet their memory still!
But they have left an aching void,
    The world can never fill.

Return, O holy Dove, return,
    Sweet messenger of rest:

I hate the sins that made Thee mourn,
And drove Thee from my breast.

The dearest idol I have known,
Whate'er that idol be,
Help me to tear it from Thy throne,
And worship only Thee.

So shall my walk be close with God,
Calm and serene my frame;
So purer light shall mark the road
That leads me to the Lamb.

WILLIAM COWPER

**Duty makes us do things well,
But love makes us do them beautifully.**

PHILLIPS BROOKS

Who shall separate us from the love of
Christ?
shall tribulation, or distress, or per-
secution, or famine, or nakedness, or
peril, or sword?

ROMANS 8:35

SHALL I COMPARE THEE TO A
SUMMER'S DAY?

Shall I compare thee to a summer's day?
Thou art more lovely and more
temperate:
Rough winds do shake the darling buds of
May,
And summer's lease hath all too short a
date:
Sometime too hot the eye of heaven
shines,
And often is his gold complexion dimm'd;
And every fair from fair sometime
declines,
By change or nature's changing course
untrimm'd;

But thy eternal summer shall not fade
Nor lose possession of that fair thou
owest;
Nor shall Death brag thou wander'st in
his shade,
When in eternal lines to time thou
growest;
So long as men can breathe or eyes can
see,
So long lives this and this gives life
to thee.

WILLIAM SHAKESPEARE

Thy love divine hath led us in the
past;
In this free land by Thee our lot
is cast;
Be Thou our Ruler, Guardian,
Guide and Stay;
Thy Word our law, thy paths
our chosen way.

DANIEL C. ROBERTS

**Nobody will know what you mean by
saying that "God is love" unless you act
it as well.**

God wants our best. He in the far-off ages
Once claimed the firstling of the flock,
the finest of the wheat;
And still He asks His own, with gentlest
leading,
To lay their highest hopes and brightest
talents at His feet.

**Love is the doorway through which man
passes from selfishness to service.**

Memories & Reflections

Come with me, and walk a way
Down the Lane of Yesterday.

Flowers beside the path are springing,
With their perfume, mem'ries bringing —
Thoughts of all those years gone by
When we loitered, you and I,
In the garden fair and sweet
Of life's springtime, full, complete;
Days in the long-ago, 'tis true,
But Memory guides our steps anew.

So, come with me and walk a way
Down the Lane of Yesterday.

ALICE C. SUTHERLAND

**God gave us memories so that we might
have roses in December.**

SIR JAMES M. BARRIE

MEMORIES

Dream with me of days gone by,
With pleasant memories
Of stardust sprinkled in the sky,
And of a balmy breeze.

Then once again we will recall
The things we loved so well . . .
The shady lanes where we would stroll
As evening shadows fell.

The park, the church, the school, the
    store,
The friendly folks back home,
The sunny brooks, the meadows, and
The hills we used to roam.

These memories are something which
My heart will always store . . .
And joys and happiness they bring
Are mine forevermore.

PATRICIA MONGEAU

●

THE HEART REMEMBERS

The heart remembers everything
    Although the mind forgets —
The raptures and the agonies,
    The hopes and the regrets.
The heart remembers April
    When the snows of winter fall —
Hearing on the bitter wind
    The sweetest song of all.

When Youth has had its shining hour
    And Love its golden day,
Time may fade the colors
    And the glory turn to gray;
But something of the magic lingers,
    Never to depart,
Deep down in the secret places
    Of the quiet heart.

PATIENCE STRONG

Memories are forget-me-nots gathered along life's way pressed close to the human heart into a perennial boquet.

CLARA SMITH REBER

Priceless little memories
Are treasures without price,
And through the gateway of the heart
They lead to paradise.

HELEN STEINER RICE

Memory is the treasure of all things and their guardian.

CICERO

MEMORY

My childhood's home I see again,
  And sadden with the view;
And still, as memory crowds my brain,
  There's pleasure in it, too.

O memory! thou midway world
  'Twixt earth and paradise,
Where things decayed and loved ones lost
  In dreamy shadows rise,

And, freed from all that's earthly, vile,
  Seem hallowed, pure and bright,
Like scenes in some enchanted isle
  All bathed in liquid light.

As dusky mountains please the eye
  When twilight chases day;
As bugle notes that, passing by,
  In distance die away;

As, leaving some grand waterfall,
  We lingering, list its roar —
So memory will hallow all
  We've known but know no more.

Near twenty years have passed away
  Since here I bid farewell

To woods and fields, and scenes of play,
  And playmates loved so well.

Where many were, but few remain
  Of old familiar things;
But seeing them to mind again
  The lost and absent brings.

The friends I left that parting day,
  How changed, as time has sped!
Young childhood grown, strong manhood
  gray;
  And half of all are dead.

I hear the loved survivors tell
  How nought from death could save,
Till every sound appears a knell
  And every spot a grave.

I range the fields with pensive tread,
  And pace the hollow rooms,
And feel (companion of the dead)
  I'm living in the tombs.

ABRAHAM LINCOLN

●

I CANNOT SING THE OLD SONGS

I cannot sing the old songs
I sang long years ago,
For heart and voice would fail me,
And foolish tears would flow;
For by-gone hours come o'er my heart
With each familiar strain.
I cannot sing the old songs,
Or dream those dreams again.

I cannot sing the old songs,
Their charm is sad and deep;
Their melodies would waken
Old sorrows from their sleep.
And though all unforgotten still,
And sadly sweet they be,
I cannot sing the old songs,
They are too dear to me!

I cannot sing the old songs,
For visions come again
Of golden dreams departed
And years of weary pain;
Perhaps when earthly fetters shall
Have set my spirit free,
My voice shall know the old songs
For all eternity.

129

I do not know what I may appear to the world, but to myself I seem to have been only like a boy playing on the seashore and diverting myself in now and then finding a smooth pebble or a prettier shell than ordinary, whilst the great ocean of truth lay all undiscovered before me.

ISAAC NEWTON

●

INSIDE AND OUT

I built myself a solid wall
    To fend me from life's care.
To keep out agonies and hurts
    I could no longer bear.

I vowed to keep away from love,
    From emotions to be free,
Believing that they brought but pain —
    How cruel I was to me!

For when the wall was strong and sound,
    And I secure inside,
I found what misery really meant —
    My friends were all outside!

There are two tragedies in life. One is not to get your heart's desire. The other is to get it.

GEORGE BERNARD SHAW

TRACINGS

Finger prints on the window,
The smear of a dog's wet nose,
Thousands of marks on the stairway
Of clattering heels and toes,
A headlong path through the garden
To a low place in the wall,
Beyond to a ring of ashes
By the boulder. That is all,
All they have left behind them —
You may search the whole place through,
Never know what the children looked like
Nor the tricks their dog could do.

BERNARD RAYMUND

Like a bird singing in the rain, let grateful memories survive in time of sorrow.

ROBERT LOUIS STEVENSON

●

LUCY

She dwelt among the untrodden ways
    Beside the springs of Dove;
A maid whom there were none to praise;
    And very few to love.

A violet by a mossy stone
    Half hidden from the eye!
Fair as a star, when only one
    Is shining in the sky.

She lived unknown, and few could know
    When Lucy ceased to be;
But she is in her grave, and O
    The difference to me!

WILLIAM WORDSWORTH

He that despiseth small things, shall fall by little and little.

ECCLESIASTICUS

THE TWO ANGELS

All is of God! If he but wave his hand,
    The mists collect, the rain falls thick
        and loud,
Till, with a smile of light on sea and land,
    Lo! he looks back from the departing
        cloud.

Angels of Life and Death alike are his;
    Without his leave they pass no
        threshold o'er;
Who, then, would wish or dare, believing
        this,
    Against his messengers to shut the
        door?

HENRY WADSWORTH LONGFELLOW

130

Memory is the cabinet of imagination, the treasury of reason, the registry of conscience, and the council chamber of thought.

BASIL

●

MEMORABILIA

My mind lets go a thousand things
Like dates of wars and deaths of kings,
And yet recalls the very hour —
'Twas noon by yonder village tower,
And on the last blue noon in May —
The wind came briskly up this way,
Crisping the brook beside the road;
Then, pausing here, set down its load
Of pine-scents, and shook listlessly
Two petals from that wild-rose tree.

THOMAS BAILEY ALDRICH

●

MUSIC

There's music in the sighing of a reed;
There's music in the gushing of a rill;
There's music in all things, if men had
ears;
The earth is but the music of the
spheres.

LORD BYRON

●

Building boys is better than mending men.

AS LONG ...

As long as there are stars to claim
From trackless heights of sky;
As long as there are seeds to throw
In fields that rear them high;
As long as streams shall end our thirst,
And weary men find rest;
As long as cures for pain exist
And faith can meet each test;
As long as peace remains our goal
And God is close above —
So long shall life be worthy of
Our living and our love!

FRANK H. KEITH

●

PERHAPS

Perhaps the dreaded future has less
bitter than I think.
The Lord may sweeten the waters
Before I stoop to drink.

●

'Tis the human touch in this world that
counts,
The touch of your hand and mine,

Which means far more to the fainting
heart
Than shelter and bread and wine;

For shelter is gone when the night is o'er
And bread lasts only a day,

But the touch of the hand,
and the sound of the voice
Sing on in the soul alway.

SPENCER MICHAEL FREE

Nature

Nature! great parent! whose unceasing hand
Rolls round the seasons of the changeful year;
How mighty, how majestic are thy works!
With what a pleasing dread they swell the soul
That sees astonished, and astonished sings!

WILL L. THOMSON

SANCTUM

Deep in the heart of the silent wood,
 Where whispering winds are free,
Where quiet shade of leaves is laid
 In patterned symmetry,
Beside the gleam of a singing brook,
 Near the roots of a beautiful tree,
I journey when the tongues of men
 Have sadly wearied me.

I lay my dreams on a mossy bank
 For the forest folk to see,
I hear purled notes from feathered
 throats,
 And the questing hum of a bee;
The stir of wings and hidden things
 Is strangely near to me,
When the vibrant song of the woodland
 throng,
 Proclaims divinity.

CLARA BERNHARDT

The daily showers rejoice the thirsty earth, and bless the flowery buds.

PRIOR

●

NATURE'S CREED

I believe in the brook as it wanders
 From hillside into glade;
I believe in the breeze as it whispers
 When evening's shadows fade.
I believe in the roar of the river
 As it dashes from high cascade;
I believe in the cry of the tempest
 'Mid the thunder's cannonade.
I believe in the light of shining stars,
 I believe in the sun and the moon;
I believe in the flash of lightning,
 I believe in the night-bird's croon.
I believe in the faith of the flowers,
 I believe in the rock and sod,
For in all of these appeareth clear
 The handiwork of God.

●

Nature is beautiful, always beautiful! Every little flake of snow is a perfect crystal, and they fall together as gracefully as if fairies of the air caught water-drops and made them into artificial flowers to garland the wings of the wind!

L. M. CHILD

TO AN INSECT

I love to hear thine earnest voice,
  Wherever thou art hid,
Thou testy-like dogmatist,
  Thou pretty Katydid!
Thou mindest me of gentlefolks —
  Old gentlefolks are they —
Thou say'st an undisputed thing
  In such a solemn way.

OLIVER WENDELL HOLMES

The country is both the philosopher's garden and library, in which he reads and contemplates the power, wisdom, and goodness, of God.

WILLIAM PENN

NATURE

As a fond mother, when the day is o'er,
  Leads by the hand her little child to
    bed,
  Half willing, half reluctant to be led,
  And leave his broken playthings on the
    floor,
Still gazing at them through the open
    door,
  Nor wholly reassured and comforted
  By promises of others in their stead,
  Which, though more splendid, may not
    please him more;
So Nature deals with us, and takes away
  Our playthings one by one, and by the
    hand
  Leads us to rest so gently, that we go
Scarce knowing if we wish to go or stay,
  Being too full of sleep to understand
  How far the unknown transcends the
    what we know.

HENRY WADSWORTH LONGFELLOW

God must be glad one loves His world so much!

ROBERT BROWNING

THE BROOK

I come from haunts of coot and hern,
  I make a sudden sally
And sparkle out among the fern,
  To bicker down a valley.

By thirty hills I hurry down,
  Or slip between the ridges,
  By twenty thorps, a little town,
  And half a hundred bridges.

Till last by Philip's farm I flow
  To join the brimming river,
For men may come and men may go,
  But I go on for ever.

I chatter over stony ways,
  In little sharps and trebles,
I bubble into eddying bays,
  I babble on the pebbles.

With many a curve my banks I fret
  By many a field and fallow,
And many a fairy foreland set
  With willow-weed and mallow.

I chatter, chatter, as I flow
  To join the brimming river,
For men may come and men may go,
  But I go on for ever.

ALFRED, LORD TENNYSON

There is a serene and settled majesty to woodland scenery that enters into the soul and delights and elevates it, and fills it with noble inclinations.

WASHINGTON IRVING

O the snow, the beautiful snow,
Filling the sky and earth below;
Over the housetops, over the street,
Over the heads of the people you meet,
Dancing, flirting, skimming along.

JAMES W. WATSON

APOSTROPHE TO THE OCEAN

There is a pleasure
   in the pathless woods,
There is a rapture
   on the lonely shore,
There is society,
   where none intrudes,
By the deep sea,
   and music in its roar.
I love not man the less,
   but Nature more,
From these our interviews,
   in which I steal
From all I may be,
   or have been before,
To mingle with
   the universe and feel
What I can ne'er express,
   Yet cannot all conceal.

LORD BYRON

WOODS IN WINTER

With solemn feet I tread the hill,
And through the hawthorn blows the
   gale;
With solemn feet I tread the hill,
That overbrows the lonely vale.

O'er the bare upland, and away
Through the long reach of desert woods,
The embracing sunbeams chastely play
And gladden these deep solitudes.

Where, twisted round the barren oak
The summer vine in beauty clung
And summer winds the stillness broke,
The crystal icicle is hung.

Where, from their frozen urns, mute
   springs
Pour out the river's gradual tide,
Shrilly the skater's iron rings,
And voices fill the woodland side.

Alas! how changed from the fair scene,
When birds sang out their mellow lay
And winds were soft, and woods were
   green,
And the song ceased not with the day!

But still wild music is abroad;

Pale, desert woods! within your crowd;
And gathering winds, in hoarse accord
Amid the vocal reeds pipe loud.

Chill airs and wintry winds! my ear
Has grown familiar with your song;
I hear it in the opening year;
I listen, and it cheers me long.

HENRY WADSWORTH LONGFELLOW

**Nature is but a name for an effect,
Whose cause is God.**

WILLIAM COWPER

To own a bit of ground, to scratch it with
a hoe, to plant seeds, and watch the
renewal of life . . . this is the commonest
delight of the race, the most satisfactory
thing a man can do.

CHARLES DUDLEY WARNER

From THE GOLDEN FLOWER

When spring is but a spendthrift's dream,
   And summer's wealth a wasted dower,
No dews nor sunshine may redeem, —
   Then autumn coins his Golden Flower.

The shadows, lengthening, stretch at
   noon;
   The fields are stripped, the groves are
     dumb;
The frost-flowers greet the icy moon, —
   Then blooms the bright
     Chrysanthemum.

OLIVER WENDELL HOLMES

**Nature does not demand that we be
   perfect.
It requires that we grow.**

JOSHUA LIEBMAN

CLOSE TO GOD

I feel so close to God outdoors
Where my ceiling is the sky,
'Neath the shelter of the leafy trees
That lift their limbs on high.

I see Him in the morning
When sparkling dewdrops cover all,
I see Him in the evening
When twilight shadows fall.

I hear Him in the rustling leaves,
Beside a shady nook,
I hear Him in the song
Of the little babbling brook.

I listen as His tender voice
Fills my very soul,
"Come unto Me, My child —
And I will make thee whole."

CLARIBEL REAM

Go forth, under the open sky, and listen to Nature's teachings.

WILLIAM CULLEN BRYANT

FOREST SYMPHONY

Oh, give me a place
    by the side of a stream,
Let pine trees wave above;
I shall not ask for any wealth
Nor shall I ask for love.

For all that I want
    of earthly things
Are the needles under my feet,
And all of heaven the patch of sky
Where green plumes meet.

I long for a spot
    where the roar of the falls
And the wind make harmony;
Where pine trees lifting giant arms
Conduct the symphony.

EDITH ADDISON THOMAS

WINDING ROAD

I like a winding road
That wanders far astray,
That twists and turns through rocks and
    ferns
And spurns the shorter way.

I like its casual mood,
The ever-changing scene,
The glad surprise that greets the eyes
Beyond each leafy screen.

I like the fragrant woods,
The birches robed in white,
The shrubs and vines, the tunneled pines,
The open fields of light.

The straightened road is fixed,
Unchangeable as truth:
Give me the gay and longer way,
It has the heart of youth.

ALFRED GRANT WALTON

Adopt the pace of nature: her secret is patience.

RALPH WALDO EMERSON

Winter's the time for woody smoke,
Bare the branch of every oak;
White is the snow for miles around;
Winter's the time for quiet sound.

MARTIN RUXBAUM

Nature is a man's teacher.
She unfolds her treasures to his search,
    unseals his eye,
    illumines his mind,
    and purifies his heart;
an influence breathes from all the sights
    and sounds of her existence.

STREET

135

Nostalgia

SOMETIMES

Across the fields of yesterday
    He sometimes comes to me,
A little lad just back from play —
    The lad I used to be.

And yet he smiles so wistfully
    Once he has crept within,
I wonder if he hopes to see
    The man I might have been.

THOMAS S. JONES, JR.

●

NOSTALGIA

To smell the scent of new-mown hay so
    wet with dew,
To hear a meadowlark when day is
    nearly through,
To hear a cowbell's distant muffled
    sound,
To see a furrow turned on fertile ground.

To see a shady lane where willows sway,
A dusty road, a lazy summer day . . .
To hear the sound of nesting cooing doves
While fleecy clouds make shadows from
    above.

To feel again the warmth of summer rain,
To walk once more a peaceful country
    lane,
Relieve this wanderlust, nostalgic pain,
And let me find the way back home again.

LAURA HOPE WOOD

A LOVELY DAY

I watched the sun begin its arc
    across the sky,
I chatted with a friend,
    I dreamed an afternoon away,
I saw the sky turn pink
    and kiss the sun good-bye,
Ah! this has been a lovely day!

BARBARA BURROW

●

WE LOVE THE VENERABLE HOUSE

We love the venerable house
Our fathers built to God;
In heaven are kept their grateful vows,
Their dust endears the sod.

Here holy thoughts a light have shed
From many a radiant face,
And prayers of humble virtue spread
The perfume of the place.

And anxious hearts have pondered here
The mystery of life,
And prayed th' Eternal Light to clear
Their doubts and aid their strife.

They live with God, their homes are dust;
Yet here their children pray,
And in this fleeting life-time trust
To find the narrow way.

RALPH WALDO EMERSON

FAMILY TIES

Family ties are precious things
 Woven through the years
Of memories of togetherness . . .
 Of laughter, love and tears.

Family ties are cherished things
 Forged in childhood days
By love of parents, deep and true,
 And sweet familiar ways.

Family ties are treasured things,
 And far though we may roam,
The tender bonds with those we love
 Still pull our hearts toward home.

VIRGINIA BLANCK MOORE

●

AT HOME

Adventure and travel haunt my dreams
And foreign names have magic glow —
Zanzibar and Mandalay
And where the trade winds blow.

So I set off when gypsy blood
Wells up and urges me to start,
I wander on and on until
Homesickness strikes my heart.

World travel has its golden days
And it is nice at times to roam,
But far the best part of adventure:
Return to Home Sweet Home.

DAWN FLANERY PARKER

**Philosophy is at bottom homesickness—
the longing to be at home everywhere.**
NOVALIS

99

TO EARTHWARD

Love at the lips was touch
As sweet as I could bear;
And once that seemed too much;
I lived on air

That crossed me from sweet things,
The flow of — was it musk
From hidden grapevine springs
Down hill at dusk?

I had the swirl and ache
From sprays of honeysuckle
That when they're gathered shake
Dew on the knuckle.

I craved strong sweets, but those
Seemed strong when I was young;
The petal of the rose
It was that stung.

Now no joy but lacks salt
That is not dashed with pain
And weariness and fault;
I crave the stain

Of tears, the aftermark
Of almost too much love,
The sweet of bitter bark
And burning clove.

When stiff and sore and scarred
I take away my hand
From leaning on it hard
In grass and sand,

The hurt is not enough:
I long for weight and strength
To feel the earth as rough
To all my length.

ROBERT FROST

●

FIRESIDE HOUR

There by the fire —
 Soft candlelight —
Curtains drawn
 Against the night.

Crackling firewood,
 Amber tea —
Light talk flowing
 Fast and free.

Nothing of false
 Pretense or sham —
Just good friends sharing
 Muffins and jam.

KATHERINE E. EDELMAN

IT IS A BEAUTEOUS EVENING

It is a beauteous evening, calm and free,
The holy time is quiet as a nun
Breathless with adoration; the broad sun
Is sinking down in its tranquillity;
The gentleness of heaven broods o'er
    the sea:
Listen! the mighty Being is awake,
And doth with his eternal motion make
A sound like thunder — everlastingly.
Dear child! dear girl! that walkest with
    me here,
If thou appear untouched by solemn
    thought,
Thy nature is not therefore less divine:
Thou liest in Abraham's bosom all the
    year;
And worship'st at the temple's inner
    shrine,
God being with thee when we know it
    not.

WILLIAM WORDSWORTH

●

I WANDERED LONELY AS A CLOUD

I wandered lonely as a cloud
    That floats on high o'er vales and hills,
When all at once I saw a crowd,
    A host of golden daffodils,
Beside the lake, beside the trees,
    Fluttering and dancing in the breeze.

Continuous as the stars that shine
    And twinkle on the milky way,
They stretched in never-ending line
    Along the margin of a bay;
Ten thousand saw I at a glance,
    Tossing their heads in sprightly dance.

The waves beside them danced, but they
    Outdid the sparkling waves in glee, —
A poet could not but be gay,
    In such a jocund company;
I gazed, and gazed, but little thought
    What wealth that show to me had
        brought.

For oft when on my couch I lie,
    In vacant or in pensive mood,
They flash upon that inward eye

Which is the bliss of solitude;
And then my heart with pleasure fills,
    And dances with the daffodils.

WILLIAM WORDSWORTH

●

STRONG BOX

I have a treasured strong box,
    Its contents are pure gold;
Where all these precious moments
    Are mine to have and hold.

Inside I've put my baby's smile
    The sound of pattering feet;
My little girl's first childish song,
    In babbling accent sweet.

There was a time when guests arrived,
    My walls were scarred and marked;
I washed the handprints all away
    But framed them in my heart.

Now when my children both have grown,
    And I am old and gray,
I'll turn the lock with mem'ry's key,
    And while the hours away.

IRENE C. WALLIS

●

THE LITTLE THINGS

It really is the little things
That mean the most of all . . .
The "let me help you with that" things
That may seem very small,
The "I'll be glad to do it" things
That make your cares much lighter,
The "laugh with me, it's funny" things
That make your outlook brighter . . .

The "never mind the trouble" things,
The "yes, I understand,"
The interest and encouragement
In everything you've planned . . .
It really is the little things,
The friendly word or smile,
That add such happiness to life
And make it more worth while.

MARY DAWSON HUGHES

138

Opportunity & Challenge

All higher motives, ideals, conceptions, sentiments in a man are of no account if they do not come forward to strengthen him for the better discharge of the duties which devolve upon him in the ordinary affairs of life.

HENRY WARD BEECHER

OPPORTUNITY

Yesterday, I dreamed of tomorrow:
In it I saw completion of little tasks;
Little duties, needing but an idle minute's
    gift of time.

I listened, in this dream of mine,
And I heard the sweet piping of tree-top
    carolers
Piping music grand enough
To make these routine cares, a joy.

And also, in this dream of mine,
I felt the peace of work well done,
Accomplished in those fleeting moments
When hand and heart were stirred by
    garden harmony.

My dream of yesterday faded:
'Twas then I realized, and knew,
That yesterday's tomorrow was today,
And I, this hour, could make my dream
    come true.

W. AUDREY P. GOOD

IT'S UP TO ME

I get discouraged now and then
When there are clouds of gray,
Until I think about the things
That happened yesterday.
I do not mean the day before
Or those of months ago,
But all the yesterdays in which
I had the chance to grow.
I think of opportunities
That I allowed to die,
And those I took advantage of
Before they passed me by.
And I remember that the past
Presented quite a plight,
But somehow I endured it and
The future seemed all right.
And I remind myself that I
Am capable and free,
And my success and happiness
Are really up to me.

JAMES J. METCALFE

WASTED OPPORTUNITY

Ruskin once said that when we fail to praise a man who deserves praise, two sad things happen; we run a chance of driving him from the right road for want of encouragement, and we deprive ourselves of one of the very happiest of our privileges, the privilege of rewarding labor that deserves a reward.

139

GIVE ME THIS DAY

A little work to occupy my mind;
A little suffering to sanctify
My spirit; and, dear Lord, if thou canst
    find
Some little good that I may do for thee,
I shall be glad, for that will comfort me.
Mind, spirit, hand — I lift them all to thee.

What a large amount of adventures may
be grasped within this little span of life
by him who interests his heart in everything, and who, having eyes to see what
time and chances are perpetually holding out to him as he journeyeth on his
way, misses nothing he can fairly lay his
sight upon.

LAURENCE STERNE

JUST THIS MINUTE

If we're thoughtful just a minute,
    In whate'er we say and do;
If we put a purpose in it
    That is honest thro' and thro',
We shall gladden life and give it
    Grace to make it all sublime;
For, though life is long, we live it
    Just a minute at a time.

Just this minute we are going
    Toward right or toward wrong;
Just this minute we are sowing
    Seeds of sorrow or of song.
Just this minute we are thinking
    On the ways that lead to God,
Or in idle dreams are sinking
    To the level of the clod.

Yesterday is gone; to-morrow
    Never comes within our grasp;
Just this minute's joy or sorrow,
    That is all our hands may clasp;
Just this minute! Let us take it
    As a pearl of precious price,
And with high endeavor make it
    Fit to shine in paradise.

JOELLE BARNES

A SACRED TRUST

Reach down your hand!
The little one who trudges by your side
Is striving hard to match your grown-up
    stride;
But oh! his feet are very tiny yet,
His arms so short — I pray you don't
    forget —
Reach down your hand!

Keep soft your voice!
For it was such a little while ago
This small one left the place where tones
    are low,
His ear still holds the cadence of that land
Where no one ever gave a stern
    command.
Keep soft your voice.

Lift up your heart.
The little child you struggle so to teach
Has resource far above the human reach;
Lift up your heart.

**When you miss an opportunity you
miss success.**

You can thank God for what is good; you
can learn something or begin a task or
finish a long-delayed piece of work. You
can cheer a friend and share a neighbor's
burden. You can forgive. You can go the
second mile. You can look for the best
and do your best and be your best . . .
and go to bed feeling that you have put
into this day and got out of it as much as
you possibly could.

Four things come not back,
The spoken word,
The sped arrow,
The past life,
The neglected opportunity.

NO SCAR?

Hast thou no scar?
No hidden scar on foot, or side, or hand?
I hear thee sung as mighty in the land,
I hear them hail thy bright ascendant star,
Hast thou no scar?

Hast thou no wound?
Yet I was wounded by the archers, spent,
Leaned Me against a tree to die; and rent
By ravening beasts that compassed Me,
  I swooned:
Hast thou no wound?

No wound? no scar?
Yet, as the Master shall the servant be,
And pierced are the feet that follow Me;
But thine are whole: can he have
  followed far
Who has not wound nor scar?

AMY CARMICHAEL

●

The potential of a child is the most intriguing thing in all creation.

RAY LYMAN WILBUR

The great pleasure in life is doing what people say you cannot do.

WALTER BAGEHOT

●

You and I cannot determine what other
  men shall think and say about us.
We can only determine what they ought
  to think of us and say about us.

The doors of opportunity are marked "push."

No opportunity is ever lost—someone else picks up the ones you miss.

●

When opportunity does knock
By some uncanny quirk
It often goes unrecognized —
It so resembles work!

Others

There is no loving others without living for others.

You will find, as you look back upon your life, that the moments that stand out are the moments when you have done things for others.

HENRY DRUMMOND

OTHERS

Lord, help me live from day to day
In such a self forgetful way
That even when I kneel to pray,
My prayer shall be for others.

Help me in all the work I do
To ever be sincere and true
And know that all I'd do for You,
Must needs be done for others.

Let "self" be crucified and slain
And buried deep, and all in vain
May efforts be to rise again,
Unless to live for others.

And when my work on earth is done
And my new work in heaven's begun,
May I forget the crown I've won
While thinking still of others.

Others, Lord, yes others,
Let this my motto be —
Help me to live for others
That I may live for Thee.

C. D. MEIGS

One of the sanest, surest, and most generous joys of life comes from being happy over the good fortune of others.

ARCHIBALD RUTLEDGE

Behave toward everyone as if receiving a great guest.

CONFUCIUS

Love demands the loving deed,
    Pass it on!
Look upon your brother's need —
    Pass it on!
Live for self, you live in vain;
Live for Christ, with Him you reign —
    Pass it on!

HENRY BURTON

142

WORKING WITH GOD

If I can put one touch of rosy sunset into the life of any man or woman, I shall feel that I have worked with God.

GEORGE MACDONALD

There is a destiny that makes us brothers;
  None goes his way alone.
All that we send into the lives of others
  Comes back into our own.

EDWIN MARKHAM

God has not called us to see through each other, but to see each other through.

HORACE MOODY

DON'T FIND FAULT

Pray don't find fault with the man who
    limps
  Or stumbles along the road,
Unless you have worn the shoes that he
    wears,
  Or struggled beneath his load.
There may be tacks in the shoes that hurt,
  Though hidden away from view;
Or burdens he bears placed on your back
  Might cause you to stumble, too.
Don't sneer at the man who's down today
  Unless you have felt the blow
That caused his fall, or felt the shame
  That only the fallen know.
You may be strong but yet the blow
  That was his, if dealt to you
In the selfsame way, or at the selfsame
    time,
  Might cause you to stagger, too.
Don't be too harsh with the man who
    sins,
  Or pelt him with words or stones,
Unless you are sure — yea, doubly sure,
  That you have not sins of your own.
For you know, perhaps, if the tempter's
    voice

Should whisper as soft to you
As it did to him when he went astray
  It would cause you to falter, too.

AS I GO ON MY WAY

My life shall touch a dozen lives before
    this day is done,
Leave countless marks for good or ill ere
    sets the evening sun;
So this the wish I always wish, the prayer
    I ever pray,
Let my life help the other lives it touches
    by the way.

STRICKLAND GILLILAN

In many things it is not well to say, "Know thyself"; it is better to say, "Know others."

MENANDER

Teach me to feel another's woe,
  To hide the fault I see;
That mercy I to others show,
  That mercy show to me.

ALEXANDER POPE

Ask not what life can give to you
But seek to serve your brothers;
The richest joys that man can know
Are those he shares with others.

The woman who helps her neighbor does herself a good turn.

BRENDAN FRANCIS

143

Patience & Forbearance

O make me patient, Lord,
  Patient in daily cares;
Keep me from thoughtless words,
  That slip out unawares,
And help me, Lord, I pray,
  Still nearer thee to live,
And as I journey on,
  More of thy presence give.

●

A CREED FOR EVERYONE

Patience *when your neighbor's curt.*
Silence *when your words would hurt.*
Deafness *when the scandal flows.*
Thoughtfulness *for others' woes.*
Promptness *when stern duty calls.*
Courage *when misfortune falls.*

●

THE RULE OF THREE

Three things to govern:
  temper, tongue, conduct
Three things to love:
  courage, gentleness, affection.
Three things to hate:
  cruelty, arrogance, ingratitude.
Three things to wish for:
  health, friends, a cheerful spirit.
Three things to fight for:
  honor, country, home.

With time and patience the mulberry leaf becomes satin.

ORIENTAL PROVERB

●

If you your lips would save from slips,
Five things observe with care;
Of whom you speak
To whom you speak
And how and when and where.

If you your ears would save from jeers,
These things keep meekly hid;
Myself and I
And mine or my
And what I do or did.

●

Consider the hammer —
  It keeps its head.
  It doesn't fly off the handle.
  It keeps pounding away.
  It finds the point and then drives it
    home.
  It looks at the other side, too, and thus
    often clinches the matter.
  It makes mistakes, but when it does
    it starts all over.
  It is the only knocker in the world that
    does any good.

144

It is not necessary for all men to be great in action. The greatest and sublimest power is often simple patience.

HORACE BUSHNELL

●

ON HIS BLINDNESS

When I consider how my light is spent,
  Ere half my days, in this dark world
      and wide,
  And that one Talent which is death to
      hide,
  Lodg'd with me useless, though my
      soul more bent
To serve therewith my Maker, and
      present
  My true account, lest he returning
      chide,
  Doth God exact day-labour, light
      deny'd,
  I fondly ask; But Patience, to prevent
That murmur, soon replies, God doth not
      need
  Either man's work or his own gifts:
      who best
  Bear his mild yoke, they serve him
      best: his State
Is kingly. Thousands at his bidding speed
  And post o'er land and ocean without
      rest:
  They also serve who only stand and
      wait.

JOHN MILTON

●

What a superb thing it would be if we were all big enough in mind to see no slights, accept no insults, cherish no jealousies and admit into our heart no hatred!

ELBERT HUBBARD

Let nothing disturb thee;
Let nothing afright thee;
All things are passing;
God never changes.

Patience gains all things;
Who has God wants nothing;
God alone suffices.

ST. TERESA OF AVILA

●

IT IS HARD

To forget
To apologize
To save money
To be unselfish
To avoid mistakes
To keep out of a rut
To begin all over again
To make the best of all things
To keep your temper at all times
To think first and act afterwards
To maintain a high standard
To keep on keeping on
To shoulder blame
To be charitable
To admit error
To take advice
To forgive
But it pays!

DAILY CREED

Let me be a little kinder,
Let me be a little blinder
To the faults of those about me,
Let me praise a little more.

Let me be, when I am weary,
Just a little bit more cheery;
Let me serve a little better
The God we would adore.

Let me be a little meeker
With the brother who is weaker;
Let me strive a little harder
To be all that I should be.

Let me be more understanding,
And a little less demanding,
Let me be the sort of friend
That you have always been to me.

JOHN GRAY

145

THE NIGHTINGALE AND GLOW-WORM

A nightingale, that all day long
Had cheered the village with his song,
Nor yet at eve his note suspended,
Nor yet when eventide was ended,
Began to feel — as well he might —
The keen demands of appetite;
When, looking eagerly around,
He spied, far off, upon the ground,
A something shining in the dark,
And knew the glow-worm by his spark;
So, stooping down from hawthorn top,
He thought to put him in his crop.

The worm, aware of his intent,
Harangued him thus, quite eloquent,
"Did you admire my lamp," quoth he,
"As much as I your minstrelsy,
You would abhor to do me wrong,
As much as I to spoil your song;
For 'twas the self-same Power divine
Taught you to sing, and me to shine;
That you with music, I with light,
Might beautify and cheer the night."
The songster heard his short oration,
And, warbling out his approbation,
Released him, as my story tells,
And found a supper somewhere else.

●

I had a little daughter,
    And she was given to me
To lead me gently backward
    To the Heavenly Father's knee,
That I, by the force of nature,
    Might in some dim wise divine
The depth of His infinite patience
    To this wayward soul of mine.

JAMES RUSSELL LOWELL

But still remember, if you mean to please,
To press your point with modesty and
    ease.

WILLIAM COWPER

●

Happy homes
are built
of blocks
of patience.

HAROLD E. KOHN

●

Endeavor to be always patient of the faults and imperfections of others, for thou hast many faults and imperfections of thy own that require a reciprocation of forbearance. If thou art not able to make thyself that which thou wishest to be, how canst thou expect to mould another in conformity to thy will?

THOMAS A KEMPIS

●

LIFE

Life is a burden; bear it.
Life is a duty; dare it.
Life is a thorn crown; wear it.
Though it break your heart in twain,
Though the burden crush you down,
Close your lips and hide the pain;
First the cross and then the crown.

Peace, Serenity, & Contentment

Lord, make me an instrument of Thy
    peace;
Where there is hatred,
  let me sow love;
Where there is doubt,
  faith;
Where there is despair,
  hope;
Where there is darkness,
  light;
and where there is sadness,
  joy.

O Divine Master, grant that I may not so
    much
  seek to be consoled,
  as to console;
to be understood,
  as to understand;
to be loved,
  as to love;
for it is in giving that we receive,
it is in pardoning that we are pardoned,
and it is in dying that we are born to
    eternal life.

ST. FRANCIS OF ASSISI

●

PEACE

With eager heart and will on fire,
I fought to win my great desire
"Peace shall be mine," I said; but life
Grew bitter in the weary strife.

My soul was tired, and my pride
Was wounded deep: to Heaven I cried,
"God grant me peace or I must die;"
The dumb stars glittered no reply.

Broken at last, I bowed my head,
Forgetting all myself, and said,
"Whatever comes, His will be done;"
And in that moment peace was won.

HENRY VAN DYKE

The secret of contentment
is knowing how to enjoy what you have.

99

Lift up your eyes to the mountains,
Breathe deeply the crisp sweet air.
Listen to the murmuring waters . . .
The spirit of peace is there.

D. A. HOOVER

●

Not that I speak in respect of want:
for I have learned,
in whatsoever state I am,
therewith to be content.

PHILIPPIANS 4:11

147

LITTLE GUIDEPOSTS

To be glad of life because it gives you
    the chance to love and to work
    and to play and to look up at the stars,

To be satisfied with your possessions
    but not contented with yourself
    until you have made the best of them,

To despise nothing in the world
    except falsehood and meanness
    and to fear nothing except cowardice,

To be governed by your admirations
    rather than by your disgusts,

To covet nothing that is your neighbor's
    except his kindness of heart
    and gentleness of manners,

To think seldom of your enemies,
    often of your friends . . .

    These are little guide-posts
    on the footpath to peace.

HENRY VAN DYKE

●

IN ACCEPTANCE LIETH PEACE

He said, "I will forget the dying faces;
The empty places,
They shall be filled again.
O voices mourning deep within me,
    cease."
But, vain the word; vain, vain:
Not in forgetting lieth peace.

He said, "I will crowd action upon action,
The strife of faction
Shall stir me and sustain;
O tears that drown the fire of manhood
    cease."
But, vain the word; vain, vain:
Not in endeavour lieth peace.

He said, "I will withdraw me and be
    quiet,
Why meddle in life's riot?
Shut be my door to pain.
Desire, thou dost befool me, thou shalt
    cease."
But, vain the word; vain, vain:
Not in aloofness lieth peace.

He said, "I will submit; I am defeated.
God hath depleted
My life of its rich gain.
O futile murmurings, why will ye not
    cease?"
But, vain the word; vain, vain:
Not in submission lieth peace.

He said, "I will accept the breaking
    sorrow
Which God to-morrow
Will to His son explain."
Then did the turmoil deep within him
    cease.
Not vain the word, not vain;
For in acceptance lieth peace.

AMY CARMICHAEL

●

Thou wilt keep him in perfect peace,
    whose mind is stayed on thee;
    because he trusteth in thee.

ISAIAH 26:3

●

TO ME, MY FARM IS . . .

My farm to me is not just land
Where bare, unpainted buildings stand.
To me my farm is nothing less
Than all created loveliness.

My farm is not where I must soil
My hands in endless, dreary toil,
But where, through seed and swelling
    pod,
I've learned to walk and talk with God.

My farm to me is not a place
Outmoded by a modern race.
I like to think I just see less
Of evil, greed and selfishness.

My farm's not lonely, for all day
I hear my children shout and play,
And here, when age comes, free from
    fears,
I'll live again, long joyous years.

My farm's a heaven — here dwells rest,
Security and happiness.

Whate'er befalls the world outside
Here faith and hope and love abide.

And so my farm is not just land
Where bare, unpainted buildings stand.
To me my farm is nothing less
Than all God's hoarded loveliness.

•

I built a chimney for a comrade old,
  I did the service, not for hope of hire —
And then I traveled on in winter's cold,
  Yet all the day I glowed before the fire.

EDWIN MARKHAM

•

THE HOUSE BY THE SIDE
OF THE ROAD

There are hermit souls that live
    withdrawn
  In the place of their self-content;
There are souls like stars, that dwell
    apart,
  In a fellowless firmament;
There are pioneer souls that blaze their
    paths
  Where highways never ran —
But let me live by the side of the road
  And be a friend to man.

Let me live in a house by the side of the
    road,
  Where the race of men go by —
The men who are good and the men who
    are bad,
  As good and as bad as I.
I would not sit in the scorner's seat,
  Or hurl the cynic's ban —
Let me live in a house by the side of the
    road
  And be a friend to man.

I see from my house by the side of the
    road,
  By the side of the highway of life,
The men who press with the ardor of
    hope,
  The men who are faint with the strife.
But I turn not away from their smiles nor
    their tears,
  Both parts of an infinite plan —

Let me live in a house by the side of the
    road
  And be a friend to man.

I know there are brook-gladdened
    meadows ahead
  And Mountains of wearisome height;
That the road passes on through the long
    afternoon
  And stretches away to the night.
But still I rejoice when the travelers
    rejoice,
  And weep with the strangers that
    moan,
Nor live in my house by the side of the
    road
  Like a man who dwells alone.

Let me live in my house by the side of the
    road —
  It's here the race of men go by.
They are good, they are bad, they are
    weak, they are strong
  Wise, foolish — so am I;
Then why should I sit in the scorner's
    seat,
  Or hurl the cynic's ban?
Let me live in my house by the side of the
    road
  And be a friend to man.

SAM WALTER FOSS

•

Even a fool, when he holdeth his peace,
is counted wise.

PROVERBS 17:28

•

COMPENSATION

Who never wept knows laughter but a
    jest;
Who never failed, no victory has sought;
Who never suffered, never lived his best;
Who never doubted, never really thought;
Who never feared, real courage has not
    shown;
Who never faltered, lacks a real intent;
Whose soul was never troubled has not
    known
The sweetness and the peace of real
    content.

E. M. BRAINARD

149

I DO NOT ASK, O LORD

I do not ask, O Lord, that life may be
    A Pleasant road;
I do not ask that thou wouldst take from
    me
        Aught of its load.

I do not ask that flowers should always
    spring
        Beneath my feet;
I know too well the poison and the sting
        Of things too sweet.

For one thing only, Lord, dear Lord,
    I plead:
        Lead me aright.
Though strength should falter and though
    heart should bleed,
        Through peace to light.

I do not ask, O Lord, that thou shouldst
    shed
        Full radiance here;
Give but a ray of peace, that I may tread
        Without a fear.

I do not ask my cross to understand,
        My way to see;
Better in darkness just to feel thy hand,
        And follow Thee.

Joy is like restless day; but peace divine
        Like quiet night.
Lead me, O Lord, till perfect day shall
    shine
        Through peace to light.

ADELAIDE ANNE PROCTER

●

Go placidly amid the noise & haste, & remember what peace there may be in silence. As far as possible without surrender be on good terms with all persons. Speak your truth quietly & clearly; and listen to others, even the dull & ignorant; they too have their story.

Avoid loud & aggressive persons, they are vexatious to the spirit. If you compare yourself with others, you may become vain & bitter; for always there will be greater & lesser persons than yourself. Enjoy your achievements as well as your plans.

Keep interested in your own career, however humble; it is a real possession in the changing fortunes of time. Exercise caution in your business affairs; for the world is full of trickery. But let this not blind you to what virtue there is; many persons strive for high ideals; and everywhere life is full of heroism.

Be yourself. Especially, do not feign affection. Neither be cynical about love; for in the face of all aridity & disenchantment it is perennial as the grass.

Take kindly the counsel of the years, gracefully surrendering the things of youth. Nurture strength of spirit to shield you in sudden misfortune. But do not distress yourself with imaginings. Many fears are born of fatigue & loneliness. Beyond a wholesome discipline, be gentle with yourself.

You are a child of the universe, no less than the trees & the stars; you have a right to be here. And whether or not it is clear to you, no doubt the universe is unfolding as it should.

Therefore be at peace with God, whatever you conceive Him to be, and whatever your labors & aspirations, in the noisy confusion of life keep peace with your soul.

With all its sham, drudgery & broken dreams, it is still a beautiful world. Be careful. Strive to be happy.

FOUND IN OLD SAINT PAUL'S CHURCH, BALTIMORE: DATED 1692

A heart full of thankfulness,
A thimbleful of care;
A soul of simple hopefulness,
An early morning prayer;
A smile to greet the morning with,
A kind word as a key
To open the door and greet the day,
Whate'er it brings to thee.
A patient trust in Providence
To sweeten all the way . . .
All these, combined with thoughtfulness
Will make a happy day.

GOD IS NIGH

Day is done, gone the sun
From the lake, from the hills, from the
sky.
Safely rest, all is well! God is nigh.

To be content with little is difficult:
to be content with much—impossible.

MARIE VON EBNER-ESCHENBACH

The day is long and the day is hard;
We are tired of the march and of keeping
guard;
Tired of the sense of a fight to be won,
Of days to live through, and of work to be
done;
Tired of ourselves and of being alone.

And all the while, did we only see,
We walk in the Lord's own company;
We fight, but 'tis he who nerves our arm;
He turns the arrows which else might
harm,
And out of the storm he brings a calm.

SUSAN COOLIDGE

●

I am looking from life's west window
Out toward the dreaming hills,
And a peace that is rare and precious
My heart's deep chambers fills.

GEORGE CHACE

●

If the wren can cling
To a spray a-swing
In the mad May wind, and sing and sing
As if she'd burst for joy —

Why cannot I
Contented lie
In his quiet arms, beneath his sky,
Unmoved by life's annoy.

ROBERT HAVEN SCHAUFFLER

I saw Him there,
    where mountains brushed the sky.
I saw Him there
    where trees and grass grace the dawn.
I saw Him there
    where rippling brooks don the green.
I saw Him there
    where waving flowers toss and speak.
I saw Him there
    where eyes of man reflect His peace
    within.

LIFE'S LOVELY THINGS

The paths we tread abound with lovely
things,
The homing drift of birds on eager wings,
The birth of dawn, flamed robes of dying
day
Recalling tender hopes long stored away.

Surf, pearly-plumed abreast a sapphire
wave,
Lush golden hills that shadows oft
engrave,
Hushed snowfall on a peaceful
countryside,
The glory-beaming stars at eventide.

A simple maiden, calm in winsome grace,
The dawning wonder in a baby's face,
The steeple of the old white church
Whose shade becomes a giant sundial
o'er the glade.

The gift of friendliness that warms a
heart
A magic boon that humans can impart,
The paths we tread are eased when
beauty brings
Us to remember only lovely things.

LILLIAN C. BUSBY

●

Under the leaves, amid the grass, lazily
the day shall pass, yet not be wasted.
From my drowsy ease I borrow health
and strength to bear my boat through the
great life ocean.

CHARLES MACKAY

151

True contentment is the power of getting out of any situation all that there is in it.

GILBERT KEITH CHESTERTON

It hain't no use to grumble and complane;
   It's jest as cheap and easy to rejoice, —
When God sorts out the weather and
   sends rain,
   W'y, rain's my choice.

JAMES WHITCOMB RILEY

It means humility and charity, a
generous appreciation of others, and a
modest opinion of self.

Cheerfulness means a contented spirit;
a pure heart, a kind and loving disposition;
it means humility and charity, a
generous appreciation of others, and a
modest opinion of self.

WILLIAM MAKEPEACE THACKERAY

SONNET OF CONTENTMENT

To one who has been long in city pent
'Tis very sweet to look into the fair
And open face of heaven, to breathe a
   prayer
Full in the smile of the blue firmament.
Who is more happy, when, with heart's
   content,
Fatigued he sinks into some pleasant lair
Of wavy grass, and reads a debonair
And gentle tale of love and
   languishment?
Returning home at evening, with an ear
Catching the notes of Philomel, an eye

Watching the sailing cloudlet's bright
   career,
He mourns that day so soon has glided by,
Even like the passage of an angel's tear
That falls through the clear ether silently.

JOHN KEATS

Fortify yourself with contentment, for this is an impregnable fortress.

EPICTETUS

CONTENTMENT

It's a small world I live in . . .
The miles I travel are few,
With always familiar faces
And a sameness each day in my view.

I know each highway and byway
And every valley and hill,
The landmarks that down through the
   ages
Are standing staunch and still.

And every tree has its place,
And I know each country lane,
Where each mailbox on the corner
Bears a familiar name.

Yes, it's a small world I live in,
But my vision reaches the sky,
And in fancy I've seen distant places
That seem real as time passes by.

Yes, mine is a simple and beautiful world,
And mine is a lucky star,
And I am contented and happy to live
In my world with things as they are.

LAURA HOPE WOOD

Perseverance & Determination

The leading rule for a man of every calling is diligence; never put off until tomorrow what you can do today.

ABRAHAM LINCOLN

●

PERSEVERANCE

Say, the man's not a man
  Who can quit when he can;
Who will cast down the load
  In the heat of the road
And not share in the sweat of the fray.
No! — the man is a man
  Who will stay.

There are cowards who fight
  When the going is right;
But the cause is forgot
  When the battle is hot —
And the foe takes the spoils of the day.
But the man is a man
  Who will stay!

Many soldiers have fought
  Where their efforts found naught
But the smile of the brave
  O'er the sod of their grave:
All their trophies were taken away —
Yet the man is a man
  Who will stay!

So let others disdain
  All the torture and pain

That must come with the fight
  Against forces of night:
All our loss He will richly repay!
He loves men — stubborn men —
  Who will stay!

And when God meets His men
  At the roll call in Heav'n
And the crown and the throne
  Shall belong to His own,
Then with glory and grace He will say,
"You are mine! You are men
  Who will stay!"

●

If you wish success in life, make perseverance your bosom friend, experience your wise counselor, conscience your elder brother, and hope your guardian genius.

JOSEPH ADDISON

●

THE PLACE OF DEFEAT

There's no defeat in life
  Save from within,
Unless you're beaten there
  You're bound to win.

HENRY AUSTIN

153

Perseverance gives power to weakness, and opens to poverty the world's wealth. It spreads fertility over the barren landscape, and bids the choicest flowers and fruits spring up and flourish in the desert abode of thorns and briars.

S. G. GOODRICH

KEEP ON

Do the best you can with what you
  possess,
Though it isn't much, yet it could be
  less.
He invites defeat who gives up to
  sighing.
But the battle is won if you keep on
  trying.

ISLA PASCHAL RICHARDSON

Diamonds are pieces of coal that stuck to their jobs.

If a man can write a better book, preach a better sermon, or make a better mousetrap than his neighbor, though he build his house in the woods, the world will make a beaten path to his door.

RALPH WALDO EMERSON

I will not hurry through this day!
Lord, I will listen by the way,
To humming bees and singing birds,
To speaking trees and friendly words;
And for the moments in between
Seek glimpses of the great Unseen.
I will not hurry through this day!
I will take time to think and pray!
I will look into the sky,
Where fleecy clouds and swallows fly;
And somewhere in the day, maybe
I will catch whispers, Lord, from Thee.

Perseverence is failing nineteen times and succeeding the twentieth.

J. ANDREWS

●

I RESOLVE

To keep my health;
To do my work;
To live;
To see to it that I grow and gain and give;
Never to look behind me for an hour;
To wait in meekness, and to walk in
  power;
But always fronting onward, to the light,
Always and always facing toward the
  right.
Robbed, starved, defeated, fallen,
  wide-astray —
On, with what strength I have —
Back to the way.

CHARLOTTE PERKINS STETSON

NATURE'S PLAN

It is easy to drift
  with the current swift —
Just to lie in your boat and dream,
But in nature's plan
  it takes a real man
To paddle the boat upstream.

Few things are impossible to diligence and skill.

SAMUEL JOHNSON

●●

O Lord God, when Thou givest to Thy servants to endeavor any great matter, grant us also to know that it is not the beginning but the continuing of the same until it be thoroughly finished which yieldeth the true glory.

SIR FRANCIS DRAKE

154

IF

If you can keep your head when all about
       you
    Are losing theirs and blaming it on you;
If you can trust yourself when all men
       doubt you,
    And make allowance for their
       doubting, too;

If you can wait and not be tired of
       waiting,
    Or being lied about, don't deal in lies;
Or, being hated, don't give way to hating;
    And yet don't look too good, nor talk
       too wise;

If you can dream, and not make dreams
       your master;
    If you can think, and not make
       thoughts your aim;
If you can meet with Triumph and
       Disaster,
    And treat those two imposters just the
       same;

If you can bear to hear the truth you've
       spoken
    Twisted by knaves to make a trap for
       fools,
Or watch the things you gave your life to,
       broken,
    And stoop, and build them up with
       worn-out tools;

If you can make one heap of all your
       winnings
    And risk it on one turn of
       pitch-and-toss,
And lose, and start again at your
       beginnings
    And never breathe a word about your
       loss;

If you can force your heart and nerve and
       sinew
    To serve your turn long after they are
       gone,
And so hold on when there is nothing in
       you
    Except the Will which says to them:
       "Hold on!"

If you can walk with crowds and keep
       your virtue,
    Or walk with Kings — nor lose the
       common touch —

If neither foes nor loving friends can hurt
       you,
    If all men count with you — but none
       too much;

If you can fill the unforgiving minute
    With sixty seconds' worth of distance
       run,
Yours is the Earth and everything that's
       in it,
    And — which is more — you'll be a
       Man, my son!

RUDYARD KIPLING

The greatest thing in this world is not so much where we stand, as in what direction we are moving.

OLIVER WENDELL HOLMES

REST

Rest is not quitting the busy career;
Rest is the fitting of self to one's sphere;
It's loving and serving the highest and
    best;
It's onward, unswerving; and this is true
    rest.

JOHANN WOLFGANG VON GOETHE

Great works are performed, not by strength but by perseverance.

SAMUEL JOHNSON

As streams of water turn mill-wheels, night and day, themselves slender, yet powerful in their accumulation, so trickling heart-streams turn the great wheel of life's purposes.

HENRY WARD BEECHER

155

BE STRONG!

Be strong!
We are not here to play, to dream, to
  drift,
We have hard work to do, and loads to
  lift.
Shun not the struggle, face it, 'tis God's
  gift.
          Be strong!
Say not the days are evil — who's to
  blame?
And fold the hands and acquiesce — O
  shame!
Stand up, speak out, and bravely, in
  God's name.
          Be strong!
It matters not how deep intrenched the
  wrong,
How hard the battle goes, the day, how
  long;
Faint not, fight on! To-morrow comes the
  song.

MALTBIE D. BABCOCK

The rung of a ladder was never meant to rest upon, but only to hold a man's foot long enough to enable him to put the other one higher.

You will never find time for anything. If you want time you must make it.

CHARLES BUXTON

Brethren, I count not myself to have apprehended: but this one thing I do, forgetting those things which are behind, and reaching forth unto those things which are before, I press toward the mark for the prize of the high calling of God in Christ Jesus.

PHILIPPIANS 3:13-14

Perspective

LEND A HAND

I am only one,
But still I am one.
I cannot do everything,
But still I can do something;
And because I cannot do everything
I will not refuse to do the something that
   I can do.

EDWARD EVERETT HALE

MUCH FOR LITTLE

How little it costs if we give a thought,
  To make some heart happy each day!
Just one kind word or a tender smile
  As we go on our daily way.

Perhaps a look will suffice to clear
  The cloud from a neighbor's face;
And the press of a hand in sympathy
  A sorrowful tear efface.

It costs so little; I wonder why
  We give it so little thought.
A smile, kind words, a glance, a touch —
  What magic by them is wrought!

If none were sick and none were sad,
  What service could we render?

I think if We were always glad,
  We scarcely could be tender.
If sorrow never claimed our heart,
  And every wish were granted,
Patience would die and hope depart —
  Life would be disenchanted.

Without the Way there is no going; without the Truth there is no knowing; without the Life there is no living.

THOMAS A KEMPIS

ENOUGH NOT ONE

The poor have little,
  Beggars none;
The rich too much,
  Enough not one.

BENJAMIN FRANKLIN

There is so much good in the worst of us,
And so much bad in the best of us,
That it hardly becomes any of us
To talk about the rest of us.

EDWARD WALLIS HOCH

A man would do nothing, if he waited until he could do it so well that no one would find fault with what he has done.

JOHN HENRY NEWMAN

SO LONG AS THERE ARE HOMES

So long as we have homes to which men
  turn
  At the close of day,
So long as we have homes where children
  are
  And women stay,
If love and loyalty and faith be found
  Across these sills,
A stricken nation can recover from
  Its gravest ills,
So long as we have homes where fires
  burn
  And there is bread,
So long as we have homes where lamps
  are lit
  And prayers are said,
Altho a people falter thru the dark
  And nations grope,
With God, Himself, back of these little
  homes,
  We still have hope.

GRACE NOLL CROWELL

Measure your mind's height by the shade it casts!

ROBERT BROWNING

WHAT A TEACHER NEEDS

The education of a college president,
The executive ability of a financier,
The humility of a deacon,
The adaptability of a chameleon,
The hope of an optimist,
The courage of a hero,
The wisdom of a serpent,
The gentleness of a dove,
The patience of Job,
The grace of God, and
The persistence of the Devil.

To love at all is to become vulnerable. Love anything, and your heart will certainly be wrung, and possibly broken. If you want to make sure of keeping it intact you must give it to no one, not even an animal. Wrap it carefully around with hobbies and little luxuries; avoid all entanglements; lock it up safe in the coffin or casket of your selfishness. But in that casket, safe, dark, motionless, airless, it will change. It will not be broken; it will become unbreakable, impenetrable, irredeemable. The alternative to true tragedy, or at least to the risk of tragedy, is damnation. The only place outside of Heaven where you can be perfectly safe from all dangers and perturbations of love is in Hell.

C. S. LEWIS

Our business in life is not to get ahead of other people, but to get ahead of ourselves.

MALTBIE D. BABCOCK

A boy is a bank where you can deposit your most precious treasures—the hard-won wisdom, the dreams of a better world. A boy can guard and protect these, and perhaps invest them wisely and with a profit — a profit larger than you ever dreamed. A boy will inherit your world. All the work will be judged by him. Tomorrow he will take your seat in Congress, own your company, run your town. The future is his and through him the future is yours. Perhaps he deserves a little more attention now.

All sunny skies would be too bright,
All morning hours mean too much light,
All laughing days too gay a strain;
There must be clouds, and night, and rain,
And shut-in days, to make us see
The beauty of life's tapestry.

The reason why most men do not achieve more is because they do not attempt more.

I count this thing to be grandly true:
That a noble deed is a step toward God.

JOSIAH GILBERT HOLLAND

Every human being has a work to carry on within, duties to perform abroad, influence to exert, which are peculiarly his, and which no conscience but his own can teach.

WILLIAM ELLERY CHANNING

PESSIMISM

If it wasn't for the optimist, the pessimist would never know how happy he wasn't.

If you have built castles in the air,
Your work need not be lost;
that is where they should be.
Now put foundations under thee.

HENRY DAVID THOREAU

Prayer

MORE THINGS ARE WROUGHT BY PRAYER

More things are wrought by prayer
Than this world dreams of. Wherefore let
  thy voice
Rise like a fountain for me night and day.
For what are men better than sheep or
  goats
That nourish a blind life within the brain,
If, knowing God, they lift not hands of
  prayer
Both for themselves and those who call
  them friend?
For so the whole round earth is every way
Bound by gold chains about the feet
  of God.

ALFRED, LORD TENNYSON

A HUMBLE HEART

I would not ask Thee that my days
  Should flow quite smoothly on and on,
Lest I should learn to love the world
  Too well, ere all my time was done.

I would not ask Thee that my work
  Should never bring me pain nor fear;
Lest I should learn to work alone,
  And never wish thy presence near.

I would not ask Thee that my friends
  Should always kind and constant be;

Lest I should learn to lay my faith
  In them alone, and not in thee.

But I would ask a humble heart,
  A changeless will to work and wake,
A firm faith in Thy providence,
  The rest — 'tis thine to give or take.

ALFRED NORRIS

O gracious and holy Father,
Give us wisdom to perceive Thee,
intelligence to understand Thee,
diligence to seek Thee,
patience to wait for Thee,
eyes to behold Thee,
a heart to meditate upon Thee,
and a life to proclaim Thee;
through the power of the Spirit of Jesus
  Christ our Lord.

ST. BENEDICT OF NURSIA

Saviour, I've no one else to tell
And so I trouble Thee,
I am the one forgot Thee so.
Dost Thou remember me?

EMILY DICKINSON

THE TASTE OF PRAYER

Lord, lay the taste of prayer upon my
tongue,
And let my lips speak banquets unto
Thee;
Then may this richest feast, when once
begun,
Keep me in hunger through eternity.

RALPH W. SEAGER

My voice shalt thou hear in the morning,
O Lord;
in the morning will I direct my prayer
unto thee,
and will look up.

PSALM 5:3

Help us, O God, to receive each new day
with joy—a gift from Thee.

DEAR LORD AND FATHER
OF MANKIND

Dear Lord and Father of mankind!
Forgive our foolish ways!
Reclothe us in our rightful mind,
In purer lives Thy service find,
In deeper reverence, praise.

In simple trust like theirs who heard,
Beside the Syrian sea,
The gracious calling of the Lord,
Let us, like them, without a word,
Rise up and follow Thee.

O Sabbath rest by Galilee!
O calm of hills above,
Where Jesus knelt to share with Thee
The silence of eternity
Interpreted by love!

With that deep hush subduing all
Our words and works that drown
The tender whisper of Thy call,
As noiseless let Thy blessing fall
As fell Thy manna down.

Drop Thy still dews of quietness,
Till all our strivings cease;
Take from our souls the strain and stress,
And let our ordered lives confess
The beauty of Thy peace.

Breathe through the heats of our desire
Thy coolness and Thy balm;
Let sense be dumb, let flesh retire;
Speak through the earthquake, wind and
fire,
O still small voice of calm!

JOHN GREENLEAF WHITTIER

PRAYER AT MORNING

The day returns and brings us the petty
round of irritating concerns and duties.
Help us to play the man, help us to perform them with laughter and kind faces,
let cheerfulness abound with industry.
Give us to go blithely on our business all
this day, bring us to our resting beds
weary and content and undishonored,
and grant us in the end the gift of sleep.

ROBERT LOUIS STEVENSON

WHO, ME?

I need to be forgiven, Lord
So many times a day
So often do I slip and fall
Be merciful, I pray!
And help me not be critical
When other's faults I see;
For so many times, my Lord,
The same faults are in me.

God, give me sympathy and sense,
And help me keep my courage high;
God, give me calm and confidence,
And — please — a twinkle in my eye.
                              Amen.

MARGARET BAILEY

PROOF

If radio's slim fingers
Can pluck a melody
From night, and toss it over
A continent or sea —

If the petaled white notes
Of a violin
Are blown across a mountain
Or a city's din —

If songs, like crimson roses
Are culled from thin blue air,
Why should mortals wonder
If God hears prayer?

EDITH ROMIG FULLER

PRAYER AT EVENING

The service of the day is over, and the hour come to rest. We resign into Thy hands our sleeping bodies, our cold hearths and open doors. Give us to awake with smiles, give us to labor smiling. As the sun returns in the east, so let our patience be renewed with dawn; as the sun lightens the world, so let our loving-kindness make bright this house of our habitations.

ROBERT LOUIS STEVENSON

Prayer can be as quiet
As a falling petal,
Fragrant as a flower,
But strong as metal.

Prayer can be a crying,
As in Gethsemane.
And he who heard his Son, the Christ,
Will he not hear me?

Prayer can be the music
Of his song divine,
The miracle of harmony,
His counterpoint with mine.

And always to the Spirit-fed
Prayer can bring the Living Bread.

GWYNNYTH GIBSON

ABOVE MEDIOCRITY

Lord, save me
From mediocrity.

Average, I know,
Is far too low.

Help me to climb
To heights sublime;

Never at rest
Below my best.

My best in Thee,
Thy best for me.

Life's real success
Can be nothing less.

Lord, save me
From mediocrity.

CARLTON C. BUCK

O Lord Jesus, may we not think of Thy coming as a distant event that took place once and has never been repeated. May we know that Thou art still here walking among us, by our sides, whispering over our shoulders, tugging at our sleeves, smiling upon us when we need encouragement and help.

PETER MARSHALL
from The Prayers of Peter Marshall
by Catherine Marshall

Oh, God — when I have food
Help me to remember the hungry;
When I have work,
Help me to remember the jobless;
When I have a warm home,
Help me to remember the homeless;
When I am without pain,
Help me to remember those who suffer;
And remembering,
Help me to destroy my complacency,
And bestir my compassion.
Make me concerned enough to help,
By word and deed, those who cry out —
For what we take for granted.

162

MORTAR

**Prayer is the mortar
that holds our house
together.**

ST. TERESA

●

*Set us afire, Lord; stir us, we pray!
While the world perishes we go our way.
Purposeless, passionless, day after day,
Set us afire, Lord; stir us, we pray!*

●

A PRAYER

Let me do my work each day; and if the darkened hours of despair overcome me, may I not forget the strength that comforted me in the desolation of other times.

May I still remember the bright hours that found me walking over the silent hills of my childhood, or dreaming on the margin of the quiet river, when a light glowed within me, and I promised early my God to have courage amid the tempests of the changing years. Spare me from bitterness and from the sharp passions of unguarded moments. May I not forget that poverty and riches are of the spirit. Though the world know me not, may my thought and actions be such as shall keep me friendly with myself.

Lift my eyes from the earth, and let me forget the uses of the stars. Forbid that I should judge others lest I condemn myself. Let me not follow the clamor of the world, but walk calmly in my path.

Give me a few friends who will love me for what I am; and keep ever burning before my vagrant steps the kindly light of hope. And though age and infirmity overtake me, and I come not within sight of the castle of my dreams, teach me still to be thankful for life, and for time's olden memories that are good and sweet; and may the evening's twilight find me gentle still.

MAX EHRMANN

*Prayer is the simplest form of speech
    That infant lips can try —
Prayer the sublimest strains that reach
    The majesty on high.*

*Nor prayer is made by man alone —
    The Holy Spirit pleads —
And Jesus, on the eternal throne,
    For sinners intercedes.*

JAMES MONTGOMERY

●

Confess your faults one to another,
and pray one for another,
that ye may be healed.
The effectual fervent prayer of a
    righteous man availeth much.

JAMES 5:16

●

*The parent-pair their secret homage pay,
And proffer up to heaven the warm
    request,
That He who stills the raven's clamorous
    nest,
And decks the lily fair in flow'ry pride,
Would, in the way His wisdom sees the
    best,
For them and for their little ones provide;
But chiefly in their hearts with grace
    divine preside.*

ROBERT BURNS

●

O Holy Spirit of God, abide with us;
    inspire all our thoughts;
    pervade our imaginations;
    suggest all our decisions;
    order all our doings.
Be with us in our silence and in our
        speech,
    in our haste and in our leisure,
    in company and in solitude,
    in the freshness of the morning and in
        the weariness of the evening;
    and give us grace at all times humbly
        to rejoice in Thy mysterious
        companionship.

JOHN BAILLIE

163

Lord Jesus, make Thyself to me
A Living Bright Reality;
More present to faith's vision keen
Than any outward object seen;
More Dear, more intimately nigh,
Than e'en the sweetest earthly tie.

HOWARD TAYLOR

•

In a world where
there is so much to ruffle the spirit,
how needful that entering into the
secret of God's pavilion, which will
alone bring it back to composure and
peace!

In a world where
there is so much to sadden and depress, how blessed the communion
with Him in whom is the one true
source and fountain of all true gladness
and abiding joy!

In a world where
so much is ever seeking to unhallow
our spirits, to render them common
and profane, how high the privilege of
consecrating them anew in prayer to
holiness and to God.

ARCHBISHOP RICHARD CHENEVIX TRENCH

A PRAYER

Grant us the will to fashion as we feel
Grant us the strength to labor as we know
Grant us the purpose, ribbed and edged
with steel
To strike the blow.
Knowledge we ask not, for knowledge
Thou has lent,
But Lord, the will, there lies our bitter
need.
Give us to build upon the deep intent
The deed, the deed.

JOHN DRINKWATER

Promises

WHAT GOD HATH PROMISED

God hath not promised
   Skies always blue,
Flower-strewn pathways
   All our lives through;
God hath not promised
   Sun without rain,
Joy without sorrow,
   Peace without pain.

But God hath promised
   Strength for the day,
Rest for the labor,
   Light for the way,
Grace for the trials,
   Help from above,
Unfailing sympathy,
   Undying love.

ANNIE JOHNSON FLINT

●

In the breast of a bulb
Is the promise of spring;

In the little blue egg
Is a bird that will sing;

In the soul of a seed
Is the hope of the sod;

In the heart of a child
Is the Kingdom of God.

WILLIAM L. STIDGER

He shall call upon me, and I will answer
   him:
I will be with him in trouble; I will deliver
   him and honor him.
With long life will I satisfy him, and show
   him my salvation.

PSALM 91:15,16

●

GOD IS OUR REFUGE

(PSALM 46)

God is our refuge, our strong tow'r,
Securing by His mighty pow'r,
When dangers threaten to devour.

Thus arm'd no fears shall chill our blood,
Tho' earth no longer steadfast stood,
And shook her hills into the flood;

Although the troubled ocean rise
In foaming billows to the skies,
And mountains shake with horrid noise.

Clear streams purl from a crystal spring,
Which gladness to God's city bring,
The mansion of th' Eternal King;

He in her centre takes His place,
What foe can her fair tow'rs deface,
Protected by His early grace?

Tumultuary nations rose,
And armed troops our walls enclose,
But His fear'd Voice unnerv'd our foes.

An acre of performance is worth the whole world of promise.

JAMES HOWELL

•

HIS WAYS

God has a thousand ways
Where I can see not one;
When all my means have reached their
    end
Then His have just begun.

ESTHER GUYOT

•

When I hear a young man spoken of as giving promise of high genius, the first question I ask about him is always, does he work.

JOHN RUSKIN

THE HOLY SPIRIT OF PROMISE

Lord, what a change within us one short
    hour
Spent in Thy presence will prevail to
    make!
What heavy burdens from our bosoms
    take,
What parched grounds refresh as with a
    shower!
We kneel, and all around us seems to
    lower;
We rise, and all, the distant and the near,
Stands forth in sunny outline brave and
    clear;
We kneel, how weak! we rise, how full of
    power!
Why, therefore, should we do ourselves
    this wrong,
Or others, that we are not always strong,
That we are ever overborne with care,
That we should ever weak or heartless be,
Anxious or troubled, when with us is
    prayer,
And joy and strength and courage are
    with Thee!

ARCHBISHOP RICHARD CHENEVIX TRENCH

ABUNDANT LIFE

To do God's will from day to day,
To follow Christ and not to stray,
To have the Spirit's power alway,
    This is abundant life!

HENRY W. FROST

•

UPHILL

Does the road wind uphill all the way?
    Yes, to the very end.
Will the day's journey take the whole
    long day?
    From morn to night, my friend.

But is there for the night a resting-place?
    A roof for when the slow, dark hours
        begin.
May not the darkness hide it from my
    face?
    You cannot miss that inn.

Shall I meet other wayfarers at night?
    Those who have gone before.
Then must I knock, or call when just in
    sight?
    They will not keep you waiting at that
        door.

Shall I find comfort, travel-sore and
    weak?
    Of labour you shall find the sum.
Will there be beds for me and all who
    seek?
    Yea, beds for all who come.

CHRISTINA ROSSETTI

•

"Day by day," the promise reads;
Daily strength for daily needs.

STEPHEN F. WINWARD

•

Our Lord has written the promise of the resurrection, not in books alone, but in every leaf of springtime.

MARTIN LUTHER

166

God makes a promise.
Faith believes it.
Hope anticipates it
Patience quietly awaits it.

●

STOPPING BY WOODS ON A SNOWY EVENING

Whose woods these are I think I know.
His house is in the village though;
He will not see me stopping here
To watch his woods fill up with snow.

My little horse must think it queer
To stop without a farmhouse near
Between the woods and frozen lake
The darkest evening of the year.

He gives his harness bells a shake
To ask if there is some mistake.
The only other sound's the sweep
Of easy wind and downy flake.

The woods are lovely, dark and deep.
But I have promises to keep,
And miles to go before I sleep,
And miles to go before I sleep.

ROBERT FROST

167

Quietness & Solitude

In times of quietness our hearts should
  be like trees,
Lifting their branches to the sky to draw
  down strength
Which they will need to face the storms
That will surely come.

TOYOHIKO KAGAWA

•

I NEEDED THE QUIET

I needed the quiet so He drew me aside.
Into the shadows where we could
  confide.
Away from the bustle where all the day
  long
I hurried and worried when active and
  strong.

I needed the quiet tho at first I rebelled
But gently, so gently, my cross He upheld
And whispered so sweetly of spiritual
  things
Tho weakened in body, my spirit took
  wings
To heights never dreamed of when active
  and gay.
He loved me so greatly He drew me away.

I needed the quiet. No prison my bed,
But a beautiful valley of blessings
  instead —
A place to grow richer in Jesus to hide.
I needed the quiet so He drew me aside.

ALICE HANSCHE MORTENSON

The holy time is quiet . . .
Breathless with adoration . . .
The gentleness of heaven broods o'er the
  sea;
Listen! . . .

WILLIAM WORDSWORTH

Be silent, O all flesh, before the Lord:
  for he is raised up out of his holy
  habitation.

ZECHARIAH 2:13

•

What is the use of worrying
And flurrying and scurrying
  And breaking up one's rest;
When all the world is teaching us
And praying and beseeching us
  That quiet ways are best.

•

BEGIN THE DAY WITH GOD

Every morning lean thine arms awhile
Upon the window sill of heaven
And gaze upon thy Lord.
Then, with the vision in thy heart,
Turn strong to meet thy day.

168

THE LITTLE GATE TO GOD

In the castle of my soul
Is a little postern gate,
Whereat, when I enter,
I am in the presence of God.
In a moment, in the turning of a thought,
I am where God is.
This is a fact.

With God is a great silence.
But that silence is a melody
Sweet as the contentment of love,
Thrilling as a touch of flame.

In this world my days are few
And full of trouble.
I strive and have not;
I seek and find not;
I ask and learn not . . .
When I enter into God,
All life has a meaning.
Without asking I know;
My desires are even now fulfilled,
My fever is gone
In the great quiet of God,
My troubles are but pebbles on the road,
My joys are like the everlasting hills.

WALTER RAUSCHENBUSCH

But all the pleasures that I find
Is to maintain a quiet mind.

EDWARD DYER

●

I knelt beside a lonely lake
    Where all was green and blue;
I asked the Lord to take my life
    And fashion it anew.
And as I knelt, a stir I felt
    Of glory in that place;
The Spirit of the living God
    Came down in power and Grace.

The wind soughed gently through the
        trees;
    No other sound was heard,
But as of yore Christ walked the shore
    And broke to me his Word;

And angel trumpets filled the air
    In praise to God the Son,
And all the pine trees clapped their hands
    At what the Lord had done.

SHERWOOD ELIOT WIRT

●

I LOVE TO STEAL AWHILE AWAY

I love to steal awhile away
    From every cumbering care,
And spend the hours of setting day
    In humble, grateful prayer.

I love in solitude to shed
    The penitential tear,
And all his promises to plead,
    Where none but God can hear.

I love to think on mercies past,
    And future good implore,
And all my cares and sorrows cast
    On him whom I adore.

PHOEBE H. BROWN

●

He is brave whose tongue is silent
Of the trophies of this world,
He is great whose quiet bearing
Marks his greatness well assured.

EDWIN ARNOLD

Conversation enriches the understanding, but solitude is the school of genius!

EDWARD GIBBON

Oh, how great peace and quietness would he possess who should cut off all vain anxiety and place all his confidence in God.

THOMAS A KEMPIS

SLOW ME DOWN

Slow me down, Lord!
Ease the pounding of my heart by the
quieting of my mind.
Steady my hurried pace with a vision of
the eternal reach of time.
Give me amid the confusion of each day,
The calmness of the everlasting hills.
Break the tension of my nerves with the
soothing music
Of the singing streams that live in my
memory.
Help me to know the magical restoring
power of sleep.
Teach me the art of taking minute
vacations:
To look at a flower; to chat with a friend;
To walk in the woods; to watch a spider
build a web;
To smile at a child; to wipe her tears.
Remind me each day,
That the race is not always to the swift,
That there is more to life than increasing
speed.
Let me look upward to the clouds and
sky,
To the towering oak, and know that it
grew great and strong,
Because it grew slowly under Thy
life-giving sun.
So, slow me down Lord! That I may take
time to commune with Thee,
And find peace and rest . . . My deepest
need.

Let thy soul walk slowly in thee,
  As a saint in heaven unshod,
For to be alone with Silence
  Is to be alone with God.

SAMUEL MILLER HAGEMAN

●

ALTARS

Let every corner of this day
Become an altar, Lord, for Thee,
A quiet place where I can pray
And hear Thee talk to me.

The bright expectancy of dawn
Will not endure the noonday heat,
Unless refreshing strength is drawn
Where altars touch Thy feet.

SYBIL LEONARD ARMES

●

Be still, and know that I am God.
I will be exalted among the heathen,
I will be exalted in the earth.

PSALM 46:10

Sincerity

A gesture of a hand, a look upon a face, the silent message sensed in a chance glimpse of another's eyes often speak more eloquently than the finest prose or poetry, the most stirring music, or all the words in the dictionary.

A man may be very sincere in good principles, without having good practice.

SAMUEL JOHNSON

THINK THROUGH ME

Think through me, Thoughts of God,
* My Father, quiet me,*
Till in Thy holy presence, hushed,
* I think Thy thoughts with Thee.*

Think through me, Thoughts of God,
* That always, everywhere,*
The stream that through my being flows,
* May homeward pass in prayer.*

Think through me, Thoughts of God,
* And let my own thoughts be*
Lost like the sand-pools on the shore
* Of the eternal sea.*

AMY CARMICHAEL

The first virtue of all really great men is that they are sincere.

ANATOLE FRANCE

ADMITTING MISTAKES

How often when we blunder, and are
* filled with guilty shame,*
Do we invent excuses, and attempt to
* shift the blame!*
But when we make mistakes, I find it's
* sensible and wise*
To honestly admit them, and omit the
* alibis.*

MARY HAMLETT GOODMAN

Be sincere—you cannot sell anything you don't believe in.

I have never had a policy.
I have simply tried
to do what seemed best each day,
as each day came.

ABRAHAM LINCOLN

171

GIVE THE FLOWERS TO THE LIVING

Give the flowers to the living,
Let sweet fragrance fill the air,
Blessings follow with the giving,
Pure and sweet as lily fair;
Give the toilers oft a token
Of the love you would bestow,
Give the flowers to the living, —
If you love them, tell them so.

WILL L. THOMPSON

Let us, then, be what we are, and speak what we think, and in all things keep ourselves loyal to truth and the sacred professions of friendship.

HENRY WADSWORTH LONGFELLOW

The true secret of happiness lies in the taking of a genuine interest in all the details of daily life.

WILLIAM MORRIS

I say, the acknowledgment of God in
   Christ accepted by thy reason, solves
   for thee
All questions in the earth and out of it,
And has so far advanced thee to be wise.

ROBERT BROWNING

Come in the evening,
Or come in the morning,
Come when you're looked for
Or come without warning.

THOMAS OSBORNE DAVIS

BE TRUE

To thine own self be true,
And it must follow, as night the day,
Thou canst not then be false to any man.

WILLIAM SHAKESPEARE

There is no man so friendless
   but what he can find
   a friend sincere enough
   to tell him disagreeable truths.

BARON LYTTON

O Lord my God,
   Rescue me from myself, and give me to
      Thee;
   Take away from me everything which
      draws me from Thee;
   Give me all those things which lead me
      to Thee;
   for Jesus Christ's sake.

PRECATIONES PIAE

Strength & Courage

THE COURAGEOUS

They on the heights are not the souls
  who never erred nor went astray
Who trod unswerving toward their goals
  Along a smooth, rose-bordered way.
Nay! Those who stand where first comes
    dawn
  Are those who stumbled — but went
    on!

No sanctity is there therefore, if Thou, O Lord, withdraw Thine hand.

No wisdom availeth, if Thou cease to guide.

No courage helpeth, if Thou leave off to preserve.

No chastity is secure, if Thou do not protect it.

No custody of our own availeth, if Thy sacred watchfulness be not present.

For left to ourselves, we sink and perish; but being visited of Thee, we are raised up and live.

Unstable truly are we, but through Thee we are strengthened; we wax lukewarm, but by Thee we are inflamed.

THOMAS A KEMPIS

A NATION'S STRENGTH

Not gold, but only man can make
A people great and strong . . .
Men who stand for truth and honor's sake
Stand fast and suffer long.

Brave men who work while others sleep,
Who dare while others fly . . .
They build a nation's pillars deep
And lift them to the sky.

RALPH WALDO EMERSON

It is only through labor and painful effort, by grim energy and resolute courage, that we move on to better things.

THEODORE ROOSEVELT

TRUST

Sure, it takes a lot of courage
  To put things in God's hands,
To give ourselves completely,
  Our lives, our hopes, our plans;

To follow where He leads us
  And make His will our own,
But all it takes is foolishness
  To go the way alone.

BETSEY KLINE

GOD'S BEST

God has His best thing for the few
    That dare to stand the test;
God has His second choice for those
    Who will not have His best.

It is not always open ill
    That risks the Promised Rest;
The better, often, is the foe
    That keeps us from the best.

Some seek the highest choice,
    But, when by trials pressed
They shrink, they yield, they shun the
      cross
    And so they lose the best.

Give me, O Lord, Thy highest choice;
    Let others take the rest.
Their good things have no charm for me,
    I want Thy very best.

I want, in this short life of mine,
    As much as can be pressed
Of service true for God and man:
    Make me to be Thy best.

A. B. SIMPSON

Strength is born in the deep silence of long-suffering hearts; not amidst joy.

FELICIA HEMANS

I SHALL WALK TODAY

I shall walk today
    upon a high green hill,
I shall forget the walls
    and the roofs of the town;
This burden, strapped to my back,
    shall be unloosed,
And I shall leave it there
    when I come down.

Warm is the hill upon which
    I shall walk today;
Gold is the sun upon
    the close-cropped grass,
And something of the peace
    of grazing sheep

Shall permeate my being
    as I pass.

Something of the look
    within their eyes
Of upland pastures, and
    of clean wind blown —
The tranquil, trusting look
    of those who know
A shepherd watches,
    I shall make my own.

And I shall gather the
    little windflowers there,
And press their sweetness
    upon my heart to stay;
Then I shall go back
    to the walls and roofs
    of the town,
Stronger than I have been
    for many a day.

GRACE NOLL CROWELL

Courage is the first of human qualities because it is the quality which guarantees all the others.

SIR WINSTON CHURCHILL

DO AND BE BLEST

Dare to think, though others frown;
    Dare in words your thoughts express;
Dare to rise, though oft cast down;
    Dare the wronged and scorned to bless.

Dare from custom to depart;
    Dare the priceless pearl possess;
Dare to wear it next your heart;
    Dare, when others curse, to bless.

Dare forsake what you deem wrong;
    Dare to walk in wisdom's way;
Dare to give where gifts belong,
    Dare God's precepts to obey.

Do what conscience says is right,
    Do what reason says is best,
Do with all your mind and might;
    Do your duty and be blest.

SURRENDER

I said, "Let me walk in the field,"
He said: "Nay, walk in the town,"
I said, "There are no flowers there,"
He said: "No flowers, but a crown."

I said, "But the air is thick,
And fogs are veiling the sun."
He said, "Yet souls are sick
And souls in the dark are undone."

I said, "But the skies are black,
There is nothing but noise and din,"
He wept as He sent me back
"There is more," He said, "There is sin."

I said, "I shall miss the light,
And friends will miss me, they say."
He said, "Choose thou tonight
If I am to miss you or they."

I pleaded for time to be given,
He said, "Is it hard to decide?
It will not seem hard in Heaven,
To have followed the steps of your
    Guide."

I cast one look on the field,
Then turned my face to the town.
He said, "My child, do you yield?
Will you leave the flowers for a crown?"

Then into His hand went mine,
And into my heart came He;
And I walk by a light divine
The path I had feared to see.

GEORGE MACDONALD

Courage is fear that has said its prayers.

Bravely to do whate'er the time demands,
    Whether with pen or sword, and not to
        flinch,
This is the task that fits heroic hands;
    So are Truth's boundaries widened,
        inch by inch.

JAMES RUSSELL LOWELL

**Keep your fears to yourself, but share
your courage with others.**

ROBERT LOUIS STEVENSON

●

THE OLD STOIC

Riches I hold in light esteem,
    And Love I laugh to scorn;
And lust of fame was but a dream
    That vanish'd with the morn:

And, if I pray, the only prayer
    That moves my lips for me
Is, 'Leave the heart that now I bear,
    And give me liberty!'

Yea, as my swift days near their goal,
    'Tis all that I implore:
In life and death a chainless soul,
    With courage to endure.

EMILY BRONTE

RESISTANCE

**Courage is resistance to fear, mastery of
fear—not absence of fear.**

MARK TWAIN

ROUND OUR RESTLESSNESS

Oh, the little birds sang east, and the little
    birds sang west,
And I smiled to think God's greatness
    flowed around our incompleteness, —
Round our restlessness, his rest.

ELIZABETH BARRETT BROWNING

●

WHAT COUNTS

**'Tisn't life that matters! It's the courage
you bring to it.**

HUGH WALPOLE

175

Today

Today is the first day of your future.

●

NEW EVERY MORNING

Every day is a fresh beginning,
  Every morn is the world made new;
You who are weary of sorrow and
    sinning,
  Here is a beautiful hope for you —
  A hope for me and a hope for you.

All the past things are past and over,
  The tasks are done and the tears are
    shed;
Yesterday's errors let yesterday cover;
  Yesterday's wounds, which smarted
    and bled,
  Are healed with the healing which
    night has shed.

Yesterday is a part of forever,
  Bound up in a sheaf, which God holds
    tight;
With glad days, and sad days, and bad
    days, which never
  Shall visit us more with their bloom
    and their blight,
  Their fullness of sunshine or sorrowful
    night.

Let them go, since we cannot relieve
    them;
  Cannot undo, and cannot atone;

God in his mercy, receive, forgive them!
  Only the new days are our own.
  Today is ours, and today alone.

Here are the skies all burnished brightly,
  Here is the spent earth all reborn;
Here are the tired limbs springing lightly
  To face the sun, and to share with the
    morn
  In the chrism of dew and the cool of
    dawn.

Every day is a fresh beginning;
  Listen, my soul, to the glad refrain,
And, spite of all sorrow and old sinning,
  And puzzles forecasted, and possible
    pain,
  Take heart with the day, and begin
    again.

SUSAN COOLIDGE

●

Finish every day and be done with it. You have done what you could. Some blunders and absurdities no doubt crept in; forget them as soon as you can. Tomorrow is a new day; begin it well and serenely and with too high a spirit to be cumbered with your old nonsense. This day is all that is good and fair. It is too dear, with its hopes and invitations, to waste a moment on the yesterdays.

RALPH WALDO EMERSON

JUST FOR TODAY

Lord, for to-morrow and its needs,
  I do not pray:
Keep me, my God, from stain of sin,
  Just for to-day;
Let me no wrong or idle word
  Unthinking say:
Set Thou a seal upon my lips,
  Just for to-day.

Let me both diligently work,
  And duly pray;
Let me be kind in word and deed,
  Just for to-day;
Let me in season, Lord, be grave,
  In season, gay;
Let me be faithful to Thy grace,
  Just for to-day.

In pain and sorrow's cleansing fires,
  Brief be my stay;
Oh, bid me if to-day I die,
  Come home to-day;
So, for to-morrow and its needs,
  I do not pray;
But keep me, guide me, love me, Lord,
  Just for to-day.

SYBIL F. PARTRIDGE

TODAY

Just for today I will try to live through this day only, not to tackle my whole life problem at once. I can do things for 24 hours that would appall me if I had to keep them up for a life time.

Just for today I will be happy. This assumes what Abraham Lincoln said is true, that "Most folks are about as happy as they make up their minds to be." Happiness is from within; it is not a matter of externals.

Just for today I will try to adapt myself to the present, and not attempt to adjust everything to my own desires. I will take my family, my business, and my licks as they come and fit myself to them.

Just for today I will take care of my body. I will exercise it, care for it, nourish it, not abuse it nor neglect it, so that it will be a perfect machine for my bidding.

Just for today I will try to strengthen my mind. I will learn something useful. I will not be a mental loafer; I will read some thing that requires effort, thought and concentration.

Just for today I will exercise my soul in three ways. I will help somebody by a good turn and not get found out; I will do at least two things I don't want to do . . . "Just for exercise."

Just for today I will be agreeable. I will appear as well as I can, dress as becomingly as possible, talk low, act courteously, be liberal with praise, criticize not at all, nor find fault with anything and not try to regulate nor improve anyone.

Just for today I will have a program. I will write down what I expect to do. I may not follow it exactly but I will have it. It will eliminate two pests — hurry and indecision.

Just for today I will be unafraid, especially I will not be afraid to be happy, to enjoy what is beautiful, to love, and to believe that those I love, love me.

Just for today I will have a quiet half hour all by myself. In this half hour I will give thanks to Almighty God for the abundance that is mine.

SCHOOL PICTURES, INC.

PERHAPS TODAY

Look up, God's child,
  This world of tragic sorrow
Might weigh thee down
  With its increasing woes!
Look up, and onward
  To that golden morrow,
To all the glory
  Which it will disclose.

Look up, and long for
  Our dear Lord's returning:
Look up and cry,
  "Lord Jesus, come, we pray!"
Look up — until for Him
  The heart is burning!
Look up! Look up!
  Perhaps He'll come today!

J. DANSON SMITH

177

Dear Lord, help me to live this day
    Quietly,
        Easily;
To lean upon Thy great strength
    Trustfully,
        Restfully;
To wait for the unfolding of Thy will
    Patiently,
        Serenely;
To meet others
    Peacefully,
        Joyously;
To face tomorrow
    Confidently,
        Courageously.

TODAY

So here hath been dawning
  Another blue day:
Think, wilt thou let it
  Slip useless away?

Out of Eternity
  This new day is born;
Into Eternity,
  At night, will return.

Behold it aforetime
  No eye ever did;
So soon it forever
  From all eyes is hid.

Here hath been dawning
  Another blue day:
Think, wilt thou let it
  Slip useless away?

THOMAS CARLYLE

●

ONE DAY AT A TIME

There are two days in every week about which we should not worry . . .

Two days which should be kept free from fear and apprehension.

One of these days is yesterday, with its mistakes and cares, it faults and blunders, its aches and pains. Yesterday has passed forever beyond our control.

All the money in the world cannot bring back yesterday. We cannot undo a single act we performed. We cannot erase a single word said. Yesterday is gone!

The other day we should not worry about is tomorrow, with its possible adversities, its burdens, it large promise and poor performance. Tomorrow is beyond our immediate control. Tomorrow's sun will rise, whether in splendor or behind a mask of clouds. But it will rise. Until it does we have no stake in tomorrow, for it is yet unborn.

This leaves only one day . . . today. Any man can fight the battles of just one day. It is when you and I add the burdens of two awful eternities — yesterday and tomorrow, that we break down.

It is not necessarily the experiences of today that disturb one's peace of mind. It is oftentimes the remorse or bitterness for something which happened yesterday and the dread of what tomorrow may bring.

Let us therefore live one day at a time.

CONSIDER

Is anybody happier
  Because you passed his way?
Does anyone remember
  That you spoke to him today?
This day is almost over,
  And its toiling time is through;
Is there anyone to utter now,
  A friendly word for you?

Can you say tonight in passing,
  With the day that slipped so fast,
That you helped a single person,
  Of the many that you passed?
Is a single heart rejoicing,
  Over what you did or said?
Does one whose hopes were fading
  Now with courage look ahead?

Did you waste the day, or lose it?
  Was it well or poorly spent?
Did you leave a trail of kindness,
  Or a scar of discontent?

Think not on yesterday, nor trouble
  borrow
On what may be in store for you
  tomorrow;
But let today be your incessant care —
The past is past, tomorrow's in the air.
Who gives today the best that in him lies
Will find the road that leads to clearer
  skies.

JOHN KENDRICK BANGS

TODAY

Fill it with gladness,
With courage, and love, and trust.
Treat it not lightly,
For it is a part of life
That, when spent, can never return.

AGNES DAVENPORT BOND

THREE DAYS

Yesterday . . .
Like mintage spent, is past recall;
Its echo dimmed beyond time's wall.

Tomorrow . . .
Is never promised earthly man,
Nor does it often fit a plan.

Today . . .
Is gold that covers hill and dell,
And rich are they who use it well.

JUST NOW

Never mind about tomorrow —
  It always is today;
Yesterday has vanished.
  Wherever, none can say.
Each minute must be guarded —
  Make worth the while somehow;
There are no other moments;
  It's always, Just Now.

Just now is the hour that's golden,
  The moment to defend.

Just now is without beginning;
  Just now can never end.
Then never mind tomorrow —
  'Tis today you must enjoy
With all that's true and noble;
  And the time for this is —
NOW!

Listen to the Exhortation of the Dawn!
Look to this Day!
For it is Life, the very Life of Life.

In its brief Course lie all the
Verities and Realities of your Existence:

The Bliss of Growth,
The Glory of Action,
The Splendour of Beauty;
For Yesterday is but a Dream
And Tomorrow is only a Vision;
But Today well-lived makes
Every Yesterday a Dream of Happiness,
And every Tomorrow a Vision of Hope.

Look well therefore to this Day!
Such is the Salutation of the Dawn!

FROM THE SANSKRIT

Tomorrow's fate, though thou be wise,
Thou canst not tell nor yet surmise;
Pass, therefore, not today in vain,
For it will never come again.

OMAR KHAYYAM

**Do your best today and tomorrow you
will be able to do better.**

MARTIN VANBEE

This is the day which the Lord hath made;
we will rejoice and be glad in it.

PSALM 118:24

TODAY

Today is mine, a gift from God,
New hours, new way, new everything . . .
A time in which no foot has trod,
A time when hopes and prayers take
   wing.

The past has ended with lessons learned;
God's sun will keep its shadows out.
New faith and strength are now discerned
To meet each test and dispel each doubt.

I'll make today the best I can
So I will seek to know God's will
And always follow well His plan
To make tomorrow better still.

LESLIE E. DUNKIN

●

THIS DAY

This day was made in heaven,
   A jewel for you and me,
The angels fashioned it with love
And sweet tranquility.

They took a lovely azure sky
And launched cloud ships of white,
Then bade the merry sunbeams
To shed their golden light.

They found the softest, sweetest breeze
And set it free this day,
To be as gentle as their kiss
While floating on its way.

They whispered to each little bird
To sing his merry song,
And bade the brilliant flowers
To bloom the whole day long.

This day was made in heaven,
Beautiful and rare . . .
The angels sent it down to earth
For you and me to share.

LAVERNE P. LARSON

Treasures & Possessions

SURRENDER

Let me hold lightly
Things of this earth;
Transient treasures,
What are they worth?
Moths can corrupt them,
Rust can decay;
All their bright beauty
Fades in a day.
Let me hold lightly
Temporal things,
I, who am deathless,
I, who wear wings!
Let me hold fast, Lord,
Things of the skies,
Quicken my vision,
Open my eyes!
Show me Thy riches,
Glory and grace,
Boundless as time is,
Endless as space!
Let me hold lightly
Things that are mine —
Lord, Thou hast giv'n me
All that is Thine!

MARTHA SNELL NICHOLSON

●

THESE I'VE LOVED

These I've loved since I was little:
Wood to build with or to whittle,

Wind in the grass and falling rain,
First leaves along an April lane,
Yellow flowers, cloudy weather,
River-bottom smell, old leather,
Fields newly plowed, young corn in rows,
Back-country roads and cawing crows,
Stone walls with stiles going over,
Daisies, Queen Anne's lace, and clover,
Night tunes of crickets, frog songs, too,
Starched cotton cloth, the color blue,
Bells that ring from white church steeple,
Friendly dogs and friendly people.

ELIZABETH-ELLEN LONG

●

HEART GIFTS

It's not the things that can be bought
    that are life's richest treasure,
It's just the little "heart gifts"
    that money cannot measure . . .
A cheerful smile, a friendly word,
    a sympathetic nod
Are priceless little treasures
    from the storehouse of our God . . .
They are the things that can't be bought
    with silver or with gold,
For thoughtfulness and kindness
    and love are never sold . . .
They are the priceless things in life
    for which no one can pay,
And the giver finds rich recompense
    in Giving Them Away.

HELEN STEINER RICE

TREASURE

I am rich today, a baby ran to meet me,
And put her tiny hand within my own
And smiled, her rosy lips a flower,
The light within her eyes, from heaven
    shone.
And when I crossed the fields the birds
    were singing,
A golden blossom in my pathway lay,
It wasn't much; but, oh, the joy there's
    in it,
To have a baby smile at you
    In just that way.

MARGUERITE A. GUTSCHOW

BORROWED TREASURES

I thank you, God
For all you've given me.
Your sun,
Your beach,
Your ocean's roar;
Your trees upon the cool
Green shore.
I thank You for the rose
Within my garden;
That is Yours.
The starlit skies,
The twinkle in my infant's
Eyes —
The world.

EVALENA FISHER

TRULY GREAT TREASURES

He who is young can be thankful that he still has all the exciting experiences of life before him.

He who is old can be thankful that he has attained judgment and understanding and has learned to be tranquil about problems which once troubled him.

He who is in good health can be thankful for a treasure greater than gold.

He who is ill or physically disabled can be thankful for the loving care of family and friends, and for a chance to be an inspiring example of patience and fortitude.

He who dwells in the country can be thankful for the wide open beauty of God's handiwork, where Nature's artistry is manifest on every hand.

He who resides in the city can be thankful for the warmth of human relationships and the opportunity to serve one's fellowman at every turn.

He who has riches of gold and silver can be thankful that life's bounty has given him the privilege and joy of sharing with those less fortunate.

He who is without worldly wealth can be thankful that the truly great treasures of life are free — kindness, friendship, love, appreciation.

He who worships can be thankful that he lives in a country where he may worship according to the dictates of his own conscience.

He who lives in a free country can be thankful that his opportunities are many, and that his chance of success is not hampered by regimentation.

For these things we should be thankful.

A CHILD IS COMPENSATION

You are the trip I did not take,
You are the pearls I cannot buy,
You are my blue Italian lake,
You are my piece of foreign sky.

You are my Honolulu moon,
You are the books I did not write,
You are my heart's unuttered tune,
You are a candle in my night.

You are a flower beneath the snow,
In my dark skies a bit of blue,
Answering disappointments' blow,
With, "I am happy," I love you.

ANNE CAMPBELL

There are few greater treasures to be acquired in youth than great poetry — and prose — stored in the memory. At the time one may resent the labor of storing. But they sleep in the memory and awake in later years, illuminated by life and illuminating it.

RICHARD W. LIVINGSTONE

182

I TASTE A LIQUOR NEVER BREWED

I taste a liquor never brewed,
From tankards scooped in pearl;
Not all the vats upon the Rhine
Yield such an alcohol!

Inebriate of air am I,
And debauchee of dew,
Reeling, through endless summer days,
From inns of molten blue.

When landlords turn the drunken bee
Out of the foxglove's door,
When butterflies renounce their drams,
I shall but drink the more!

Till seraphs swing their snowy hats,
And saints to windows run,
To see the little tippler
Leaning against the sun!

EMILY DICKINSON

TREASURE

A happy man or woman is a better thing
to find than a five-pound note. He or she
is a radiating focus of good-will; and their
entrance into a room is as though another
candle had been lighted. We need not
care whether they could prove the forty-
seventh proposition; they do a better
thing than that—they practically demon-
strate the great Theorem of the Livable-
ness of Life.

ROBERT LOUIS STEVENSON

REAL RICHES

If all the world were yours to win,
And all the wealth and land therein;
If coffers heaped with golden store
Would line your walls and gilt your door;
If men would loudly sing your praise
And children would bedeck your ways;
You still would be a beggared lot
If honor somehow was forgot.

If you had naught but daily bread,
A humble cot, a path which led
To where your friends and loved ones
  wait

With eager smile and open gate;
If none but friends e'er hear your name,
If you are ne'er to taste of fame;
But if self-respect is your creed,
You are a millionaire, indeed.

The unpolished pearl can never shine —
'Tis sorrow makes the soul divine.

FROM THE JAPANESE
Translated by FREDERIC ROWLAND MARVIN

TREASURES

One by one He took them from me,
  All the things I valued most;
Until I was empty-handed,
  Every glittering toy was lost.
And I walked earth's highways, grieving,
  In my rags and poverty
Till I heard His voice inviting,
  "Lift your empty hands to Me!"
So I held my hands toward heaven
  And He filled them with a store
Of His own transcendent riches
  Till they could hold no more.
And at last I comprehended
  With my stupid mind and dull
That God could not pour His riches
  Into hands already full!

MARTHA SNELL NICHOLSON

HOW TO POSSESS

If you want to possess something, help
create it. If you want to possess a landscape, try to reproduce it. To others it
may seem very crude and ugly, but to you
it will hold all the beauty of the original
and more, for you have put your life into
it. If you want to possess a flower, help
it grow. If you want a share in the life of
another, do something to make that life
larger and better. So shall you become a
part of the creative energy of God and
share with Him as a son and heir a
portion of His divine life.

FRANK O. HALL

183

GOD IMMEDIATE

I looked for Heaven high on a hill,
Heaven where mighty towers stand;
Then emptied my hands of gold to fill
The empty hands of others — and still
Had gold, with Heaven in my hand.

RAYMOND KRESENSKY

TREASURES

Out of this life I shall never take
Things of silver and gold I make.
All that I cherish and hoard away
After I leave, on this earth must stay.
Tho' I have toiled for a painting rare
To hang on the wall, I must leave it there.
Tho' I call it mine, and boast its worth,
I must give it up when I leave this earth.
All that I gather, and all that I keep
I must leave behind when I fall asleep.

And I often wonder what I shall own
In that other life, when I pass alone.
What shall they find, and what
Shall they see, in the soul that
Answers the call for me?
Shall the Great Judge learn
When my task is through,
That my spirit has gathered some riches
too?
Or shall at last it be mine to find
That all I'd worked for I'd left behind.

There is nothing that makes men rich and strong but that which they carry inside of them. True wealth is of the heart, not of the hand.

JOHN MILTON

FINER THAN GOLD

Be not afraid! — For your heart can hold
Riches far finer than any gold,
Treasures more precious than costly gem,
Inheritance greater than diadem.
Faith you can have that is shining and
clear,
Hope that is bright with the brightness of
cheer;

Love you can have, uplifting and wise,
And Friendship's light in a dear one's
eyes;
Truth you can have like a prayer in your
heart —
Fountain of literature, music, and art;
The grace of the flowers, the solace of
trees.
Be not afraid, for any of these
Are yours to gather and yours to hold,
Wealth that is greater than any gold.
With Faith and Love your heart is at ease;
Count any man rich possessed of these.

NORA CARTER

What I spent, I lost;
What I possessed is left to others;
What I gave away remains with me.

JOSEPH ADDISON

That's the wise thrush; he sings each song
twice over,
Lest you should think he never could
recapture
The first fine careless rapture!

ROBERT BROWNING

A faithful friend is a strong defense; and he that hath found such a one hath found a treasure.

ECCLESIASTICUS

THE BEST TREASURE

There are veins in the hills where jewels
hide,
And gold lies buried deep;
There are harbor-towns where the
great ships ride,
And fame and fortune sleep;
But land and sea though we tireless rove,
And follow each trail to the end,
Whatever the wealth of our treasure-
trove,
The best we shall find is a friend.

JOHN J. MOMENT

True Values

THE THINGS I PRIZE

These are the things I prize
And hold of deepest worth:
Light of the sapphire skies,
Peace of the silent hills,
Shelter of forest, comfort of the grass,
Shadow of clouds that swiftly pass,
And after showers
The smell of flowers,
And of the good brown earth,
And best of all, along the way,
Friendship and mirth.

HENRY VAN DYKE

●

What matters supremely to our soul's growth is how we lay hold of life; whether we let it just go on without giving it significance, or whether we so respond to the mesh of circumstance, that through and in it we find God. Our job, our environment, however narrow, is always adequate to this, because there is no place or circumstance where God is not.

It is consoling to remember that circumstances can do nothing to us, to our deepest selves, because they can neither help nor hinder, save in so far as we do or do not direct our will through them to God. We are not required to adjust ourselves to circumstances by some awful wrench; but to let circumstances be, let them happen, be quiet in them and do our best without fuss; and then God will come to us in them, however hostile to our own notion of spiritual life, peace and happiness, they may be. . . . It was not (Martha's) usefulness, it was her spirit of fuss that spoilt her capacity for Him. . . . The real remedy for the spirit of fuss lies much deeper . . . it lies . . . in a stern and faithful setting-in-order of our love, getting the proportion of existence right. In modern jargon, get your scale of values right, and whatever the job you are called to, it will help your soul to grow towards God.

EVELYN UNDERHILL

Nobody ever added up
The value of a smile;
We know how much a dollar's worth
And how much is a mile;
We know the distance to the sun,
The size and weight of earth —
But no one's ever told us yet
How much a smile is worth.

●

He is no fool who gives what he cannot keep to gain what he cannot lose.

JAMES ELLIOTT

185

SMALL THINGS

Blessed is the man who can enjoy the small things, the common beauties, the little day-by-day events; sunshine on the fields, birds on the bough, breakfast, dinner, supper, the daily paper on the porch, a friend passing by. So many people who go afield for enjoyment leave it behind them at home.

DAVID GRAYSON

BETTER THINGS

Better to smell the violet cool than sip the
   glowing wine;
Better to hark a hidden brook than watch
   a diamond shine.

Better the love of gentle heart than
   beauty's favors proud,
Better the rose's living seed than roses
   in a crowd.

Better to love in loneliness than bask in
   love all day;
Better the fountain in the heart than the
   fountain by the way.

Better be fed by a mother's hand than eat
   alone at will;
Better to trust in God than say, My goods
   my storehouse fill.

Better to be a little wise than in
   knowledge to abound;
Better to teach a child than toil to fill
   perfection's round.

Better sit at a master's feet than thrill a
   listening state;
Better suspect that thou art proud than be
   sure that thou art great.

Better to walk in the realm unseen than
   watch the hour's event;
Better the well done at the last than the
   air with shoutings rent.

Better to have a quiet grief than a
   hurrying delight;
Better the twilight of the dawn than the
   noonday burning bright.

Better to sit at the water's birth than a sea
   of waves to win;
To live in the love that floweth forth than
   the love that cometh in.

Better a death when work is done than
   earth's most favored birth;
Better a child in God's great house than
   the king of all the earth.

GEORGE MACDONALD

You will never be sorry —
   for thinking before acting,
   for hearing before judging,
   for forgiving your enemies,
   for being candid and frank,
   for helping a fallen brother,
   for being honest in business,
   for thinking before speaking,
   for being loyal to your church,
   for standing by your principles,
   for stopping your ears to gossip,
   for bridling a slanderous tongue,
   for harboring only pure thoughts,
   for sympathizing with the afflicted,
   for being courteous and kind to all.

Friendship is Love without his wings!

LORD BYRON

THE LITTLE THINGS

The little things
Are most worth-while —
A quiet word,
A look, a smile,
A listening ear
That's quick to share
Another's thoughts,
Another's care . . .
Though sometimes they may seem
Quite small,
These little things
Mean most of all.

MARGARET LINDSEY

There is beauty in homely things which
    many people have never seen:
Sunligh through a jar of peach-plum
    jelly;
A rainbow in soapsuds in dishwater;
An egg yolk in a blue bowl;
White ruffled curtains sifting moonlight;
The color of cranberry glass;
A little cottage with blue shutters;
Crimson roses in an old stone crock;
The smell of newly baked bread;
Candlelight on old brass;
The soft brown of a cocker's eyes.

PETER MARSHALL

If we made God a little more real than
otherwise he would be to any single
human being, we have not wasted our
little lives in a large world or lived in vain.

WILLARD L. SPERRY

MAKE FRIENDS

He who has a thousand friends has not a
    friend to spare,
And he who has one enemy shall meet
    him everywhere.

ALI BEN ABU TALEB

LITTLE THINGS

Oh, it's just the little, homely things,
The unobtrusive, friendly things,
The "Won't-you-let-me-help-you" things
That make the pathway light.
And it's just the jolly, joking things,
The "Laugh-with-me-it's-funny" things,
The "Never-mind-the-trouble" things
That make our world seem bright.

For all the countless, famous things,
The wondrous, record-breaking things,
Those "Never-can-be-equalled" things
That all the papers cite,
Can't match the little, human things,

The "Just-because-I-like-you" things,
Those "Oh-it's-simply-nothing" things,
That make us happy, quite.

So here's to all the little things
The every-day-encountered things,
The "Smile-and-face-your-trouble"
    things,
"Trust God to put it right,"
The "Done-and-then-forgotten" things,
The "Can't-you-see-I-love-you" things,
The hearty "I-am-with-you!" things
That make life worth the fight.

EVA M. HINCKLEY

THE TESTING

To walk when others are running,
To whisper when others are shouting;
To sleep when others are restless,
To smile when others are angry;
To work when others are idle,
To pause when others are hurrying;
To pray when others are doubting,
To think when others are in confusion;
To face turmoil, yet feel composure;
To know inner calm in spite of
    everything —
This is the test of serenity.

DORIS LACASSE

LIFE'S COMPLETENESS

A love that lasts forever:
A friendship naught can sever;
A courage never failing,
Though evil seems prevailing;
And joyous, radiant living,
Made glorious by its giving;
A faith strong and enduring,
Unworthy thoughts obscuring;
And eyes for seeing beauty
In work, in play, in duty;
Life ever onward flowing
And more abundant growing;
Love, courage, faith, and sweetness
To make up life's completeness.

S. G. FISHER

Wisdom & Understanding

Look not mournfully into the Past. It comes not back again. Wisely improve the Present. It is thine. Go forth to meet the shadowy Future, without fear, and with a manly heart.

HENRY WADSWORTH LONGFELLOW

WISDOM

When I was young, and very young,
    Say seventeen or so,
I said, "I'll sail the seven seas,
    And every port I'll know.
I'll seek for fame, I'll seek for gold,
    And hoard and pile it high —"
When I was young, and very young,
    At seventeen, said I.

Now I am old, and very old,
    And this is what I say:
"Fame will dim, and gold will fade,
    And glory pass away;
And love, alone, of all I sought,
    A hearthfire leaping bright,
A roof that holds a robin's song,
    Comfort me tonight."

So all ye lads who sail the seas,
    Put into port today,
And hear the words that wisdom
    speaks —
    These are the words I say:
"Build ye a roof beneath the trees,

A new moon swinging high,
And kiss your love and latch the door
    And let the world go by!"

DANIEL W. HICKY

When angry count ten before you speak; if very angry, count a hundred.

Wisdom is before him that hath understanding.

PROVERBS 17:24

TWELVE THINGS TO REMEMBER
1. The value of time.
2. The success of perseverance.
3. The dignity of simplicity.
4. The pleasure of working.
5. The worth of character.
6. The influence of example.
7. The obligation of duty.
8. The power of kindness.
9. The wisdom of economy.
10. The improvement of talent.
11. The joy of originating.
12. The virtue of patience.

MARSHALL FIELD

A wise man will desire no more than he may
get justly,
use soberly,
distribute cheerfully,
and leave contentedly.

JEREMY TAYLOR

Wisdom is ofttimes nearer when we stoop than when we soar.

WILLIAM WORDSWORTH

FEAR NOT

Don't you trouble trouble
Till trouble troubles you.
Don't you look for trouble;
Let trouble look for you.

Don't you borrow sorrow;
You'll surely have your share.
He who dreams of sorrow
Will find that sorrow's there.

Don't you hurry worry
By worrying lest it come.
To flurry is to worry,
'Twill miss you if you're mum.

If care you've got to carry
Wait till 'tis at the door;
For he who runs to meet it
Takes up the load before.

If minding will not mend it,
Then better not to mind;
The best thing is to end it
Just leave it all behind.

Behold, how good and how pleasant it is
for brethren to dwell together in unity!
It is like the precious ointment upon the
head,
that ran down upon the beard, even

Aaron's beard:
that went down to the skirts of his
garments;
As the dew of Hermon,
and as the dew that descended
upon the mountains of Zion:
for there the Lord commanded the
blessing,
even life for evermore.

PSALM 133

God, grant me the serenity
To accept the things I cannot change,
The courage to change the things I can;
And the wisdom to know the difference.

REINHOLD NIEBUHR

Every person is worth understanding.

CLYDE M. NARRAMORE

Sometimes, looking deep into the eyes
of a child, you are conscious of meeting
a glance full of wisdom. The child has
known nothing yet but love and beauty —
all this piled-up world knowledge you
have acquired is unguessed at by him.
And yet you meet this wonderful look that
tells you in a moment more than all the
years of experience have seemed to
teach.

HILDEGARDE HAWTHORNE

He who knows not, and knows not that he
knows not, is a fool — shun him.
He who knows not, and knows that he
knows not, is a child — teach him.
He who knows, and knows not that he
knows, is asleep — wake him.
He who knows, and knows that he knows,
is wise — follow him.

THE PERSIAN

We look along the shining ways,
  to see the angel faces;
They come to us in darkest days
  And in the blackest places,
The strongest hearts have strongest
    need,
  To them the fiery trial;
Who walks a saint in word and deed
  Is saint by self-denial.

If you mean to act nobly and seek to know the best things God has put within reach of men, you must learn to fix your mind on that end, and not on what will happen to you because of it.

GEORGE ELIOT

Lord, if I dig a pit for others
Let me fall into it;
But if I dig it for myself
Give me sense enough to walk around.

SHERWOOD ELIOT WIRT

A man should never be ashamed to say he has been in the wrong, which is but saying in other words that he is wiser today than he was yesterday.

ALEXANDER POPE

Prudence is the footprint of wisdom.

A. BRONSON ALCOTT

A penny saved is as good as a penny earned.

If it is not right,
Do not do it:
If it is not true,
Do not say it.

MARCUS AURELIUS

●

But where shall wisdom be found?
and where is the place
of understanding?

Man knoweth not the price thereof;
neither is it found in the land
of the living.

The depth saith, It is not in me:
and the sea saith,
It is not with me,
It cannot be gotten for gold,
neither shall silver be weighed
for the price thereof.
It cannot be valued with the gold
of Ophir,
with the precious onyx,
or the sapphire.
The gold and the crystal
cannot equal it: and the exchange of it
shall not be for jewels of fine gold.
No mention shall be made of coral,
or of pearls:
for the price of wisdom
is above rubies.

Whence then cometh wisdom?
and where is the place of understanding?

God understandeth the way thereof,
and He knoweth the place thereof.
For He looketh to the ends
of the earth, and seeth
under the whole heaven;

And unto man He said,
Behold, the fear of the Lord,
that is wisdom;
and to depart from evil
is understanding.

JOB 28:12-18,20,23,24,28

Wonder

PETE AT THE ZOO

I wonder if the elephant
Is lonely in his stall
When all the boys and girls are gone
and there's no shout at all,
And there's no one to stamp before,
No one to note his might.
Does he hunch up, as I do,
Against the dark of night?

GWENDOLYN BROOKS

**The man who cannot wonder is but a pair
of spectacles behind which there is no
eye.**

THOMAS CARLYLE

WONDERS TO SHARE

She never said, "Run out and play
For Mother's busy now."
Housework will wait for one all day;
But little boys, somehow
Find wonders in the out-of-doors
About which mothers know;
Far better leave some daily chores
To help a young mind grow.

There's only one first butterfly
Afloat on airborne wings;

First boblink that hurries by
In flight, the while he sings;
First dandelions like precious gold
Will tempt his eager hands
To gather all that they will hold ...
Yes, mother understands,

Remembering that childhood joys
Will always, always be
The heritage for girls and boys ...
They were for you and me.

ETHEL E. MANN

Happiness is a sunbeam which may pass
through a thousand bosoms without losing a particle of its original ray; nay, when
it strikes a kindred heart, like the con-
verged light upon a mirror, it reflects
itself with redoubled brightness. — It is
not perfected till it is shared.

JANE PORTER

!

To see a World in a Grain of Sand
And a Heaven in a Wild Flower,
Hold Infinity in the palm of your hand
And Eternity in an hour.

WILLIAM BLAKE

WONDER OF LIFE

Children are the most wholesome part of the race, the sweetest, for they are freshest from the hand of God. Whimsical, ingenious, mischievous, they fill the world with joy and good humor. We adults live a life of apprehension as to what they will think of us; a life of defense against their terrifying energy; a life of hard work to live up to their great expectations. We put them to bed with a sense of relief — and greet them in the morning with delight and anticipation. We envy them the freshness of adventure and the discovery of life. In all these ways, children add to the wonder of being alive. In all these ways, they help to keep us young.

HERBERT HOOVER

INTERLACED WITH WONDER

Blessed with two childhoods, mine and
   hers,
The space between them often blurs . . .
I can't be sure who caught and dressed
The bullfrog in a satin vest;
Who went to school in pinafores
And named her love by apple cores.
The dollhouse underneath the vine,
The acorn dishes . . . Mother's? Mine?
Impossible to tear asunder
These childhoods interlaced with
   wonder!

F. B. JACOBS

Wonder is the feeling of a philosopher and philosophy begins in wonder.

WHERE DID YOU COME FROM?

Where did you come from, baby dear?
Out of the everywhere into here.

Where did you get those eyes so blue?
Out of the sky as I came through.

What makes the light in them sparkle and
   spin?
Some of the starry spikes left in.

Where did you get that little tear?
I found it waiting when I got here.

What makes your forehead so smooth
   and high?
A soft hand stroked it as I went by.

What makes your cheek like a warm
   white rose?
I saw something better than any one
   knows.

Whence that three-cornered smile of
   bliss?
Three angels gave me at once a kiss.

Where did you get this pearly ear?
God spoke, and it came out to hear.

Where did you get those arms and hands?
Love made itself into bonds and bands.

Feet, when did you come, you darling
   things?
From the same box as the cherubs' wings.

How did they all just come to be you?
God thought about me, and so I grew.

But how did you come to us, you dear?
God thought about you, and so I am here.

GEORGE MACDONALD

LOOK UP

Some people pass through this wonderful
   world
And never look up at the sky . . .
It's nothing to them that the lark sings
   there
While the great white clouds sail by.

It's nothing to them that the millions of
   stars
Weave a silver web at night . . .
They do not know of the hush that falls
When the dawn gives birth to light.

Oh, pity the people with all your heart,
Who never look up at the sky . . .
So many beautiful sights they miss
As the pageant of God goes by.

GOD'S MERCY

For the love of God is broader
Than the measure of man's mind,
And the heart of the Eternal
Is most wonderfully kind.
If our faith were but more simple,
We should take him at his Word,
And our lives would be all sunshine
In the sweetness of our Lord.

FREDERICK WILLIAM FABER

When I consider thy heavens,
   the work of thy fingers,
   the moon and the stars,
which thou hast ordained;
What is man,
   that thou art mindful of him?
and the son of man, that thou visitest
   him?
O Lord our Lord,
how excellent is thy name in all the earth!
Thou hast beset me behind and before,
and laid thine hand upon me.
Such knowledge is too wonderful for me;
it is high,
I cannot attain unto it.
O sing unto the Lord a new song;
for he hath done marvellous things:
his right hand, and his holy arm,
   hath gotten him the victory.
The Lord hath made known his salvation:
his righteousness hath he openly shewed
   in the sight of the heathen.

PSALMS 8:3, 4, 9; 139:5, 6; 98:1, 2

WHO HAS SEEN THE WIND?

Who has seen the wind?
   Neither I nor you:
But when the leaves hang trembling,
   The wind is passing through.

Who has seen the wind?
   Neither you nor I:
But when the trees bow down their heads,
   The wind is passing by.

CHRISTINA ROSSETTI

FLOWER IN THE CRANNIED WALL

Flower in the crannied wall,
I pluck you out of the crannies,
I hold you here, root and all, in my hand,
Little flower — but if I could understand
What you are, root and all, and all in all,
I should know what God and man is.

ALFRED, LORD TENNYSON

When man ceases to wonder, God's secrets remain unrevealed.

APRIL RAIN

It isn't raining rain to me,
It's raining daffodils;
In every dimpled drop I see
Wild flowers on the hills.

The clouds of gray engulf the day
And overwhelm the town;
It isn't raining rain to me,
It's raining roses down.

It isn't raining rain to me,
But fields of clover bloom,
Where any buccaneering bee
Can find a bed and room.

A health unto the happy,
A fig for him who frets!
It isn't raining rain to me,
It's raining violets.

ROBERT LOVEMAN

Sometimes a light surprises
   The Christian while he sings;
It is the Lord who rises
   With healing in his wings.

God moves in a mysterious way
   His wonders to perform;
He plants his footsteps on the sea
   And rides upon the storm.

WILLIAM COWPER

Wonders are many, and none is more wonderful than Man.

SOPHOCLES

●

THE BEAUTIFUL SNOW

Oh, the snow, the beautiful snow
Filling the sky and the earth below.
Over the housetops and over the street,
Over the heads of the people you meet,
Dancing — flirting — skimming along.

It lights on the face and it sparkles the eye
And even the dogs with a bark and a
  bound
Snap at its crystals that eddy around.
The town is alive and its heart aglow
To welcome the coming of the beautiful
  snow.

Over the crest of the beautiful snow,
Snow so pure when it falls from the sky
To be trampled in mud by the crowds
  rushing by.
To be trampled and tracked by thousands
  of feet
Till it blends with the horrible filth in the
  street.

Once I was pure as the snow; but I fell,
Fell like the snowflakes from heaven to
  hell,
Fell to be scoffed at, to be spit on and
  beat,
Pleading — cursing — dreading to die,

Selling my soul to whomever would buy;
Dealing in shame for a morsel of bread,

Hating the living and fearing the dead.
Merciful God! Have I fallen so low
And Yet I was once like this beautiful
  snow.

How strange it should be that the
  beautiful snow
Should fall on a sinner with nowhere to
  go.
How strange it would be, when the night
  comes again
If the snow and the ice struck my
  desperate brain
Fainting — freezing — dying alone.

Helpless and foul as the trampled snow.
Sinner, despair not; Christ stoopeth low
To rescue the soul that is steeped in sin
And lift it to life and enjoyment again.
Groaning — bleeding — dying for thee,

The Crucified died on the cursed tree.
Is there mercy for me? Will He hear my
  weak call?
O God, in the blood that for sinner did
  flow,
Wash me and I shall be whiter than snow!

●

To a darning-needle once exclaimed
  the kitchen sieve,
"You've a hole right through your body,
  and I wonder how you live."
But the needle (who was sharp) replied,
  "I too have wondered
That you notice my one hole,
  when in you there are a hundred!"

SAADI
TRANSLATED BY JAMES FREEMAN CLARKE

194

Work, Service, & Deeds

SOMEBODY

Somebody did a golden deed;
Proving himself a friend in need.
Somebody sang a cheerful song;
Bright'ning the skies the whole day long,
Somebody thought, "Tis sweet to live,"
Willingly said, "I'm glad to give."
Somebody fought a valiant fight;
Bravely he lived to shield the right.
Somebody filled the day with light,
Constantly chased away the night.
Somebody's work bore joy and peace,
Surely his life shall never cease.

JOHN R. CLEMENTS

●

THE JOY OF WORK

Give us, oh, give us, the man who sings at his work! He will do more in the same time, — he will do it better, — he will persevere longer. One is scarcely sensible of fatigue whilst he marches to music. The very stars are said to make harmony as they revolve in their spheres. Wondrous is the strength of cheerfulness, altogether past calculation in its powers of endurance. Efforts, to be permanently useful, must be uniformly joyous, a spirit all sunshine, graceful from very gladness, beautiful because bright.

THOMAS CARLYLE

Small deeds done are better than great deeds planned.

PETER MARSHALL

●

Question not, but live and labor
   Till yon goal be won,
Helping every feeble neighbor,
   Seeking help from none;
Life is mostly froth and bubble,
   Two things stand like stone —
Kindness in another's trouble,
   Courage in our own.

ADAM LINDSAY GORDON

●

Small service is true service while it lasts.
Of humblest friends, bright creature!
   scorn not one:
The daisy, by the shadow that it casts,
Protects the lingering dewdrop from
   the sun.

WILLIAM WORDSWORTH

●

Work for some good, be it ever so slowly,
Cherish some flower, be it ever so lowly,
Labor — all labor is noble and holy.

FRANCES SARGENT OSGOOD

Every now and then go away, have a little relaxation, for when you come back to your work your judgment will be surer; since to remain constantly at work will cause you to lose power of judgment . . . Go some distance away because then the work appears smaller, and more of it can be taken in at a glance, and a lack of harmony or proportion is more readily seen.

LEONARDO DA VINCI

Let me but find it in my heart to say,
When vagrant wishes beckon me astray,
    "This is my work; my blessing, not my
        doom;
    Of all who live, I am the one by whom
This work can best be done in the right
        way."

HENRY VAN DYKE

The best things are nearest . . . breath in your nostrils, light in your eyes, flowers at your feet, duties at your hand, the path of right just before you. Then do not grasp at the stars, but do life's plain, common work as it comes, certain that daily duties and daily bread are the sweetest things of life.

ROBERT LOUIS STEVENSON

No Race can prosper till it learns that there is as much dignity in tilling a field as in writing a poem.

BOOKER T. WASHINGTON

DO IT NOW

If you have hard work to do,
    Do it now.
Today the skies are clear and blue,
Tomorrow clouds may come in view,
Yesterday is not for you;
    Do it now.

If you have a song to sing,
    Sing it now.

Let the notes of gladness ring
Clear as song of bird in spring,
Let every day some music bring;
    Sing it now.

If you have kind words to say,
    Say them now.
Tomorrow may not come your way,
Do a kindness while you may;
Loved ones will not always stay;
    Say them now.

If you have a smile to show,
    Show it now.
Make hearts happy, roses grow,
Let the friends around you know
The love you have before you go;
    Show it now.

From NOW

This for the day of life I ask:
Some all-absorbing, useful task;
And when 'tis wholly, truly done,
A tranquil rest at set of sun.

O TO BE UP AND DOING

O to be up and doing, O
Unfearing and unshamed to go
In all the uproar and the press
About my human business! . . .
For still the Lord is Lord of might:
In deeds, in deeds he takes delight;
The plough, the spear, the laden barks,
The field, the founded city, marks;
He marks the smiler of the streets,
The singers upon garden seats, . . .
Those he approves that ply the trade,
That rock the child, that wed the maid,
That with weak virtues, weaker hands,
Sow gladness on the peopled lands,
And still with laughter, song and shout,
Spin the great wheel of earth about.

ROBERT LOUIS STEVENSON

Depend upon it, God's work done in God's way will never lack God's supplies.

J. HUDSON TAYLOR

In order that people may be happy in their work, these three things are needed: They must be fit for it; They must not do too much of it; And they must have a sense of success in it.

JOHN RUSKIN

What secret trouble stirs thy heart?
Why all this fret and flurry?
Dost thou not know that what is best
In this too restless world is rest
From over-work and hurry?

HENRY WADSWORTH LONGFELLOW

Find out what God would have you do
And do that little well;
For what is great and what is small
'Tis only He can tell.

BUILDERS

When we build, let us think that we build forever. Let it not be for present delight nor for present use alone. Let it be such work as our descendants will thank us for, and let us think, as we lay stone on stone, that a time is to come when those stones will be held sacred because our hands have touched them, and that men will say as they look upon the labor and wrought substance of them, "See! This our Fathers did for us."

JOHN RUSKIN

O give me the joy of living
  And some glorious work to do!
A spirit of thanksgiving,
  With loyal heart and true;
Some pathway to make brighter,
  Where tired feet now stray;
Some burden to make lighter,
  While 'tis day.

Let us be content in work
To do the thing we can, and not presume
To fret because it's little.

ELIZABETH BARRETT BROWNING

Our deeds are like stones cast into the pool of time, though they themselves may disappear, their ripples extend to eternity.

OUR DAILY BREAD

In the deed that no man knoweth
Where no praiseful trumpet bloweth,
Where he may not reap who soweth,
  There, Lord, let my heart serve thee.

O keep us building, Master; may our
  hands
Ne'er falter when the dream is in our
  hearts
When to our ears there come divine
  commands.

PURD E. DEITZ

Praise not thy work, but let thy work
  praise thee;
For deeds, not words, make each man's
  memory stable.
If what thou dost is good, its good all men
  will see;
  Musk by its smell is known, not by its
  label.

197

Worship

I was glad when they said unto me,
Let us go into the house of the Lord.
Our feet shall stand within thy gates,
  O Jerusalem.
Jerusalem is builded as a city that is
  compact together:
Whither the tribes go up, the tribes of the
  Lord,
Unto the testimony of Israel,
To give thanks unto the name of the Lord.
For there are set thrones of judgment,
The thrones of the house of David.
Pray for the peace of Jerusalem:
They shall prosper that love thee.
Peace be within thy walls,
And prosperity within thy palaces.
For my brethren and companions' sakes,
  I will now say,
Peace be within thee.
Because of the house of the Lord our God
I will seek thy good.

PSALM 122

●

WORSHIP

O holy God, undone by guilt depressing,
We come to Thee, our every sin
* confessing;*
Grant us, we pray, Thy cleansing and Thy
* blessing;*
*   We worship Thee, O God!*

Look down on us as low we bend before
* Thee;*

Hear Thou our prayer, we fervently
* implore Thee;*
Accept our praise, as our fond hearts
* adore Thee;*
*   We worship Thee, O God!*

Keep Thou our souls entirely true and
* holy;*
Preserve our spirits deeply pure and
* lowly;*
Add strength to strength that we may
* serve Thee wholly;*
*   We worship Thee, O God!*

Give us, at last, the house of Thy
* preparing,*
That face to face, Thy heavenly glory
* sharing,*
We may praise Thee, our love for e'er
* declaring;*
*   We worship Thee, O God!*

HENRY W. FROST

●

We adore Thee, God, because Thou hast
empowered man to create beauty. Our
every sense is conscious of beauty in
  the graceful column,
  the sound of a tuneful violin,
  the touch of soft linen,
  the odor of choice perfume
  the flavor of good food.
All show beauty to the sensitive soul.

MARIE WELLES CLAPP

A room of quiet,
A temple of peace,
The home of faith
Where doubtings cease;
A house of comfort
Where hope is given,
A source of strength
To make earth heaven;
A shrine of worship,
A place to pray —
I found all this
In my church today.

CYRUS E. ALBERTSON

Worship is fellowship with God.

THE SECRET PLACE

Each soul has its secret place,
Where none may enter in
Save it and God — to them alone
What goeth on therein is known —
To it and God alone.

JOHN OXENHAM

Make a joyful noise unto the Lord, all ye
   lands.
Serve the Lord with gladness:
  come before his presence with singing.
Know ye that the Lord, he is God:
    it is he that hath made us,
      and not we ourselves;
        we are his people,
          and the sheep of his pasture.
Enter into his gates with thanksgiving,
   and into his courts with praise:
     be thankful unto him,
      and bless his name.
For the Lord is good;
   his mercy is everlasting;
     and his truth endureth to all
       generations.

PSALM 100

WORSHIP

God made my cathedral
  Under the stars;
He gave my cathedral
  Trees for its spires;
He hewed me an altar
  In the depth of a hill
He gave for a hymnal
  A rock-bedded rill;
He voiced me a sermon
  Of heavenly light
In the beauty around me —
  The calmness of night;
And I felt as I knelt
  On the velvet-like sod
I had supped of the Spirit
  In the Temple of God.

RUTH FURBEE

Worship is the exposing of the whole person to reality.
Worship is the entire self's response to
  God, requiring a unity of mind, will, and
  feelings.
Worship entails work, but work cannot
  take its place.
Worship demands thought, but no thinking can substitute for it.
Worship engenders emotion, but no feeling as such is ever worship.
Worship is the rooting of life in reality;
  it is man's exposing himself to the
  rightness of God; it is finding God real
  and religion rich for every need.
Worship is finding meaning in life within
  the depths of eternity.

NELS F. S. FERRE

SUNDAY SERVICE

He ruffles through his hymnbook,
He fumbles with his tie,
He laces up his oxfords,
He overworks a sigh,
He goes through all his pockets,
Engrossed in deep research —
There's no one quite so busy as
A little boy in church.

THELMA IRELAND

NOT BY BREAD ALONE

The soul, in order to be strong,
Should take some time for looking long
Into the vast, star-sequined night.
The heavens declare the power and might
Of God; the day sings out His praise
In cloud and sky and woodland ways
Where song birds carol melodies —
There should be time to savor these.
There should be time for friends, for
*   smiles,*
Along the hectic hurrying miles
Of living. And with each new day
The soul that seeks to grow will pray
And meditate upon the Word,
Wherein the voice of God is heard.
For, understanding hearts will own,
Man does not live by bread alone.

CORDELIA SPITZER

Worship is the highest act of which man
is capable. It not only stretches him
beyond all the limits of his finite self to
affirm the divine depth of mystery and
holiness in the living and eternal God,
but it opens him at the deepest level of
his being to an act which unites him most
realistically with his fellow man.

SAMUEL H. MILLER

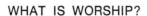

THE CHURCH IN THE HEART

Who builds a church within his heart
And takes it with him everywhere
Is holier far than he whose church
Is but a one-day house of prayer.

MORRIS ABEL BEER

WHAT IS WORSHIP?

It is the exposure of what man is to what
he ought to become.
It is the knife of conscience removing that
which offends.
It is the medicine of the Great Physician
for tired bodies and weary souls.
It is the door into the abundant life.
It is the hand of a small child seeking the
hand of his Father.
It is permitting our bodies to rest while
our souls catch up.
It is the book of memories and aspirations.
It is our little soul seeking the bigness
of God.

You can worship God in the woods . . .
but you don't!
You can worship God on the lakes . . .
but you don't!
You can worship God in your auto . . .
but you don't
You can worship God in a different
church each Sunday . . . but you don't!
You can worship God by sending the
children to Sunday school . . . but you
don't!
The best place to worship God on Sunday
is at your church!

THE ONE THOUSANDTH PSALM

O God, we thank Thee for everything.
For the sea and its waves, blue, green
and gray and always wonderful;
For the beach and the breakers and the
spray and the white foam on the rocks;
For the blue arch of heaven; for the
clouds in the sky, white and gray and
purple;
For the green of the grass; for the forests
in their spring beauty; for the wheat
and corn and rye and barley.
We thank Thee for all Thou hast made
and that Thou hast called it good;
For all the glory and beauty and wonder
of the world to subdue all things to
Thy glory,
And to use all things for the good of Thy
children.

EDWARD EVERETT HALE

True family worship is a vase of perfume that sheds fragrance over all. It softens harshness; it quells anger; it quiets impatience; it settles differences; it subdues evil passions. Hearts that are drawn together at God's feet every day cannot wander far apart. The altar in the midst wonderfully hallows and sweetens the home fellowship. It smooths out the wrinkles of care. It keeps the fire burning on every heart's altar.

WORSHIP AND THANKS TO HIM BELONG

Come, let us tune our loftiest song,
And raise to Christ our joyful strain;
Worship and thanks to Him belong,
Who reigns, and shall forever reign.

His sovereign power our bodies made;
Our souls are His immortal breath;
And when His creatures sinned, He bled,
To save us from eternal death.

Extol the Lamb with loftiest song,
Ascend for Him our cheerful strain;
Worship and thanks to Him belong,
Who reigns, and shall forever reign.

ROBERT A. WEST

To worship is to quicken the conscience
   by the holiness of God,
to feed the mind with the truth of God,
to purge the imagination by the beauty
   of God,
to open the heart to the love of God,
to devote the will to the purpose of God.

WILLIAM TEMPLE

Youth & Old Age

I shall grow old,
  but never lose life's zest,
Because the road's last turn
  will be the best.

HENRY VAN DYKE

ON YOUTH

The whole secret of remaining young in spite of years, and even of gray hairs, is to cherish enthusiasm in oneself, by poetry, by contemplation, by charity, — that is, in fewer words, by the maintenance of harmony in the soul. When everything is in its right place within us, we ourselves are in equilibrium with the whole work of God. . . . Deep and grave enthusiasm for the eternal beauty and the eternal order, reason touched with emotion and a serene tenderness of heart — these surely are the foundations of wisdom.

HENRI FREDERIC AMIEL

AGE IS A QUALITY OF MIND

Age is a quality of mind —
If you have left your dreams behind,
If hope is lost,

If you no longer look ahead,
If your ambitions' fires are dead —
  Then you are old.

But if from life you take the best
And if in life you keep the jest,
If love you hold —
No matter how the years go by,
No matter how the birthdays fly,
  You are not old!

To be seventy years young is sometimes far more cheerful and hopeful than to be forty years old.

OLIVER WENDELL HOLMES

LET ME GROW LOVELY

Let me grow lovely, growing old —
  So many fine things do:
Laces, and ivory, and gold,
  And silks need not be new;
And there is healing in old trees,
  Old streets a glamour hold;
Why may not I, as well as these,
Grow lovely, growing old?

KARLE WILSON BAKER

Count your garden by the flowers,
Never by the leaves that fall.
Count your days by golden hours,
Don't remember clouds at all.

Count your night by stars, not shadows;
Count your life with smiles not tears.
And with joy on every birthday,
Count your age by friends, not years.

DIXIE LEE

Oh, talk not to me of a name great in
    story;
The days of our youth are the days of our
    glory;
And the myrtle and ivy of sweet
    two-and-twenty
Are worth all your laurels, though ever
    so plenty.

LORD BYRON

**So long as enthusiasm lasts, so long is
youth still with us.**

DAVID STARR JORDAN

BIRTHDAYS ARE A GIFT FROM GOD

Where does TIME go in its endless
    flight —
Spring turns to fall and day to night,
And birthdays come and birthdays go
And where they go we do not know ...
But God who planned our life on earth
And gave our mind and body birth
And then enclosed a living soul
With heaven as the spirit's goal
Has given man the gift of choice
To follow that small inner voice
That speaks to us from year to year
Reminding us we've naught to fear ...
For BIRTHDAYS are a STEPPINGSTONE
To endless joys as yet unknown,
So fill each day with happy things
And may your burdens all take wings

And fly away and leave behind
Great joy of heart and peace of mind ...
For BIRTHDAYS are THE GATEWAY to
An ENDLESS LIFE OF JOY FOR YOU
If you but pray from day to day
That He will show you the TRUTH and
    THE WAY.

HELEN STEINER RICE

Youth is happy because it has the ability
to see beauty. Anyone who keeps the
ability to see beauty never grows old.

FRANZ KAFKA

AS I GROW OLD

God keep my heart attuned to laughter
    When youth is done;
When all the days are gray days, coming
    after
    The warmth, the sun.
God keep me then from bitterness, from
    grieving,
    When life seems cold;
God keep me always loving and believing
    As I grow old.

The error of youth is to believe that intelli-
    gence is a substitute for experience,
while the error of age is to believe that ex-
    perience is a substitute for intelligence.

SUCH BEAUTIFUL HANDS

Such beautiful, beautiful hands!
They are growing feeble now,
For time and pain have left their mark
On hand, and heart, and brow.
I've looked on hands whose form and hue
A sculptor's dream might be.
Yet are those aged, wrinkled hands
More beautiful to me.

THE BRIDGE BUILDER

An old man going a lone highway
Came at the evening, cold and gray,
To a chasm vast and wide and steep,
With waters rolling cold and deep.
The old man crossed in the twilight dim,
The sullen stream had no fears for him;
But he turned when safe on the other side,
And built a bridge to span the tide.
"Old man," said a fellow pilgrim near,
"You are wasting your strength with
    building here.
Your journey will end with the ending
    day,
You never again will pass this way.
You've crossed the chasm, deep and wide,
Why build you this bridge at eventide?"

The builder lifted his old gray head.
"Good friend, in the path I have come,"
    he said,
"There followeth after me today
A youth whose feet must pass this way.
The chasm that was as nought to me
To that fair-haired youth may a pitfall be;
He, too, must cross in the twilight dim —
Good friend, I am building this bridge
    for him."

WILL ALLEN DROMGOOLE

**The three ages of man are
school tablet,
aspirin tablet,
and stone tablet.**

WARREN C. WOOD

BRINGING UP FATHER

When I was a boy of 14, my father was so ignorant I could hardly stand to have the old man around. But when I got to be 21, I was astonished at how much the old man had learned in seven years.

MARK TWAIN

GROWING OLDER

A little more tired at close of day;
A little less anxious to have our way;
A little less ready to scold and blame;
A little more care of a brother's name;
And so we are nearing the journey's end,
Where time and eternity meet and blend.
And so we are faring down the way
That leads to the gates of a better day.
A little more laughter, a few more tears,
And we shall have told our increasing
    years.
The book is closed and the prayers are
    said,
And we are part of the countless dead.
And so we are going, where all must go,
To the place the living may never know.
Thrice happy if then some soul can say,
"I'm better because he passed my way."

ROLLIN J. WELLS

●

**I grow old learning something
new every day.**

SOLON

**When saving for old age, be sure to put
away a few pleasant thoughts.**

GROW OLD ALONG WITH ME!

Grow old along with me!
The best is yet to be;
The last of life, for which the first was
    made;
Our times are in his hand who saith,
    "A whole I planned,
Youth shows but half; trust God: See all,
    nor be afraid!"

ROBERT BROWNING

Acknowledgments

Grateful acknowledgment is made
to the following who have granted
permission to reprint copyrighted material:

July 1967 issue of *Decision*.

DODD, MEAD & COMPANY, INC. for an excerpt from *My Utmost for His Highest* by Oswald Chambers; "Home at Last" and "Inspiration" from *Collected Poems by G. K. Chesterton* by Gilbert Keith Chesterton; "The Lost Master" from *Rhymes of a Rolling Stone* by Robert W. Service and a verse from *The Land of Beyond* by Robert W. Service; "Tonight" by Arthur Symons. Reprinted by permission by Dodd, Mead & Company.

DOUBLEDAY & COMPANY, INC. for "If," copyright 1910 by Rudyard Kipling; "L'Envoi," and "The Recessional" by Rudyard Kipling. All reprinted by permission of Mrs. George Bambridge and Doubleday & Company, Inc. "Cause and Effect," "Moments of Awareness," "Dare to Be Happy," and "Generosity" (titled "The Song and The Echo") from *Dare to Be Happy* by Helen Lowrie Marshall, copyright © 1964 by Helen Lowrie Marshall; "The House You Call Home" and "Aim for a Star" from *Bright Horizons* by Helen Lowrie Marshall, copyright © 1962 by Helen Lowrie Marshall. Reprinted by permission of Doubleday and Company, Inc. Excerpts from "Small Things" by David Grayson from *Possessions; Up From Slavery* by Booker T. Washington, and *The Story of My Life* by Helen Keller.

WILLIAM B. EERDMANS, JR. for "Sanctum" from *Open Windows* by Clara Bernhardt and excerpts from *Thoughts Afield* by Harold E. Kohn.

NORMA MILLAY ELLIS for "God's World" from *Collected Poems* by Edna St. Vincent Millay, Harper & Row, Publishers. Copyright © 1913, 1940 by Edna St. Vincent Millay, c/o Norma Millay Ellis.

EVANGELICAL PUBLISHERS for the following poems by Annie Johnson Flint: "What God Hath Promised," "One Day At a Time," and "The World's Bible."

FABER AND FABER, LTD. for the poem "The Mind is an Enchanting Thing" from *The Complete Poems of Marianne Moore*. Reprinted by permission of Faber and Faber, Ltd.

FIRST CHURCH OF CHRIST, SCIENTIST, Maywood, Illinois, for permission to reprint "A Song of Service" by Marguerite Few from *Poems for Daily Needs* edited by Thomas Curtis Clark; "Building a Temple" by Thomas Curtis Clark.

SAMUEL FRENCH INC. for "A Prayer" by John Drinkwater from *Collected Poems by John Drinkwater*, copyright 1919 by John Drinkwater.

FRIENDSHIP PRESS for the poem beginning "In times of quietness our hearts should be like trees" by Toyohiko Kagawa from *Songs from the Land of Dawn* by Toyohiko Kagawa and other Japanese Poets, Friendship Press, New York. Used by permission.

N. CARR GRACE, executor for estate of Frances Frost, for "Of a Small Daughter Walking Outdoors."

ZANE GREY INC. for "Recipe for Greatness" by Zane Grey.

GROSSET AND DUNLAP, INC. for materials by Bessie A. Stanley.

HARCOURT, BRACE & WORLD, INC. for an Excerpt from *The Family Reunion*, copyright 1939 by T. S. Eliot — renewed 1967 by Esme Valerie Eliot. Reprinted by permission of Harcourt, Brace and World, Inc.

HARPER & ROW, PUBLISHERS, INC. for "The Crazy Woman" from *Selected Poems* by Gwendolyn Brooks, copyright © 1960 by Gwendolyn Brooks; "Pete at the Zoo" from *The Bean Eaters* by Gwendolyn Brooks, copyright © 1960 by Gwendolyn Brooks; "I Shall Walk Today" from *Poems of Inspiration and Courage* (1965) by Grace Noll Crowell, copyright 1930 by Harper & Brothers — renewed 1958 by Grace Noll Crowell; "So Long As There Are Homes" from *Light of the Years* by Grace Noll Crowell, copyright 1936 by Harper & Brothers — renewed 1964 by Grace Noll Crowell; "I Shall Be Glad," copyright 1938 by Harper & Brothers — renewed 1966 by Grace Noll Crowell; "To One in Sorrow" from *Songs of Hope* by Grace Noll Crowell, copyright 1938 by Harper Brothers — renewed 1966 by Grace Noll Crowell. Reprinted by permission of Harper & Row, Publishers. Excerpt from *Making Religion Real* by Nels F. S. Ferre, copyright Harper & Row, Publishers; excerpt by James Elliott from *Shadow of the Almighty* by Elizabeth Elliott, copyright by Harper & Row, Publishers; and excerpt from *Dr. Schweitzer of Lambarene*

HENRY REGNERY COMPANY for "Sermons We See" and an excerpt from "From My Books & I" from *Collected Verse* by Edgar A. Guest, copyright 1934 by Reilly & Lee Company, Chicago.

FLEMING H. REVELL COMPANY for poems by Sherwood Eliot Wirt from the book *The Quiet Corner*, copyright © 1965 by Sherwood Eliot Wirt and published by Fleming H. Revell Company, Old Tappan, N.J.; and an excerpt from the book *Mr. Jones, Meet the Master, Sermons and Prayers of Peter Marshall*, copyright 1949, 1950 by Fleming H. Revell Company. All rights reserved.

HELEN STEINER RICE, GIBSON GREETING CARDS, INC., DOUBLEDAY & COMPANY, INC. and the FLEMING H. REVELL COMPANY for the following poems: "Thank God for Little Things," "Birthdays Are a Gift from God," "On the Wings of Prayer," "Heart Gifts," "After the Winter," and excerpts from two other poems.

RAND McNALLY for "The Winds of Fate," "The Goal," and "Faith" by Ella Wheeler Wilcox.

THE RODEHEAVER COMPANY for an excerpt from "As I Go On My Way," published by The Rodeheaver Company in *Gillilan, Finnigin & Company*. Used by permission.

MRS. ALMA J. SARRETT for "Wind in the Pine" from *Covenant with Earth, a Selection from the Poems of Lew Sarett*, edited and copyrighted 1956, by Alma Johnson Sarett. Gainesville: University of Florida Press, 1956. Reprinted by permission.

SCHOOL PICTURES, INC. and JOE HUGHES, JR. for the poem "Today."

CHARLES SCRIBNER'S SONS for an excerpt of twelve lines from "Morning Prayer," reprinted with the permission of Charles Scribner's Sons from *A Diary of Private Prayer*, page 89, by John Baillie, copyright 1949 Charles Scribner's Sons; an excerpt from *The Complete Works of John Galsworthy* by John Galsworthy; "Be Strong" from *This Is My Father's World* by Maltbie D. Babcock, Charles Scribner's Sons (1901); an excerpt from *The Irony of American History* by Reinhold Niebuhr; the following poems of Henry van Dyke: "Peace" and "Little Guideposts" from *The Builders and Other Poems*; "Time Is" and "Work" from *Music and Other Poems*; "The Things I Prize," "These Are the Gifts I Ask," "I Shall Grow Old," and "Four Things" from *The Poems of Henry van Dyke and Chosen Poems*.

RALPH W. SEAGER for "The Extravagance of God" and "The Taste of Prayer" from *Beyond the Green Gate*, copyright © and published by Wake-Brook House.

SIMON & SCHUSTER, INC. for excerpts from *Hope for Man* by Joshua Liebman, copyright © 1966; and excerpts from *The Art of Living* by Wilferd A. Peterson, copyright © 1960.

SINGSPIRATION, INC. for the chorus of "Got Any Rivers" by Oscar Eliason, copyright 1945 by Singspiration, Inc. All rights reserved. Used by permission.

LUCI SHAW for "Hundredfold."

DR. OSWALD J. SMITH for "A Wedding Prayer" and "In the Morning" from *Poems of a Lifetime*, copyright 1965.

THE SOCIETY FOR PROMOTING CHRISTIAN KNOWLEDGE, London, for the following poems by Amy Carmichael: "In Acceptance Lieth Peace" in *Gold Cord;* "Put Forth by the Moon," "Come, Lord Jesus," "Light in the Cell," "Think Through Me," "Cornered by Angels," and "No Scar" from *Toward Jerusalem*. Used by permission.

THE SOCIETY OF AUTHORS for a quotation from *Man and Superman* by George Bernard Shaw; a paragraph by Walter de la Mare from *Early One Morning in the Spring;* sixteen lines from "The Everlasting Mercy" by John Masefield from *The Collected Poems of John Masefield*, permission granted by the Society of Authors as literary representative of the estate of John Masefield.

STANDARD PUBLISHING for "Others" and "What is Home?" by C. D. Meigs.

IRA STANPHILL for "My Life Is Like a River," 1914.

CHARLES L. WALLIS for "The Housewife" by Catherine C. Coblentz from *Treasury of Poems for Worship and Devotion*, edited by Dr. Charles L. Wallis and reprinted by permission of Harper & Row, Publishers; "Proof" by Ethil Romig Fuller from *Kitchen Sonnets*, edited by J. D. Morrison and reprinted by permission of Harper & Row, Publishers; and "The Captain," now known by the title "The Conqueror of My Soul," by Dorothea Day from *Masterpieces of Religious Verse*, edited by J. D. Morrison and reprinted by permission of Harper & Row, Publishers.

WATCHMAN EXAMINER for "Sunday Service" by Thelma Ireland.

DR. WALTER L. WILSON for the quotation from his writing.

LON R. WOODRUM for "Lord, Help Me To Be a Man" from *Souvenir Poems of Lon R. Woodrum*.

YALE UNIVERSITY PRESS for "Tracings" from *Hidden Waters* by Bernard Raymund, copyright © 1922 by Yale University Press.

ZONDERVAN PUBLISHING HOUSE for excerpts from *Sermons* and *Christ Above All* by Robert G. Lee; "I Met the Master" from *212 Victory Poems* by Clifford Lewis; excerpt from *Day by Day* by Andrew Murray; and two lines from "Gossip" by Mabel H. Nance.

Diligent effort has been made to locate the original source of all copyrighted materials in this book and to secure permission for their inclusion. If such acknowledgments have been inadvertently omitted, the compiler and publisher would appreciate receiving full information so that proper credit may be given in future editions.

Index of Titles and First Lines*

* The first lines of Scripture are italicized.

212

Index of Authors and Sources

Index of Topics

ISBN 0-310-23790-4/0995